# JDBC™ Database Access with Java™

# JDBC™ Database Access with Java™

## A Tutorial and Annotated Reference

**Graham Hamilton**
**Rick Cattell**
**Maydene Fisher**

## ADDISON-WESLEY

**An imprint of Addison Wesley Longman, Inc.**
Reading, Massachusetts • Harlow, England • Menlo Park, California
Berkeley, California • Don Mills, Ontario • Sydney
Bonn • Amsterdam • Tokyo • Mexico City

The publisher offers discounts on this book when ordered in quantity for special sales. For more information, please contact:

CORPORATE AND PROFESSIONAL PUBLISHING GROUP
ADDISON WESLEY LONGMAN, INC.
ONE JACOB WAY
READING, MASSACHUSETTS 01867

ISBN   0-201-30995-5

2  3  4  5  6  7─MA   00 99 98 97

2nd Printing  September, 1997

# Acknowledgments

MARK Hapner has been responsible for JavaSoft's JDBC engineering efforts over the last year, including but not limited to copious input on this book. We are indebted to him for all of his help.

We want to thank the many developers who supplied input on the JDBC specification and thereby contributed to its development.

We also want to thank our reviewers, John Goodson, Marc Loy, David Jordan, Dan McMullen, and Ken North. Their thoughtful comments helped to improve the book greatly.

Thanks are also due to Lisa Friendly, the series editor.

And, of course, none of this could have come to be without the support of our families and friends.

We will be grateful to readers who alert us to errors by sending us e-mail at

jdbc-book@wombat.eng.sun.com

Errata for this book and information on other books in the Addison-Wesley Java series will be posted at

http://www.javasoft.com/Series

v

# Contents

# Part Two

# Part One

Part One contains material that introduces JDBC. The first chapter, "Introduction," briefly explains what JDBC is, and it also presents overviews of the Java programming language and relational databases. The two tutorial chapters, "Basic Tutorial" and "MetaData Tutorial," demonstrate how to use JDBC.

# Introduction

THIS is really two books in one: a tutorial and a reference manual for JDBC, the application programming interface that makes it possible for programmers to access databases from Java. The goal is to be useful to a wide range of readers, from database novices to database experts. Therefore, we have arranged the book so that information needed only by experts is separated out from the basic material. We hope that driver developers as well as application programmers and MIS administrators will find what they need. Because different sections are aimed at different audiences, we expect that few people will read every page. We have sometimes duplicated explanations in an effort to make reading easier for those who do not read all sections.

This book will be most helpful to those who have some knowledge of the Java programming language and SQL (Structured Query Language), but one doesn't need to be an expert in either to understand the basic concepts presented here.

## 1.1    Contents of the Book

Part One includes three chapters, an introduction and two tutorial chapters. Part Two, the reference manual, has a chapter for each class or interface, a chapter on how SQL and Java types are mapped to each other, two appendices, a glossary, and an index.

**PART ONE**

Chapter 1, "Introduction," outlines the contents of the book and gives an overview of what the JDBC application programming interface (API) is and how it fits into the world of Java and SQL. The overview includes a brief description of the Java programming language and also a basic discussion of relational databases

3

and SQL. The overview of Java summarizes many concepts and is not intended to be complete. We suggest that anyone who is unfamiliar with Java refer to one of the many excellent books available. The overview of relational databases and SQL likewise covers just the highlights and presents only basic terminology and concepts.

Chapter 2, "Basic Tutorial," walks the reader through how to use the basic JDBC API, giving many examples along the way. The emphasis is on showing how to execute the more common tasks rather than on giving exhaustive examples of every possible feature.

Chapter 3, "Metadata Tutorial," shows how to use the JDBC metadata API, which is used to get information about result sets and databases. It will be of most interest to those who need to write applications that adapt themselves to the specific capabilities of several database systems or to the content of any database. Those who just need to execute standard SQL statements can safely skip this chapter.

## PART TWO

Part Two is the definitive reference manual for the JDBC API.

Chapters 4 through 20, which cover the classes and interfaces, are arranged alphabetically for easy reference. Each chapter contains an overview, a class or interface definition, and an explanation of the methods and fields.

Chapter overviews generally show how to create an instance of the class or interface and how that instance is commonly used. Overviews also present a summary of what the class or interface contains and explanatory material as needed.

The class and interface definitions list the methods and variables, grouping them in logical order.

An explanation of each method follows the class or interface definition. These method explanations are in alphabetical order to facilitate looking them up quickly. If there are any fields, their explanations follow those of the methods, and they, too, are arranged alphabetically.

Chapter 21, which explains mapping Java and SQL types, includes tables showing the various mappings.

Appendix A, "For Driver Writers," contains information for driver writers, including requirements, allowed variations, and notes on security.

Appendix B, "JDBC Design," gives a short history of JDBC, a list of the latest changes, and plans for the future. This section should answer some questions about how JDBC got to its present form and where it is going from here.

Completing the book are a glossary and an index, which we hope readers find helpful and easy to use.

A Quick Reference Card can be found inside the back cover. It includes the most commonly used methods and SQL/Java type mappings.

## 1.2    What Is JDBC ?

JDBC is a Java API for executing SQL statements. (As a point of interest, JDBC is a trademarked name and is not an acronym; nevertheless, JDBC is often thought of as standing for "Java Database Connectivity.") It consists of a set of classes and interfaces written in the Java programming language. JDBC provides a standard API for tool/database developers and makes it possible to write database applications using a pure Java API.

Using JDBC, it is easy to send SQL statements to virtually any relational database. In other words, with the JDBC API, it isn't necessary to write one program to access a Sybase database, another program to access an Oracle database, another program to access an Informix database, and so on. One can write a single program using the JDBC API, and the program will be able to send SQL statements to the appropriate database. And, with an application written in the Java programming language, one also doesn't have to worry about writing different applications to run on different platforms. The combination of Java and JDBC lets a programmer write it once and run it anywhere. (We explain more about this later.)

Java, being robust, secure, easy to use, easy to understand, and automatically downloadable on a network, is an excellent language basis for database applications. What is needed is a way for Java applications to talk to a variety of different databases. JDBC is the mechanism for doing this.

JDBC extends what can be done in Java. For example, with Java and the JDBC API, it is possible to publish a web page containing an applet that uses information obtained from a remote database. Or an enterprise can use JDBC to connect all its employees (even if they are using a conglomeration of Windows, Macintosh, and UNIX machines) to one or more internal databases via an intranet. With more and more programmers using the Java programming language, the need for easy database access from Java is continuing to grow.

MIS managers like the combination of Java and JDBC because it makes disseminating information easy and economical. Businesses can continue to use their installed databases and access information easily even if it is stored on different database management systems. Development time for new applications is short. Installation and version control are greatly simplified. A programmer can write an application or an update once, put it on the server, and everybody has access to the latest version. And for businesses selling information services, Java and JDBC offer a better way of getting out information updates to external customers.

We will discuss various ways to use JDBC in more detail later.

### 1.2.1   What Does JDBC Do?

Simply put, JDBC makes it possible to do three things:

1. establish a connection with a database

2. send SQL statements

3. process the results.

The following code fragment gives a basic example of these three steps:

```
Connection con = DriverManager.getConnection (
                    "jdbc:odbc:wombat", "login", "password");
Statement stmt = con.createStatement();
ResultSet rs = stmt.executeQuery("SELECT a, b, c FROM Table1");
while (rs.next()) {
    int x = getInt("a");
    String s = getString("b");
    float f = getFloat("c");
}
```

### 1.2.2   A Low-level API and a Base for Higher-level APIs

JDBC is a "low-level" interface, which means that it is used to invoke (or "call") SQL commands directly. It works very well in this capacity and is easier to use than other database connectivity APIs, but it was designed also to be a base upon which to build higher-level interfaces and tools. A higher-level interface is "user-friendly," using a more understandable or more convenient API that is translated behind the scenes into a low-level interface such as JDBC. At the time of this writing, two kinds of higher-level APIs are under development on top of JDBC:

1. An embedded SQL for Java. At least one vendor plans to build this. DBMSs implement SQL, a language designed specifically for use with databases.

JDBC requires that the SQL statements be passed as strings to Java methods. An embedded SQL preprocessor allows a programmer to instead mix SQL statements directly with Java: for example, a Java variable can be used in an SQL statement to receive or provide SQL values. The embedded SQL preprocessor then translates this Java/SQL mix into Java with JDBC calls.

2. A direct mapping of relational database tables to Java classes. JavaSoft and others have announced plans to implement this. In this "object/relational" mapping, each row of the table becomes an instance of that class, and each column value corresponds to an attribute of that instance. Programmers can then operate directly on Java objects; the required SQL calls to fetch and store data are automatically generated "beneath the covers." More sophisticated mappings are also provided, for example, where rows of multiple tables are combined in a Java class.

As interest in JDBC has grown, more developers have been working on JDBC-based tools to make building programs easier, as well. Programmers have also been writing applications that make accessing a database easier for the end user. For example, an application might present a menu of database tasks from which to choose. After a task is selected, the application presents prompts and blanks for filling in information needed to carry out the selected task. With the requested input typed in, the application then automatically invokes the necessary SQL commands. With the help of such an application, users can perform database tasks even when they have little or no knowledge of SQL syntax.

### 1.2.3    JDBC versus ODBC and other APIs

At this point, Microsoft's ODBC (Open DataBase Connectivity) API is probably the most widely used programming interface for accessing relational databases. It offers the ability to connect to almost all databases on almost all platforms. So why not just use ODBC from Java?

The answer is that you *can* use ODBC from Java, but this is best done with the help of JDBC in the form of the JDBC–ODBC Bridge, which we will cover shortly. The question now becomes, "Why do you need JDBC?" There are several answers to this question:

1. ODBC is not appropriate for direct use from Java because it uses a C interface. Calls from Java to native C code have a number of drawbacks in the security, implementation, robustness, and automatic portability of applications.

2. A literal translation of the ODBC C API into a Java API would not be desirable. For example, Java has no pointers, and ODBC makes copious use of them, including the notoriously error-prone generic pointer void *. You can think of JDBC as ODBC translated into an object-oriented interface that is natural for Java programmers.

3. ODBC is hard to learn. It mixes simple and advanced features together, and it has complex options even for simple queries. JDBC, on the other hand, was designed to keep simple things simple while allowing more advanced capabilities where required.

4. A Java API like JDBC is needed in order to enable a "pure Java" solution. When ODBC is used, the ODBC driver manager and drivers must be manually installed on every client machine. When the JDBC driver is written completely in Java, however, JDBC code is automatically installable, portable, and secure on all Java platforms from network computers to mainframes.

In summary, the JDBC API is a natural Java interface to the basic SQL abstractions and concepts. It builds on ODBC rather than starting from scratch, so programmers familiar with ODBC will find it very easy to learn JDBC. JDBC retains the basic design features of ODBC; in fact, both interfaces are based on the X/Open SQL CLI (Call Level Interface). The big difference is that JDBC builds on and reinforces the style and virtues of Java, and, of course, it is easy to use.

More recently, Microsoft has introduced new APIs beyond ODBC: RDO, ADO, DAO, and OLE DB. These designs move in the same direction as JDBC in many ways, for example, in being object-oriented interfaces to databases based on classes that can be implemented on ODBC. However, we did not see functionality in any of these interfaces compelling enough to make them an alternative basis to ODBC, especially with the ODBC driver market well-established. Mostly they represent a thin veneer on ODBC. This is not to say that JDBC does not need to evolve from the initial release described in this book; we discuss a few directions in "The Future of JDBC" on page 421. However, we feel that most new functionality belongs in higher-level APIs such as the object/relational mappings and embedded SQL we mentioned in "A Low-level API and a Base for Higher-level APIs" on page 6.

### 1.2.4   Two-tier and Three-tier Models

The JDBC API supports both two-tier and three-tier models for database access.

In the two-tier model, a Java applet or application talks directly to the database. This requires a JDBC driver that can communicate with the particular database management system being accessed. A user's SQL statements are delivered to the database, and the results of those statements are sent back to the user. The database may be located on another machine to which the user is connected via a network. This is referred to as a *client/server* configuration, with the user's machine as the client, and the machine housing the database as the server. The network can be an intranet, which, for example, connects employees within a corporation, or it can be the Internet.

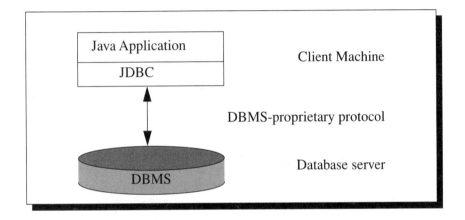

**Figure 1.1:** JDBC Two-tier Model

In the three-tier model, commands are sent to a "middle tier" of services, which then sends SQL statements to the database. The database processes the SQL statements and sends the results back to the middle tier, which then sends them to the user. MIS directors find the three-tier model very attractive because the middle tier makes it possible to maintain control over access and the kinds of updates that can be made to corporate data. Another advantage is that when there is a middle tier, the user can employ an easy-to-use higher-level API, which is translated by the middle tier into the appropriate low-level calls. Finally, in many cases the three-tier architecture can provide performance advantages.

Until now the middle tier has typically been written in languages such as C or C++, which offer fast performance. However, with the introduction of optimizing compilers that translate Java bytecode into efficient machine-specific code, it is becoming practical to implement the middle tier in Java. This is a big plus, making it possible to take advantage of Java's robustness, multithreading, and security features. Of course, JDBC is important in allowing database access from a Java middle tier.

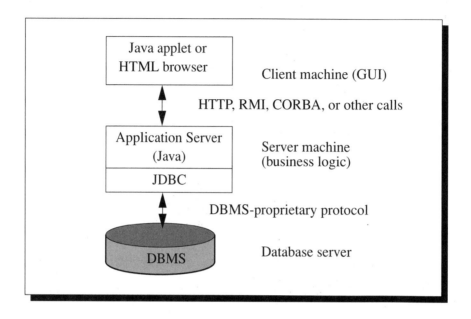

**Figure 1.2:** JDBC Three-tier Model

### 1.2.5   SQL Conformance

Structured Query Language (SQL) is the standard language for accessing relational databases. Unfortunately, SQL is not yet as standard as one would like.

One area of difficulty is that data types used by different DBMSs (DataBase Management Systems) sometimes vary, and the variations can be significant. JDBC deals with this by defining a set of generic SQL type identifiers in the class `java.sql.Types`. Note that, as used in this book, the terms "JDBC SQL type," "JDBC type," and "SQL type" are interchangeable and refer to the generic SQL type identifiers defined in `java.sql.Types`. There is a more complete discussion of data type conformance later in the book.

Another area of difficulty with SQL conformance is that although most DBMSs use a standard form of SQL for basic functionality, they do not conform to the more recently defined standard SQL syntax or semantics for more advanced functionality. For example, not all databases support stored procedures or outer joins, and those that do are not consistent with each other. It is hoped that the portion of SQL that is truly standard will expand to include more and more functionality. In the meantime, however, the JDBC API must support SQL as it is.

One way the JDBC API deals with this problem is to allow any query string to be passed through to an underlying DBMS driver. This means that an application is free to use as much SQL functionality as desired, but it runs the risk of receiving an error on some DBMSs. In fact, an application query need not even be SQL, or it may be a specialized derivative of SQL designed for specific DBMSs (for document or image queries, for example).

A second way JDBC deals with problems of SQL conformance is to provide ODBC-style escape clauses, which are discussed in "SQL Escape Syntax in Statement Objects" on page 345. The escape syntax provides a standard JDBC syntax for several of the more common areas of SQL divergence. For example, there are escapes for date literals and for stored procedure calls.

For complex applications, JDBC deals with SQL conformance in a third way. It provides descriptive information about the DBMS by means of the interface `DatabaseMetaData` so that applications can adapt to the requirements and capabilities of each DBMS. Typical end users need not worry about metadata, but experts may want to refer to "DatabaseMetaData Overview" on page 163.

Because the JDBC API will be used as a base API for developing higher-level database access tools and APIs, it also has to address the problem of conformance for anything built on it. The designation "JDBC Compliant" was created to set a standard level of JDBC functionality on which users can rely. In order to use this designation, a driver must support at least ANSI SQL-2 Entry Level. (ANSI SQL-2 refers to the standards adopted by the American National Standards Institute in 1992. Entry Level refers to a specific list of SQL capabilities.) Driver developers can ascertain that their drivers meet these standards by using the test suite available with the JDBC API.

The "JDBC Compliant" designation indicates that a vendor's JDBC implementation has passed the conformance tests provided by JavaSoft. These conformance tests check for the existence of all of the classes and methods defined in the JDBC API, and check as much as possible that the SQL Entry Level functionality is available. Such tests are not exhaustive, of course, and JavaSoft is not currently branding vendor implementations, but this compliance definition provides some degree of confidence in a JDBC implementation. With wider and wider acceptance of the JDBC API by database vendors, connectivity vendors, Internet service vendors, and application writers, JDBC is quickly becoming the standard for Java database access.

### 1.2.6   JDBC Products

The JDBC API is a natural choice for Java developers because it offers easy database access for Java applications and applets.

At the time of this writing, a number of JDBC-based products have already been deployed or are under development. The status of these products changes frequently, so the reader should consult the JDBC web page for the latest information. It can be found at the following URL:

```
http://www.javasoft.com/products/jdbc
```

### 1.2.7   JavaSoft Framework

JavaSoft provides three JDBC product components:

- the JDBC driver manager (included as part of the Java Development Kit (JDK))

- the JDBC driver test suite (available from the JDBC web site)

- the JDBC–ODBC bridge (included in the Solaris and Windows versions of the JDK)

The JDBC driver manager is the backbone of the JDBC architecture. It actually is quite small and simple; its primary function is to connect Java applications to the correct JDBC driver and then get out of the way.

The JDBC driver test suite provides some confidence that JDBC drivers will run your program. Only drivers that pass the JDBC driver test suite can be designated "JDBC Compliant."

The JDBC–ODBC bridge allows ODBC drivers to be used as JDBC drivers. It was implemented as a way to get JDBC off the ground quickly, and long term will provide a way to access some of the less popular DBMSs if JDBC drivers are not implemented for them.

### 1.2.8   JDBC Driver Types

The JDBC drivers that we are aware of at this time generally fit into one of four categories:

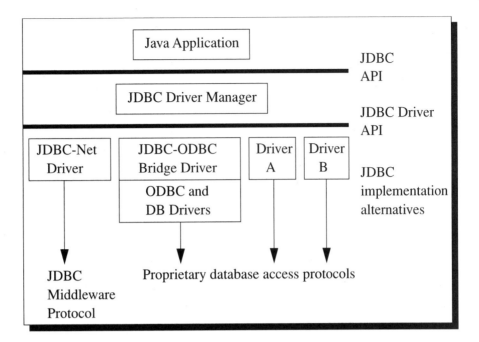

**Figure 1.3:** JDBC Driver Implementations

1. *JDBC–ODBC bridge plus ODBC driver:* The JavaSoft bridge product provides JDBC access via ODBC drivers. Note that ODBC binary code, and in many cases database client code, must be loaded on each client machine that uses this driver. As a result, this kind of driver is most appropriate on a corporate network where client installations are not a major problem, or for application server code written in Java in a three-tier architecture.

2. *Native-API partly-Java driver:* This kind of driver converts JDBC calls into calls on the client API for Oracle, Sybase, Informix, DB2, or other DBMS. Note that, like the bridge driver, this style of driver requires that some binary code be loaded on each client machine.

3. *JDBC-Net pure Java driver:* This driver translates JDBC calls into a DBMS-independent net protocol, which is then translated to a DBMS protocol by a server. This net server middleware is able to connect its pure Java clients to many different databases. The specific protocol used depends on the vendor. In general, this is the most flexible JDBC alternative. It is likely that all vendors of this solution will provide products suitable for intranet use. In order for these products to also support Internet access, they must handle the additional requirements for security, access through firewalls, and so forth, that the Web imposes.

4. *Native-protocol pure Java driver:* This kind of driver converts JDBC calls directly into the network protocol used by DBMSs. This allows a direct call from the client machine to the DBMS server and is an excellent solution for intranet access. Since many of these protocols are proprietary, the database vendors themselves will be the primary source. Several database vendors have these in progress.

The expectation is that eventually driver categories 3 and 4 will be the preferred way to access databases from JDBC. Driver categories 1 and 2 are interim solutions where direct pure Java drivers are not yet available. There are possible variations on categories 1 and 2 (not shown in the following table) that require a connector, but these are generally less desirable solutions. Categories 3 and 4 offer all the advantages of Java, including automatic installation (for example, downloading the JDBC driver with an applet that uses it).

Table 1.1 shows the four categories and their properties:

| DRIVER CATEGORY | ALL JAVA? | NET PROTOCOL |
|---|---|---|
| 1 - JDBC–ODBC Bridge | No | Direct |
| 2 - Native API as basis | No | Direct |
| 3 - JDBC-Net | Yes | Requires Connector |
| 4 - Native protocol as basis | Yes | Direct |

**Table 1.1:  Driver Categories**

### 1.2.9   Obtaining JDBC Drivers

At the time of this writing, there are dozens of drivers in Category 1: ODBC drivers that can be used with JavaSoft's bridge. There are currently about a dozen Category 2 drivers built on top of native APIs for DBMSs. There are a few Category 3 drivers. There are currently at least two Category 4 drivers, but by the end of 1997, we expect that there will be Category 4 drivers for all of the major DBMSs.

To get the latest information on drivers, check the JDBC web site at

```
http://www.javasoft.com/products/jdbc
```

JavaSoft and Intersolv, a leading database connectivity vendor, worked together to produce the JDBC–ODBC Bridge and the JDBC Driver Test Suite.

### 1.2.10  Other Products

Various JDBC application development tools are under way. Watch the JavaSoft pages for updates.

Because JDBC brings together Java and databases, the remainder of this chapter gives a brief overview of each. Readers familiar with Java can skip section 1.3; readers familiar with SQL can skip section 1.4.

## 1.3    Java Overview

Java is a powerful but lean object-oriented programming language. It has generated a lot of excitement because it makes it possible to program for the Internet by creating applets, programs that can be embedded in a web page. The content of an applet is limited only by one's imagination. For example, an applet can be an animation with sound, an interactive game (that could include various animations with sound), or a ticker tape with constantly updated stock prices. Applets can be just little decorations to liven up a web page, or they can be serious applications like word processors or spreadsheets.

But Java is more than a programming language for writing applets. It is being used more and more for writing standalone applications as well. It is becoming so popular that many people believe it will become the standard language for both general-purpose and Internet programming. There are many buzzwords associated with Java, but because of its spectacular growth in popularity, a new buzzword has appeared: *ubiquitous*. Indeed, all indications are that it will soon be everywhere.

Java builds on the strengths of C++. It has taken the best features of C++ and discarded the more problematic and error-prone parts. To this lean core it has added garbage collection (automatic memory management), multithreading (the capacity for one program to do more than one thing at a time), and security capabilities. The result is that Java is simple, elegant, powerful, and easy to use.

Java is actually a platform consisting of three components: (1) the Java programming language, (2) the Java library of classes and interfaces, and (3) the Java Virtual Machine. The following sections will say more about these components.

### 1.3.1    Java Is Portable

One of the biggest advantages Java offers is that it is portable. An application written in Java will run on all of the major platforms. Any computer with a Java-based browser can run the applications or applets written in the Java programming language. A programmer no longer has to write one program to run on a Macintosh, another program to run on a Windows machine, still another to run on a UNIX machine, and so on. In other words, with Java, developers write their programs only once.

The Virtual Machine is what gives Java its cross-platform capabilities. Rather than being compiled into a machine language, which is different for each operating system and computer architecture, Java code is compiled into bytecodes.

With other languages, program code is compiled into a language that the computer can understand. The problem is that other computers with different machine instruction sets cannot understand that language. Java code, on the other hand, is compiled into bytecodes rather than a machine language. These bytecodes go to the Java Virtual Machine, which executes them directly or translates them into the language that is understood by the machine running it.

In summary, this means that with the JDBC API extending Java, a programmer writing Java code can access all of the major relational databases on any platform that supports the Java Virtual Machine.

### 1.3.2   Java Is Object-Oriented

The Java programming language is object-oriented, which makes program design focus on *what* you are dealing with rather than on *how* you are going to do something. This makes it more useful for programming in sophisticated projects because one can break things down into understandable components. A big benefit is that these components can then be reused.

Object-oriented languages use the paradigm of classes. In simplest terms, a class includes both data and the functions to operate on that data. You can create an *instance* of a class, also called an *object*, which will have all the data members and functionality of its class. Because of this, you can think of a class as being like a template, with each object being a specific instance of a particular type of class. For example, suppose you have a very simple class called `Person`, which has three *fields* (a data member is called a *field* in Java) and one *method* (a function is called a *method* in Java). The following code illustrates creating a simplified class. Don't worry if you don't understand everything in this example; just try to get a general idea. For example, the first thing inside the beginning brace ({) is a constructor, a special kind of method that creates an instance of a class and sets its fields with their initial values.

```
class Person {
    public Person(String n, int a, String oc) {
        name = n;
```

```
        age = a;
        occupation = oc;
    }
    public void identifySelf() {
        System.out.print("I am " + name + ", a " + age );
        System.out.println("-year-old " + occupation + ".");
    }
    protected String name;      // three attributes of Person
    protected int age;
    protected String occupation;
}
```

The last three items are *fields*, which are attributes of a Person object. They are given the access specifier protected, which means that these fields can be used by subclasses of Person but not by any other classes. (We will explain subclasses later in this section.) If the access specifier had been private, only the class Person could access these fields. The access specifier public allows access by all classes.

The following code creates an instance of Person and stores it in the variable p. This means that p is of type Person—a new class is a new type. This newly created instance of Person, p, is given the name, age, and occupation that were supplied to the constructor for Person. Note that the method new is used with a constructor to create a new instance of a class.

```
Person p = new Person("Adela", 37, "astronomer");
```

The following line of code causes p to identify herself. The results follow. (Note that the curved arrow signifies a line of output and is not part of the actual output.)

```
p.identifySelf( );
```

➡ I am Adela, a 37-year-old astronomer.

The following code creates a second instance of Person and invokes identifySelf:

```
Person q = new Person("Hakim", 22, "student");
q.identifySelf( );
```

➡ I am Hakim, a 22-year-old student.

The class paradigm allows one to *encapsulate* data so that specific data values or function implementations cannot be seen by those using the class. In the class Person, the fields name, age, and occupation are all given the access modifier protected, which signifies that these fields can be assigned values only by using methods in the class that defines them or in its subclasses—in this case, class Person or a subclass of Person. In other words, the only way a user can change the value of private or protected fields in a class is to use the methods supplied by the class. In our example, the Person class does not provide any methods other than the constructor for assigning values, so in this case, a user cannot modify the name, age, or occupation of an instance of Person after its creation. Also, given the way Person is defined here, there is only one way a user can find out the values for name, age, and occupation: to invoke the method identifySelf.

To allow a user to modify, say, the field occupation, one could write a method such as the following:

```
void setOccupation(String oc) {
    occupation = oc;
}
```

The following code defines methods that will return the current values of name and occupation, respectively:

```
String getName( ) {
    return name;
}
```

```
String getOccupation( ) {
    return occupation;
}
```

Using Person p in our example, you can set the field occupation to a new value and verify its current value as follows:

```
p.setOccupation("orthodontist");
String newOccupation = p.getOccupation();
System.out.print(p.getName() + "'s new occupation is ");
System.out.println(newOccupation + ".");
```

➥ Adela's new occupation is orthodontist.

Encapsulation makes it possible to make changes in code without breaking other programs that use that code. If, for example, the implementation of a function is changed, the change is invisible to another programmer who invokes that function, and it doesn't affect his/her program, except hopefully to improve it.

Java includes *inheritance*, or the ability to derive new classes from existing classes. The *derived* class, also called a *subclass*, inherits all the data and functions of the existing class, referred to as the *parent* class. A subclass can add new data members to those inherited from the parent class. As far as methods are concerned, the subclass can reuse the inherited methods as is, change them, and/or add its own new methods. For example, the subclass VerbosePerson could be derived from the class Person, with the difference between instances of the Person class and instances of the VerbosePerson class being the way they identify themselves. The following code creates the subclass VerbosePerson and changes only the implementation of the method identifySelf:

```java
class VerbosePerson extends Person {
    public VerbosePerson(String n, int a, String oc) {
        super(n, a, oc);  //this calls the constructor for Person
    }
    identifySelf( ) {      // modifies the method in class Person
        System.out.println("Hi there! How are you doing today?");
        System.out.println("I go by the name of " + name + ".");
        System.out.print("I am " + age + " years old, and my ");
        System.out.println("occupation is " + occupation + ".");
    }
}
```

An instance of VerbosePerson will inherit the three protected data members that Person has, and it will have the method identifySelf but with a different implementation. Now an instance of the class VerbosePerson can be created:

```java
VerbosePerson happyPerson = new VerbosePerson(
                            "Buster Brown", 45, "comedian");
```

A call to the method identifySelf will produce the following results:

```java
happyPerson.identifySelf( );
```

➡ Hi there! How are you doing today?
➡ I go by the name of Buster Brown.
➡ I am 45 years old, and my occupation is comedian.

### 1.3.3    Java Makes It Easy to Write Correct Code

In addition to being portable and object-oriented, Java facilitates writing correct code. Programmers spend less time writing Java code and a lot less time debugging it. In fact, many developers have reported slashing development time by as much as two-thirds. The following is a list of some of Java's features that make it easier to write correct code:

- **Garbage collection** — automatically takes care of allocating and deallocating memory, a huge potential source of errors. If an object is no longer being used (has no references to it), then it is automatically removed from memory, or "garbage collected." Programmers don't have to keep track of what has been allocated and deallocated themselves, which makes their job a lot easier, but, more importantly, it stops memory leaks.

- **No pointers** — eliminates a big source of errors. By using object references instead of memory pointers, problems with pointer arithmetic are eliminated, and problems with inadvertently accessing the wrong memory address are greatly reduced.

- **Strong typing** — cuts down on run-time errors. Because Java enforces strong type checking, many errors are caught when code is compiled. Dynamic binding is possible and often very useful, but static binding with strict type checking is used when possible.

- **Simplicity**—makes Java easier to learn and use correctly. Java keeps it simple by having just one way to do something instead of having several alternatives, as in some languages. Java also stays lean by not including multiple inheritance, which eliminates the errors and ambiguity that arise when you create a subclass that inherits from two or more classes. To replace the capabilities multiple inheritance provides, Java lets you add functionality to a class through the use of *interfaces*. See the next section for a brief explanation of interfaces.

### 1.3.4   Java Includes a Library of Classes and Interfaces

The Java platform includes an extensive class library so that programmers can use already-existing classes as is, create subclasses to modify existing classes, or implement interfaces to augment the capabilities of classes.

Both classes and interfaces contain data members (fields) and functions (methods), but there are major differences. In a class, fields may be either variable or constant, and methods are fully implemented. In an interface, fields must be constants, and methods are just prototypes with no implementations. The prototypes give the method signature (the return type, the function name, and the number of parameters with the type for each parameter), but the programmer must supply implementations. To use an interface, a programmer defines a class, declares that it implements the interface, and then implements all of the methods in that interface as part of the class.

These methods are implemented in a way that is appropriate for the class in which the methods are being used. For example, suppose a programmer has created a class Person and wants to use an interface called Sortable, which contains various methods for sorting objects. If one wanted to be able to sort instances of the Person class, one would declare the class to implement Sortable and write an implementation for each method in the Sortable interface so that instances of Person would be sorted by the criteria the programmer supplies. For instance, Person objects could be sorted by age, by name, or by occupation, and the order could be ascending or descending. Interfaces let one add functionality to a class and give a great deal of flexibility in doing it. In other words, interfaces provide most of the advantages of multiple inheritance without its disadvantages.

A *package* is a collection of related Java classes and interfaces. The following list, though not complete, gives examples of some Java packages and what they cover:

- **java.lang** — the basic classes. This package is so basic that it is automatically included in any Java program. It includes classes dealing with numerics, strings, objects, runtime, security, and threads.

- **java.io** — classes that manage reading data from input streams and writing data to output streams

- **java.util** — miscellaneous utility classes, including generic data structures, bit sets, time, date, string manipulation, random number generation, system properties, notification, and enumeration of data structures

- **java.net** — classes for network support

- **java.awt** — classes that manage user interface components such as windows, dialog boxes, buttons, checkboxes, lists, menus, scrollbars, and text fields; the "awt" stands for Abstract Window Toolkit

- **java.awt.image** — classes for managing image data, including color models, cropping, color filtering, setting pixel values, and grabbing snapshots

- **java.applet** — the Applet class, which provides the ability to write applets; this package also includes several interfaces that connect an applet to its document and to resources for playing audio

- **java.sql**—the JDBC API, classes and interfaces that access databases and send SQL statements

The first three packages listed, `java.lang`, `java.io`, and `java.util`, form the foundation; they are the basic classes and interfaces for general-purpose programming. The Java Development Kit version 1.1 added some new packages, with JDBC being one of them. Other new packages include such things as remote method invocation, security, and JavaBeans, the new API for creating reusable components.

In Java, packages serve as a foundation for building other packages, as discussed in the following section.

### 1.3.5    Java Is Extensible

A big plus for Java is the fact that it can be extended. It was purposely written to be lean with the emphasis on doing what it does very well; instead of trying to do everything from the beginning, it was written so that extending it is easy. Programmers can modify existing classes or write their own new classes, or they can write a whole new package. The JDBC API, the java.sql package, is one example of a foundation upon which extensions are being built. Other extensions are being added or worked on in areas such as multimedia, Internet commerce, conferencing, and telephony. Check the JavaSoft web page (`http://www.javasoft.com`) to find a current list.

In addition to extensions, there are also many tools being developed to make existing capabilities easier to use. For example, there is already a tool that greatly simplifies creating and laying out graphical user interfaces, such as menus, dialog boxes, and buttons.

### 1.3.6 Java Is Secure

It is important that a programmer not be able to write subversive code for applications or applets. This is especially true with the Internet being used more and more extensively for services such as electronic commerce and electronic distribution of software and multimedia content.

The Java platform builds in security in four ways:

- **The way memory is allocated and laid out.** In Java, an object's location in memory is not determined until run time, as opposed to C and C++, where the compiler makes memory layout decisions. As a result, a programmer cannot look at a class definition and figure out how it might be laid out in memory. Also, since Java has no pointers, a programmer cannot forge pointers to memory.

- **The way incoming code is checked.** The Java Virtual Machine does not trust any incoming code and subjects it to what is called bytecode verification. The bytecode verifier, part of the Virtual Machine, checks that (1) the format of incoming code is correct, (2) incoming code doesn't forge pointers, (3) it doesn't violate access restrictions, and (4) it accesses objects as what they are (for example, an InputStream object is used only as an InputStream object).

- **The way classes are loaded.** The Java bytecode loader, another part of the Virtual Machine, checks whether classes loaded during program execution are local or from across a network. Imported classes cannot be substituted for built-in classes, and built-in classes cannot accidentally reference classes brought in over a network.

- **The way access is restricted for untrusted code.** The Java security manager allows users to restrict untrusted Java applets so that they cannot access the local network, local files, and other resources.

### 1.3.7 Java Performs Well

Java's performance is better than one might expect. Java's many advantages, such as having built-in security and being interpreted as well as compiled, do have a cost attached to them. However, various optimizations have been built in, and the bytecode interpreter can run very fast because it does not have to do any checking. As a result, Java has done quite respectably in performance tests. Its performance numbers for interpreted bytecodes are usually more than adequate to run interactive graphical end-user applications. For situations that require unusually high performance, bytecodes can be translated on the fly, generating the final machine code for the particular CPU on which the application is running, at run time.

High-level interpreted scripting languages generally offer great portability and fast prototyping but poor performance. Low-level compiled languages like C and C++ offer great performance but require large amounts of time for writing and debugging code because of problems with areas such as memory management, pointers, and multiple inheritance. Java offers good performance with the advantages of high-level languages but without the disadvantages of C and C++. In the world of design trade-offs, you can think of Java as providing a very attractive middle ground.

### 1.3.8    Java Scales Well

The Java platform is designed to scale well, from portable consumer electronic devices (PDAs) to powerful desktop and server machines. The Java Virtual Machine takes a small footprint, and Java bytecode is optimized to be small and compact. As a result, Java accommodates the need for low storage and for low bandwidth transmission over the Internet. In addition, the JavaOS (Java Operating System) offers a standalone Java platform that eliminates host operating system overhead while still supporting the full Java platform API. This makes Java ideal for low-cost network computers whose sole purpose is to access the Internet.

### 1.3.9    Java Is Multithreaded

Multithreading is simply the ability of a program to do more than one thing at a time. For example, an application could be faxing a document at the same time it is printing another document. Or a program could process new inventory figures while it maintains a feed of current prices. Multithreading is particularly important in multimedia: a multimedia program might often be running a movie, running an audio track, and displaying text all at the same time.

## 1.4    Relational Database Overview

A database is a means of storing information in such a way that information can be retrieved from it. In simplest terms, a *relational* database is one that presents information in tables with rows and columns. (A table is referred to as a *relation*, which explains the term *relational database*.) A Database Management System (DBMS) handles the way data is stored, maintained, and retrieved. In the case of a relational database, a Relational Database Management System (RDBMS) performs these tasks. DBMS as used in this book is a general term that includes RDBMS.

### 1.4.1 Integrity Rules

Relational tables follow certain integrity rules to ensure that the data they contain stay accurate and are always accessible. First, the rows in a relational table should all be distinct. If there are duplicate rows, there can be problems resolving which of two possible selections is the correct one. For most DBMSs, the user can specify that duplicate rows are not allowed, and if that is done, the DBMS will prevent the addition of any rows that duplicate an existing row. A second integrity rule is that column values cannot be repeating groups or arrays. A third aspect of data integrity involves the concept of a *null* value. A database has to take care of situations where data may not be available: a null value indicates that a value is missing. It does not equate to a blank or zero. A blank is considered equal to another blank, a zero is equal to another zero, but two null values are not considered equal.

When each row in a table is different, it is possible to use one or more columns to identify a particular row. This unique column or group of columns is called a *primary key*. Any column that is part of a primary key cannot be null; if it were, the primary key containing it would no longer be a complete identifier. This rule is referred to as *entity integrity*. (The rule for *referential integrity* is discussed in the section entitled "Joins" on page 28.)

Table 1.2 illustrates some of these relational database concepts:

| Employee_ Number | First_Name | Last_Name | Date_of_Birth | Car_ Number |
|---|---|---|---|---|
| 10001 | Axel | Washington | 28-AUG-43 | 5 |
| 10083 | Arvid | Sharma | 24-NOV-54 | null |
| 10120 | Jonas | Ginsburg | 01-JAN-69 | null |
| 10005 | Florence | Wojokowski | 04-JUL-71 | 12 |
| 10099 | Sean | Washington | 21-SEP-66 | null |
| 10035 | Elizabeth | Yamaguchi | 24-DEC-59 | null |

### Table 1.2: Employees

In this table of employees, there are five columns: Employee_Number, First_Name, Last_Name, Date_of_Birth, and Car_Number. There are six rows, each representing a different employee. The primary key for this table would generally be the employee number because each one is guaranteed to be different. (A number is also more efficient than a string for making comparisons.) It would also be possible to use First_Name and Last_Name because the combination of the two also identifies just one row in our sample database. Using the last name alone would not work because there are two employees with the last name of "Washington." In this particular case the first names are all different, so one could conceivably use that column as a primary key, but it is best to avoid using a column where duplicates could occur. If Elizabeth Taylor gets a job at this company, and the primary key is First_Name, the RDBMS will not allow her name to be added (if it has been specified that no duplicates be permitted). Because there is already an Elizabeth in the table, adding a second one would make the primary key useless as a way of identifying just one row.

## 1.4.2   SELECT Statements

SQL (Structured Query Language) is a language designed to be used with relational databases. There is a set of basic SQL commands that is considered standard and is used by all RDBMSs. For example, all RDBMSs use the SELECT statement.

A SELECT statement, also called a *query*, is used to get information from a table. It specifies one or more column headings, one or more tables from which to select, and some criteria for selection. The RDBMS returns rows of the column entries that satisfy the stated requirements. A SELECT statement such as the following will fetch the first and last names of employees who have company cars:

```
SELECT First_Name, Last_Name
FROM Employees
WHERE Car_Number IS NOT NULL
```

The result set (the set of rows that satisfy the requirement of not having null in the Car_Number column) follows. The first name and last name are printed for each row that satisfies the requirement because the SELECT statement (the first line) specifies the columns First_Name and Last_Name. The FROM clause (the second line) gives the table from which the columns will be selected.

```
FIRST_NAME              LAST_NAME
----------              ----------
Axel                    Washington
Florence                Wojokowski
```

The following code produces a result set that includes the whole table because it asks for all of the columns in the table `Employees` with no restrictions (no `WHERE` clause). Note that "`SELECT *`" means "`SELECT` all columns."

```
SELECT *
FROM Employees
```

### 1.4.3 WHERE Clauses

The `WHERE` clause in a `SELECT` statement provides the criteria for selecting values. For example, in the code fragment below, values will be selected only if they occur in a row in which the column `Last_Name` contains the string `'Washington'`.

```
SELECT First_Name, Last_Name
FROM Employees
WHERE Last_Name LIKE 'Washington%'
```

The keyword `LIKE` is used to compare strings, and it offers the feature that patterns containing wildcards can be used. For example, in the code fragment above, there is a percent sign (%) at the end of `'Washington'`, which signifies that any value containing the string `'Washington'` plus zero or more additional characters will satisfy this selection criterion. So `'Washington'` or `'Washingtonian'` would be matches, but `'Washing'` would not be. The other wildcard used in `LIKE` clauses is an underbar (_), which stands for any one character. For example,

```
WHERE Last_Name LIKE 'Ba_man'
```

would match `'Batman'`, `'Barman'`, `'Badman'`, `'Balman'`, `'Bagman'`, `'Bamman'`, and so on.

The code fragment below has a `WHERE` clause that uses the equal sign (=) to compare numbers. It selects the first and last name of the employee who is assigned car 12.

```
SELECT First_Name, Last_Name
FROM Employees
WHERE Car_Number = 12
```

The next code fragment selects the first and last names of employees whose employee number is greater than 10005:

```
SELECT First_Name, Last_Name
FROM Employees
WHERE Employee_Number > 10005
```

WHERE clauses can get rather elaborate, with multiple conditions and, in some DBMSs, nested conditions. This overview will not cover complicated WHERE clauses, but the following code fragment has a WHERE clause with two conditions; this query selects the first and last names of employees whose employee number is less than 10100 and who do not have a company car:

```
SELECT First_Name, Last_Name
FROM Employees
WHERE Employee_Number < 10100 and Car_Number IS NULL
```

A special type of WHERE clause involves a join, which is explained in the next section.

### 1.4.4   Joins

A distinguishing feature of relational databases is that it is possible to get data from more than one table in what is called a *join*. Suppose that after retrieving the names of employees who have company cars, one wanted to find out who has which car, including the make, model, and year of car. This information is stored in another table, Cars, shown in Table 1.3:

| Car Number | Make | Model | Year |
|:---:|:---:|:---:|:---:|
| 5 | Honda | Civic DX | 1996 |
| 12 | Toyota | Corolla | 1993 |

**Table 1.3:  Cars**

There must be one column that appears in both tables in order to relate them to each other. This column, which must be the primary key in one table, is called the *foreign key* in the other table. In this case, the column that appears in two tables is Car_Number, which is the primary key for the table Cars and the foreign key in the table Employees. If the 1996 Honda Civic were wrecked and deleted from the Cars table, then Car_ Number 5 would also have to be removed from the Employees table in order to maintain what is called *referential integrity*. Otherwise, the foreign key column (Car_Number) in Employees would contain an entry that did not refer to anything in Cars. A foreign key must either be null or equal to an existing primary key value of the table to which it refers. This is different from a primary key, which may not be null. There are several null values in the Car_Number column in the table Employees because it is possible for an employee not to have a company car.

The following code asks for the first and last names of employees who have company cars and for the make, model, and year of those cars. Note that the FROM clause lists both Employees and Cars because the requested data is contained in both tables. Using the table name and a dot (.) before the column name indicates which table contains the column.

```
SELECT Employees.First_Name, Employees.Last_Name, Cars.Make,
          Cars.Model, Cars.Year
FROM Employees, Cars
WHERE Employees.Car_Number = Cars.Car_Number
```

This returns the following result set:

| FIRST_NAME | LAST_NAME | MAKE | MODEL | YEAR |
| --- | --- | --- | --- | --- |
| Axel | Washington | Honda | CivicDX | 1996 |
| Florence | Wojokowski | Toyota | Corolla | 1993 |

### 1.4.5    Common SQL Commands

SQL commands are divided into categories, the two main ones being Data Manipulation Language (DML) commands and Data Definition Language (DDL) commands. DML commands deal with data, either retrieving it or modifying it to keep it up-to-date. DDL commands deal with creating or changing tables and other database objects such as views and indexes.

A list of the more common DML commands follows:
- SELECT—used to query and display data from a database. The SELECT statement specifies which columns to include in the result set. The vast majority of the SQL commands used in applications are SELECT statements.

- INSERT—adds new rows to a table. INSERT is used to populate a newly-created table or to add a new row (or rows) to an already-existing table.

- DELETE—removes a specified row or set of rows from a table.

- UPDATE—changes an existing value in a column of a table.

The more common DDL commands follow:

- CREATE TABLE—creates a table with the column names the user provides. The user also needs to specify a type for the data in each column. Data types vary from one RDBMS to another, so a user might need to use metadata to establish the data types used by a particular database. (See "Metadata" on page 32 for a definition of metadata. Also, we have provided a table showing the type names used by some leading DBMSs on page 399.) CREATE TABLE is normally used less often than the data manipulation commands because a table is created only once, whereas adding or deleting rows or changing individual values generally occurs more frequently.

- DROP TABLE—deletes all rows and removes the table definition from the database.

- ALTER TABLE—adds or removes a column from a table.

### 1.4.6   Result Sets and Cursors

The rows that satisfy the conditions of a query are called the *result set*. The number of rows returned in a result set can be zero, one, or many. One accesses the data in a result set one row at a time, and a *cursor* provides the means to do that. A cursor can be thought of as a pointer into a file that contains the rows of the result set, and that pointer has the ability to keep track of which row is currently being accessed. A cursor allows one to process each row of a result set from top to bottom and consequently may be used for iterative processing.

Most DBMSs create a cursor automatically when a result set is generated.

### 1.4.7   Transactions

When one is accessing data in a database, someone else may be accessing the same data at the same time. If, for instance, one user is updating some columns in a table at the same time another user is selecting columns from that table, it could be possible that the data returned is partly old data and partly updated data. For this reason,

DBMSs use *transactions* to maintain data in a consistent state (*data consistency*) while allowing more than one user to access a database at the same time (*data concurrency*).

A transaction is a set of one or more SQL statements that make up a logical unit of work. A transaction ends with either a *commit* or a *rollback*, depending on whether there are any problems with data consistency or data concurrency. The `commit` statement makes permanent the changes resulting from the SQL statements in the transaction, and the `rollback` statement undoes all changes resulting from the SQL statements in the transaction.

A *lock* is a mechanism that prohibits two transactions from manipulating the same data at the same time. For example, a table lock prevents a table from being dropped if there is an uncommitted transaction on that table. A row lock prevents two transactions from modifying the same row, or it prevents one transaction from selecting a row while another transaction is still modifying it.

The chapter "Connection" starting on page 143 has more information about transactions. See especially the sections "Transactions" on page 148 and "Transaction Isolation Levels" on page 149.

### 1.4.8    Stored Procedures

A *stored procedure* is a group of SQL statements that can be called by name. In other words, it is executable code, a mini-program, that performs a particular task that can be invoked the same way one can call a function. Once a stored procedure is written, it can be used and reused because a DBMS that supports stored procedures will, as its name implies, store it in the database. A DBMS compiles a stored procedure before storing it, so it does not have to be recompiled each time it is called, cutting down on execution time.

The following code is an example of how to create a very simple stored procedure, but since each DBMS has its own way of creating stored procedures, it is meant to give only an idea of how it might be done and is not meant to be used in actual code. This example creates a stored procedure called `Assign_Car_Num`, which updates the `Employees` table. It takes two input arguments, the number of the car to be added and the number of the employee to whom the car is being assigned. The type of each argument must be `integer`, as specified in the first line.

```
create procedure Assign_Car_Num (Car_No integer, Emp_No integer)
as begin
UPDATE Employees
```

```
SET Car_Number = Car_No
WHERE Employee_Number = Emp_No
end
```

### 1.4.9   Metadata

Databases store user data, and they also store information about the database itself. Most DBMSs have a set of system tables, which list tables in the database, column names in each table, primary keys, foreign keys, stored procedures, and so forth. Each DBMS has its own functions for getting information about table layouts and database features. JDBC uses the class `DatabaseMetaData` as a standardized way to get this information. See "DatabaseMetaData Overview" on page 163 and "ResultSetMetaData Overview" on page 319 for more information. In general, only developers writing tools and drivers normally need to be concerned with metadata.

# CHAPTER 2

# Basic Tutorial

J DBC was designed to keep simple things simple. This means that JDBC makes everyday database tasks, like simple SELECT statements, very easy. This chapter will walk you through examples of using JDBC to execute common SQL statements, letting you see for yourself how easy it is to use the basic JDBC API.

By the end of the chapter, you will know how to use JDBC to create tables, insert values into them, query the tables, retrieve the results of the queries, and update the tables. In this process, you will learn how to use simple statements and prepared statements, and you will see an example of a stored procedure. You will also learn how to perform transactions and how to catch exceptions and warnings. Finally, you will see a how to create an applet.

Chapter 3 shows how to use the metadata API, which is used in more sophisticated programs, such as applications that must dynamically discover and present the table structure of a target database.

## 2.1  Getting Started

The first thing you need to do is check that you are set up properly. This involves the following steps:

1. Install Java and JDBC on your machine.

   To install both Java and JDBC, simply follow the instructions for downloading the JDK1.1 (Java Development Kit version 1.1). When you download the JDK1.1, you will get JDBC 1.2 as well. The sample code used in the tutorials was written for JDK1.1.

You can find the latest release (JDK1.1 at the time of this writing) at the following URL:

```
http://java.sun.com/products/JDK/CurrentRelease
```

2. Install a driver on your machine.

Your driver should include instructions for installing it. For JDBC drivers written for specific DBMSs, installation consists of just copying the driver onto your machine; there is no special configuration needed.

The JDBC–ODBC Bridge driver is not quite as easy to set up. If you download either the Solaris or Windows versions of JDK1.1, you will automatically get the JDBC–ODBC Bridge driver, which does not itself require any special configuration. ODBC, however, does. If you do not already have ODBC on your machine, you will need to see your ODBC driver vendor for information on installation and configuration.

3. Install your DBMS if needed.

If you do not already have a DBMS installed, you will need to follow the vendor's instructions for installation. Most users will have a DBMS installed and will be working with an established database.

## 2.2    Setting Up a Database

We will assume that the database COFFEEBREAK already exists. (Creating a database is not at all difficult, but it requires special permissions and is normally done by a database administrator.) When you create the tables used as examples in this tutorial, they will be in the default database. We purposely kept the size and number of tables small to keep things manageable.

Suppose that our sample database is being used by the proprietor of a small coffee house called The Coffee Break, where coffee beans are sold by the pound and brewed coffee is sold by the cup. To keep things simple, also suppose that the proprietor needs only two tables, one for types of coffee and one for coffee suppliers.

First we will show you how to open a connection with your DBMS, and then, since what JDBC does is to send your SQL code to your DBMS, we will demonstrate some SQL code. After that, we will show you how easy it is to use JDBC to pass these SQL statements to your DBMS and process the results that are returned.

For your convenience, the JDBC code used in this chapter can be downloaded from our web site:

```
http://www.javasoft.com/products/jdbc/book.html
```

This code has been tested on most of the major DBMS products. However, you may encounter some compatibility problems using it with older ODBC drivers with the JDBC–ODBC Bridge.

## 2.3    Establishing a Connection

The first thing you need to do is establish a connection with the DBMS you want to use. This involves two steps: (1) loading the driver and (2) making the connection.

### 2.3.1    Loading Drivers

Loading the driver or drivers you want to use is very simple and involves just one line of code. If, for example, you want to use the JDBC–ODBC Bridge driver, the following code will load it:

```
Class.forName("sun.jdbc.odbc.JdbcOdbcDriver");
```

Your driver documentation will give you the class name to use. For instance, if the class name is jdbc.DriverXYZ, you would load the driver with the following line of code:

```
Class.forName("jdbc.DriverXYZ");
```

You do not need to create an instance of a driver and register it with the DriverManager because calling Class.forName will do that for you automatically. If you were to create your own instance, you would be creating an unnecessary duplicate.

When you have loaded a driver, it is available for making a connection with a DBMS.

### 2.3.2    Making the Connection

The second step in establishing a connection is to have the appropriate driver connect to the DBMS. The following line of code illustrates the general idea:

```
Connection con = DriverManager.getConnection(
                                url, "myLogin", "myPassword");
```

This step is also simple, with the hardest thing being what to supply for *url*. If you are using the JDBC–ODBC Bridge driver, the JDBC URL will start with `jdbc:odbc:`. The rest of the URL is generally your data source name or database system. So, if you are using ODBC to access an ODBC data source called "`Fred`," for example, your JDBC URL could be `jdbc:odbc:Fred`. In place of "`myLogin`" you put the name you use to log in to the DBMS; in place of "`myPassword`" you put your password for the DBMS. So if you log in to your DBMS with a login name of "Fernanda" and a password of "`J8`," just these two lines of code will establish a connection:

```
String url = "jdbc:odbc:Fred";
Connection con = DriverManager.getConnection(url, "Fernanda", "J8");
```

If you are using a JDBC driver, the documentation will tell you what subprotocol to use, that is, what to put after `jdbc:` in the JDBC URL. For example, if the driver developer has registered the name *acme* as the subprotocol, the first and second parts of the JDBC URL will be `jdbc:acme:`. The driver documentation will also give you guidelines for the rest of the JDBC URL. This last part of the JDBC URL supplies information for identifying the data source.

If one of the drivers you loaded recognizes the JDBC URL supplied to the method `DriverManager.getConnection`, that driver will establish a connection to the DBMS specified in the JDBC URL. The `DriverManager` class, true to its name, manages all of the details of establishing the connection for you behind the scenes. Unless you are writing a driver, you will probably never use any of the methods in the interface `Driver`, and the only `DriverManager` method you really need to know is `DriverManager.getConnection`.

The connection returned by the method `DriverManager.getConnection` is an open connection you can use to create JDBC statements that pass your SQL statements to the DBMS. In the previous example, *con* is an open connection, and we will use it in the examples that follow.

## 2.4 Setting Up Tables

### 2.4.1 Creating a Table

First, we will create one of the tables in our example database. This table, COFFEES, contains the essential information about the coffees sold at The Coffee Break, including the coffee names, their prices, the number of pounds sold the current week, and the number of pounds sold to date. The table COFFEES, which we describe in more detail later, is shown in Table 2.1:

| COF_NAME | SUP_ID | PRICE | SALES | TOTAL |
|---|---|---|---|---|
| Colombian | 101 | 7.99 | 0 | 0 |
| French_Roast | 49 | 8.99 | 0 | 0 |
| Espresso | 150 | 9.99 | 0 | 0 |
| Colombian_Decaf | 101 | 8.99 | 0 | 0 |
| French_Roast_Decaf | 49 | 9.99 | 0 | 0 |

**Table 2.1: Coffees**

The column storing the coffee name is COF_NAME, and it holds values with an SQL type of VARCHAR and a maximum length of 32 characters. Since we will use different names for each type of coffee sold, the name will uniquely identify a particular coffee and can therefore serve as the primary key. The second column, named SUP_ID, will hold a number that identifies the coffee supplier; this number will be of SQL type INTEGER. The third column, called PRICE, stores values with an SQL type of FLOAT because it needs to hold values with decimal points. (Note that money values would normally be stored in an SQL type DECIMAL or NUMERIC, but because of differences among DBMSs and to avoid incompatibility with older versions of JDBC, we are using the more standard type FLOAT for this tutorial.) The column named SALES stores values of SQL type INTEGER and indicates the number of pounds of coffee sold during the current week. The final column, TOTAL, contains an SQL INTEGER which gives the total number of pounds of coffee sold to date.

SUPPLIERS, the second table in our database, gives information about each of the suppliers. It is shown in Table 2.2:

| SUP_ID | SUP_NAME | STREET | CITY | STATE | ZIP |
|--------|----------|--------|------|-------|-----|
| 101 | Acme, Inc. | 99 Market Street | Groundsville | CA | 95199 |
| 49 | Superior Coffee | 1 Party Place | Mendocino | CA | 95460 |
| 150 | The High Ground | 100 Coffee Lane | Meadows | CA | 93966 |

**Table 2.2:  Suppliers**

The tables COFFEES and SUPPLIERS both contain the column SUP_ID, which means that these two tables can be used in SELECT statements to get data based on the information in both tables. The column SUP_ID is the primary key in the table SUPPLIERS, and as such, it uniquely identifies each of the coffee suppliers. In the table COFFEES, SUP_ID is called a foreign key. (You can think of a foreign key as being foreign in the sense that it is imported from another table.) Note that each SUP_ID number appears only once in the SUPPLIERS table; this is required for it to be a primary key. In the COFFEES table, where it is a foreign key, however, it is perfectly all right for there to be duplicate SUP_ID numbers because one supplier may sell many types of coffee. Later in this chapter, you will see an example of how to use primary and foreign keys in a SELECT statement. Such a statement, called a *join*, was explained in "Joins" on page 28.

The following SQL statement creates the table COFFEES. The entries within the outer pair of parentheses consist of the name of a column followed by a space and the SQL type to be stored in that column. A comma separates the entry for one column (consisting of column name and SQL type) from the next one. The type VARCHAR is created with a maximum length, so it takes a parameter indicating that maximum length. The parameter must be in parentheses following the type. The SQL statement shown here, for example, specifies that the name in column COF_NAME may be up to 32 characters long:

```
CREATE TABLE COFFEES
(COF_NAME VARCHAR(32),
 SUP_ID INTEGER,
 PRICE FLOAT,
 SALES INTEGER,
 TOTAL INTEGER)
```

This code does not end with a DBMS statement terminator, which can vary from DBMS to DBMS. For example, Oracle uses a semicolon (;) to indicate the end of a statement, and Sybase uses the word go. The driver you are using will automatically supply the appropriate statement terminator, and you will not need to include it in your JDBC code.

Another thing we should point out about SQL statements is their form. In the CREATE TABLE statement, key words are printed in all capital letters, and each item is on a separate line. SQL does not require either; these conventions simply make statements easier to read. The standard in SQL is that keywords are not case sensitive, so, for example, the following SELECT statement (from the relational database overview in chapter 1) can be written various ways. As an example, these two versions below are equivalent as far as SQL is concerned:

```
SELECT First_Name, Last_Name
FROM Employees
WHERE Last_Name LIKE "Washington"

select First_Name, Last_Name from Employees where
Last_Name like "Washington"
```

Quoted material, however, is case sensitive: in the name "Washington," "W" must be capitalized, and the rest of the letters must be lowercase.

Requirements can vary from one DBMS to another when it comes to identifier names. For example, some DBMSs require that column and table names be given exactly as they were created in the CREATE TABLE statement, while others do not. You can find more information in the section "String Patterns as Arguments" on page 164. To be safe, we will use all uppercase for identifiers such as COFFEES and SUPPLIERS because that is how we defined them.

So far we have written the SQL statement that creates the table COFFEES. Now let's put quotation marks around it (making it a string) and assign that string to the variable *createTableCoffees* so that we can use the variable in our JDBC code later. As just shown, the DBMS does not care about where lines are divided, but Java will not compile a String object that extends beyond one line. Consequently, when you are giving strings in Java, you need to enclose each line in quotation marks and use a plus sign (+) to concatenate them:

```
String createTableCoffees = "CREATE TABLE COFFEES " +
    "(COF_NAME VARCHAR(32), SUP_ID INTEGER, PRICE FLOAT, " +
    "SALES INTEGER, TOTAL INTEGER)";
```

The data types we used in our CREATE TABLE statement are the generic SQL types (also called JDBC types) that are defined in the class java.sql.Types. DBMSs generally use these standard types, so when the time comes to try out some JDBC applications, you can just use the application CreateCoffees.java, which uses the CREATE TABLE statement. If your DBMS uses its own local type names, we supply another application for you, which we will explain fully later.

Before running any applications, however, we are going to walk you through the basics of JDBC.

### 2.4.2    Creating JDBC Statements

A Statement object is what sends your SQL statement to the DBMS. You simply create a Statement object and then execute it, supplying the appropriate execute method with the SQL statement you want to send. For a SELECT statement, the method to use is executeQuery. For statements that create or modify tables, the method to use is executeUpdate.

It takes an instance of an active connection to create a Statement object. In the following example, we use our Connection object *con* to create the Statement object *stmt*:

```
Statement stmt = con.createStatement();
```

At this point *stmt* exists, but it does not have an SQL statement to pass on to the DBMS. We need to supply that to the method we use to execute *stmt*. For example, in the following code fragment, we supply executeUpdate with the SQL statement from the example above:

```
stmt.executeUpdate("CREATE TABLE COFFEES " +
    "(COF_NAME VARCHAR(32), SUP_ID INTEGER, PRICE FLOAT, " +
    "SALES INTEGER, TOTAL INTEGER)");
```

Since we made a string out of the SQL statement and assigned it to the variable *createTableCoffees*, we could have written the code in this alternate form:

```
stmt.executeUpdate(createTableCoffees);
```

### 2.4.3    Executing Statements

We used the method executeUpdate because the SQL statement contained in *createTableCoffees* is a DDL (data definition language) statement. Statements that create a table, alter a table, or drop a table are all examples of DDL statements and are executed with the method `executeUpdate`. As you might expect from its name, the method `executeUpdate` is also used to execute SQL statements that update a table. In practice, `executeUpdate` is used far more often to update tables than it is to create them because a table is created once but may be updated many times.

The method used most often for executing SQL statements is `executeQuery`. This method is used to execute SELECT statements, which comprise the vast majority of SQL statements. You will see how to use this method shortly.

### 2.4.4 Entering Data into a Table

We have shown how to create the table COFFEES by specifying the names of the columns and the data types to be stored in those columns, but this only sets up the structure of the table. The table does not yet contain any data. We will enter our data into the table one row at a time, supplying the information to be stored in each column of that row. Note that the values to be inserted into the columns are listed in the same order that the columns were declared when the table was created, which is the default order.

The following code inserts one row of data, with `Colombian` in the column `COF_NAME`, 101 in `SUP_ID`, 7.99 in `PRICE`, 0 in `SALES`, and 0 in `TOTAL`. (Since The Coffee Break has just started out, the amount sold during the week and the total to date are zero for all the coffees to start with.) Just as we did in the code that created the table COFFEES, we will create a `Statement` object and then execute it using the method `executeUpdate`.

Since the SQL statement will not quite fit on one line on the page, we have split it into two strings concatenated by a plus sign (+) so that it will compile. Pay special attention to the need for a space between COFFEES and VALUES. This space must be within the quotation marks and may be after COFFEES or before VALUES; without a space, the SQL statement will erroneously be read as "INSERT INTO COFFEESVALUES . . ." and the DBMS will look for the table COFFEESVALUES. Also note that we use single quotation marks around the coffee name because it is nested within double quotation marks. For most DBMSs, the general rule is to alternate double quotation marks and single quotation marks to indicate nesting.

```
Statement stmt = con.createStatement();
stmt.executeUpdate("INSERT INTO COFFEES " +
                "VALUES ('Colombian', 101, 7.99, 0, 0)");
```

The code that follows inserts a second row into the table COFFEES. Note that we can just reuse the Statement object *stmt* rather than having to create a new one for each execution.

```
stmt.executeUpdate("INSERT INTO COFFEES " +
            "VALUES ('French_Roast', 49, 8.99, 0, 0)");
```

Values for the remaining rows can be inserted as follows:

```
stmt.executeUpdate("INSERT INTO COFFEES " +
            "VALUES ('Espresso', 150, 9.99, 0, 0)");

stmt.executeUpdate("INSERT INTO COFFEES " +
            "VALUES ('Colombian_Decaf', 101, 8.99, 0, 0)");

stmt.executeUpdate("INSERT INTO COFFEES " +
            "VALUES ('French_Roast_Decaf', 49, 9.99, 0, 0)");
```

## 2.5    Getting Data from a Table

Now that the table COFFEES has values in it, we can write a SELECT statement to access those values. The star (*) in the following SQL statement indicates that all columns should be selected. Since there is no WHERE clause to narrow down the rows from which to select, the following SQL statement selects the whole table:

```
SELECT *
FROM COFFEES
```

The result, which is the entire table, will look similar to the following:

| COF_NAME | SUP_ID | PRICE | SALES | TOTAL |
|----------|--------|-------|-------|-------|
| Colombian | 101 | 7.99 | 0 | 0 |
| French_Roast | 49 | 8.99 | 0 | 0 |
| Espresso | 150 | 9.99 | 0 | 0 |
| Colombian_Decaf | 101 | 8.99 | 0 | 0 |
| French_Roast_Decaf | 49 | 9.99 | 0 | 0 |

The result above is what you would see on your terminal if you entered the SQL query directly to the database system. When we access a database through a Java application, as we will be doing shortly, we will need to retrieve the results so that we can use them. You will see how to do this in the next section.

Here is another example of a SELECT statement; this one will get a list of coffees and their respective prices per pound:

```
SELECT COF_NAME, PRICE
FROM COFFEES
```

The results of this query will look something like this:

```
COF_NAME              PRICE
------------------    -----
Colombian             7.99
French_Roast          8.99
Espresso              9.99
Colombian_Decaf       8.99
French_Roast_Decaf    9.99
```

The SELECT statement above generates the names and prices of all of the coffees in the table. The following SQL statement limits the coffees selected to just those that cost less than $9.00 per pound:

```
SELECT COF_NAME, PRICE
FROM COFFEES
WHERE PRICE < 9.00
```

The results would look similar to this:

```
COF_NAME             PRICE
---------------      -----
Colombian            7.99
French_Roast         8.99
Colombian Decaf      8.99
```

## 2.6    Retrieving Values from Result Sets

We now show how you send the above SELECT statements from a Java program and get the results we showed.

JDBC returns results in a ResultSet object, so we need to declare an instance of the class ResultSet to hold our results. The following code demonstrates declaring the ResultSet object *rs* and assigning the results of our earlier query to it:

```
ResultSet rs = stmt.executeQuery("SELECT COF_NAME, PRICE
                                  FROM COFFEES");
```

### 2.6.1    Using the Method next

The variable *rs*, which is an instance of ResultSet, contains the rows of coffees and prices shown in the result set example above. In order to access the names and prices, we will go to each row and retrieve the values according to their types. The method next moves what is called a *cursor* to the next row and makes that row (called the *current row*) the one upon which we can operate. Since the cursor is initially positioned just above the first row of a ResultSet object, the first call to the method next moves the cursor to the first row and makes it the current row. Successive invocations of the method next move the cursor down one row at a time from top to bottom. Note that JDBC does not provide a previous method; thus it is not possible to move backward in a ResultSet object. Appendix B has a note about why this is so on page 420.

### 2.6.2    Using the getXXX Methods

We use the getXXX method of the appropriate type to retrieve the value in each column. For example, the first column in each row of *rs* is COF_NAME, which stores a value of SQL type VARCHAR. The method for retrieving a value of SQL type VARCHAR is getString. The second column in each row stores a value of SQL type FLOAT, and the method for retrieving values of that type is getFloat. The following code accesses the values stored in the current row of *rs* and prints a line with the name followed by three spaces and the price. Each time the method next is invoked, the next row becomes the current row, and the loop continues until there are no more rows in *rs*.

```
String query = "SELECT COF_NAME, PRICE FROM COFFEES";
ResultSet rs = stmt.executeQuery(query);
while (rs.next()) {
    String s = rs.getString("COF_NAME");
    Float n = rs.getFloat("PRICE");
    System.out.println(s + "    " + n);
}
```

The output will look something like this:

```
➥ Colombian    7.99
➥ French_Roast    8.99
➥ Espresso    9.99
➥ Colombian_Decaf    8.99
➥ French_Roast_Decaf    9.99
```

Note that we use a curved arrow to identify output from JDBC code; it is not part of the output. The arrow is not used for results in a result set, so its use distinguishes between what is contained in a result set and what is printed as the output of an application.

Let's look a little more closely at how the getXXX methods work by examining the two getXXX statements in this code. First let's examine getString.

```
String s = rs.getString("COF_NAME");
```

The method getString is invoked on the ResultSet object *rs*, so getString will retrieve (*get*) the value stored in the column COF_NAME in the current row of *rs*. The value that getString retrieves has been converted from an SQL VARCHAR to a Java String, and it is assigned to the String object *s*. Note that we used the variable *s* in the println expression above (println(s + "    " + n)).

The situation is similar with the method getFloat except that it retrieves the value stored in the column PRICE, which is an SQL FLOAT, and converts it to a Java float before assigning it to the variable *n*.

JDBC offers two ways to identify the column from which a getXXX method gets a value. One way is to give the column name, as was done in the example above. The second way is to give the column *index* (number of the column), with 1 signifying the first column, 2 , the second, and so on. Using the column number instead of the column name looks like this:

```
String s = rs.getString(1);
float n = rs.getFloat(2);
```

The first line of code gets the value in the first column of the current row of *rs* (column COF_NAME), converts it to a Java String object, and assigns it to *s*. The second line of code gets the value stored in the second column of the current row of *rs* , converts it to a Java float, and assigns it to *n*. Note that the column number refers to the column number in the result set, not in the original table.

In summary, JDBC allows you to use either the column name or the column number as the argument to a getXXX method. Using the column number is slightly more efficient, and there are some cases where the column number is required. In general, though, supplying the column name is essentially equivalent to supplying the column number.

JDBC allows a lot of latitude as far as which getXXX methods you can use to retrieve the different SQL types. For example, the method getInt can be used to retrieve any of the numeric or character types. The data it retrieves will be converted to an int; that is, if the SQL type is VARCHAR, JDBC will attempt to parse an integer out of the VARCHAR. The method getInt is recommended for retrieving only SQL INTEGER types, however, and it cannot be used for the SQL types BINARY, VARBINARY, LONGVARBINARY, DATE, TIME, or TIMESTAMP.

The chart "Types Retrieved by ResultSet.getXXX Methods" on page 398 shows which methods can legally be used to retrieve SQL types and, more important, which methods are recommended for retrieving the various SQL types.

Note that this table uses the term "JDBC type" in place of "SQL type." Both terms refer to the generic SQL types defined in java.sql.Types, and they are interchangeable.

### 2.6.3   Using the Method getString

Although the method getString is recommended for retrieving the SQL types CHAR and VARCHAR, it is possible to retrieve any SQL type with it. Getting all values with getString can be very useful, but it also has its limitations. For instance, if it is used to retrieve a numeric type, getString will convert the numeric value to a Java String object, and the value will have to be converted back to a numeric type before it can be operated on as a number. In cases where the value will be treated as a string anyway, there is no drawback. Further, if you want an application to be able to retrieve values of any standard SQL type, the method to use is getString.

## 2.7    Updating Tables

Suppose that after a successful first week, the proprietor of The Coffee Break wants to update the SALES column in the table COFFEES by entering the number of pounds sold for each type of coffee. The SQL statement to update one row might look like this:

```
String updateString = "UPDATE COFFEES " +
                      "SET SALES = 75 " +
                      "WHERE COF_NAME LIKE 'Colombian'";
```

Using the Statement object *stmt*, this JDBC code executes the SQL statement contained in *updateString*:

```
stmt.executeUpdate(updateString);
```

The table COFFEES will now look like this:

| COF_NAME | SUP_ID | PRICE | SALES | TOTAL |
|----------|--------|-------|-------|-------|
| Colombian | 101 | 7.99 | 75 | 0 |
| French_Roast | 49 | 8.99 | 0 | 0 |
| Espresso | 150 | 9.99 | 0 | 0 |
| Colombian_Decaf | 101 | 8.99 | 0 | 0 |
| French_Roast_Decaf | 49 | 9.99 | 0 | 0 |

Note that we have not yet updated the column TOTAL, so it still has the value 0.

Now let's select the row we updated, retrieve the values in the columns COF_NAME and SALES, and print out those values:

```
String query = "SELECT COF_NAME, SALES FROM COFFEES " +
               "WHERE COF_NAME LIKE 'Colombian'";
ResultSet rs = stmt.executeQuery(query);
while (rs.next()) {
    String s = rs.getString("COF_NAME");
    int n = rs.getInt("SALES");
    System.out.println(n + " pounds of " + s + " sold this week.")
}
```

This will print the following:

➥ 75 pounds of Colombian sold this week.

Since the WHERE clause limited the selection to only one row, there was just one row in the ResultSet *rs* and one line printed as output. Accordingly, it is possible to write the code without a while loop:

```
rs.next();
String s = rs.getString(1);
int n = rs.getInt(2);
System.out.println(n + " pounds of " + s + " sold this week.")
```

Even when there is only one row in a result set, you need to use the method next to access it. A ResultSet object is created with a cursor pointing above the first row. The first call to the next method positions the cursor on the first (and in this case, only) row of *rs*. In this code, next is called only once, so if there happened to be another row, it would never be accessed.

Now let's update the TOTAL column by adding the weekly amount sold to the existing total, and then let's print out the number of pounds sold to date:

```
String updateString = "UPDATE COFFEES " +
                      "SET TOTAL = TOTAL + 75 " +
                          "WHERE COF_NAME LIKE 'Colombian'";
stmt.executeUpdate(updateString);

String query = "SELECT COF_NAME, TOTAL FROM COFFEES " +
               "WHERE COF_NAME LIKE 'Colombian'";
ResultSet rs = stmt.executeQuery(query);
while (rs.next()) {
    String s = rs.getString(1);
    int n = rs.getInt(2);
    System.out.println(n + " pounds of " + s + " sold to date.")
}
```

Note that in this example, we used the column index instead of the column name, supplying the index 1 to getString (the first column of the result set is COF_NAME), and the index 2 to getInt (the second column of the result set is TOTAL). It is important to distinguish between a column's index in the database table as opposed to its index in the result set table. For example, TOTAL is the fifth column in the table COFFEES but the second column in the result set generated by the query in the example above.

## 2.8    Milestone: The Basics of JDBC

You have just reached a milestone.

With what we have done so far, you have learned the basics of JDBC. You have seen how to create a table, insert values into it, query the table, retrieve results, and update the table. These are the nuts and bolts of using a database, and you can now utilize them in a Java program using JDBC. We have used only very simple queries in our examples so far, but as long as the driver and DBMS support them, you can send very complicated SQL queries using only the basic JDBC we have covered so far.

The rest of this chapter looks at how to use features that are a little more advanced: prepared statements, stored procedures, and transactions. It also illustrates warnings and exceptions and gives an example of how to convert a JDBC application into an applet. The final part of this chapter is sample code that you can run yourself.

## 2.9    Using Prepared Statements

Sometimes it is more convenient or more efficient to use a PreparedStatement object for sending SQL statements to the database. This special type of statement is derived from the more general class, Statement, that you already know.

### 2.9.1    When to Use a PreparedStatement Object

If you want to execute a Statement object many times, it will normally reduce execution time to use a PreparedStatement object instead.

The main feature of a PreparedStatement object is that, unlike a Statement object, it is given an SQL statement when it is created. The advantage to this is that in most cases, this SQL statement will be sent to the DBMS right away, where it will be compiled. As a result, the PreparedStatement object contains not just an SQL statement, but an SQL statement that has been precompiled. This means that when the PreparedStatement is executed, the DBMS can just run the Prepared-Statement's SQL statement without having to compile it first.

Although PreparedStatement objects can be used for SQL statements with no parameters, you will probably use them most often for SQL statements that take parameters. The advantage of using SQL statements that take parameters is that you can use the same statement and supply it with different values each time you execute it. You will see an example of this in the following sections.

### 2.9.2    Creating a **PreparedStatement** Object

As with Statement objects, you create PreparedStatement objects with a Connection method. Using our open connection *con* from previous examples, you might write code such as the following to create a PreparedStatement object that takes two input parameters:

```
PreparedStatement updateSales = con.prepareStatement(
        "UPDATE COFFEES SET SALES = ? WHERE COF_NAME LIKE ?");
```

The variable *updateSales* now contains the SQL statement, "UPDATE COFFEES SET SALES = ? WHERE COF_NAME LIKE ?", which has also, in most cases, been sent to the DBMS and been precompiled.

### 2.9.3    Supplying Values for **PreparedStatement** Parameters

You will need to supply values to be used in place of the question mark placeholders, if there are any, before you can execute a PreparedStatement object. You do this by calling one of the setXXX methods defined in the class PreparedStatement. If the value you want to substitute for a question mark is a Java int, you call the method setInt. If the value you want to substitute for a question mark is a Java String, you call the method setString, and so on. The methods you can use to set parameter values are listed in "PreparedStatement Methods" starting on page 282, but in general, there is a setXXX method for each Java type.

Using the PreparedStatement object *updateSales* from the previous example, the following line of code sets the first question mark placeholder to a Java int with a value of 75:

```
updateSales.setInt(1, 75);
```

As you might surmise from the example, the first argument given to a setXXX method indicates which question mark placeholder is to be set, and the second argument indicates the value to which it is to be set. The next example sets the second placeholder parameter to the string "Colombian":

```
updateSales.setString(2, "Colombian");
```

After these values have been set for its two input parameters, the SQL statement in *updateSales* will be equivalent to the SQL statement in the String object *updateString* that we used in the previous update example. Therefore, the following two code fragments accomplish the same thing:

Code Fragment 1:

```
String updateString = "UPDATE COFFEES SET SALES = 75 " +
                         "WHERE COF_NAME LIKE 'Colombian'";
stmt.executeUpdate(updateString);
```

Code Fragment 2:

```
PreparedStatement updateSales = con.prepareStatement(
        "UPDATE COFFEES SET SALES = ? WHERE COF_NAME LIKE ? ");
updateSales.setInt(1, 75);
updateSales.setString(2, "Colombian");
updateSales.executeUpdate():
```

We used the method executeUpdate to execute both the Statement *stmt* and the PreparedStatement *updateSales*. Notice, however, that no argument is supplied to executeUpdate when it is used to execute *updateSales*. This is true because *updateSales* already contains the SQL statement to be executed.

Looking at these examples, you might wonder why you would choose to use a PreparedStatement object with parameters instead of just a simple statement, since the simple statement involves fewer steps. If you were going to update the SALES column only once or twice, then there would be no need to use an SQL statement with input parameters. If you will be updating often, on the other hand, it might be much easier to use a PreparedStatement object, especially in situations where you can use a for loop or while loop to set a parameter to a succession of values. You will see an example of this later in this section.

Once a parameter has been set with a value, it will retain that value until it is reset to another value or the method clearParameters is called. Using the Prepared-Statement object *updateSales*, the following code fragment illustrates reusing a prepared statement after resetting the value of one of its parameters and leaving the other one the same:

```
updateSales.setInt(1, 100);
updateSales.setString(2, "French_Roast");
updateSales.executeUpdate();
// changes SALES column of French Roast row to 100


updateSales.setString(2, "Espresso");
updateSales.executeUpdate();
// changes SALES column of Espresso row to 100 (the first parameter
// stayed 100, and the second parameter was reset to "Espresso")
```

### 2.9.4    Using a Loop to Set Values

You can often make coding easier by using a for loop or a while loop to set values for input parameters.

The code fragment that follows demonstrates using a for loop to set values for parameters in the PreparedStatement object *updateSales*. The array *sales-ForWeek* holds the weekly sales amounts. These sales amounts correspond to the coffee names listed in the array *coffees*, so that the first amount in *salesForWeek* (175) applies to the first coffee name in *coffees* ("Colombian"), the second amount in *salesForWeek* (150) applies to the second coffee name in *coffees* ("French_Roast"), and so on. This code fragment demonstrates updating the SALES column for all the coffees in the table COFFEES:

```
PreparedStatement updateSales;
String updateString = "update COFFEES " +
                "set SALES = ? where COF_NAME like ?";
updateSales = con.prepareStatement(updateString);
int [] salesForWeek = {175, 150, 60, 155, 90};
String [] coffees = {"Colombian", "French_Roast", "Espresso",
                "Colombian_Decaf", "French_Roast_Decaf"};
int len = coffees.length;
for(int i = 0; i < len; i++) {
    updateSales.setInt(1, salesForWeek[i]);
    updateSales.setString(2, coffees[i]);
    updateSales.executeUpdate();
}
```

When the proprietor wants to update the sales amounts for the next week, he can use this same code as a template. All he has to do is enter the new sales amounts in the proper order in the array *salesForWeek*. The coffee names in the array *coffees* remain constant, so they do not need to be changed. (In a real application, the values would probably be input from the user rather than from an initialized Java array.)

### 2.9.5    Return Values for the Method `executeUpdate`

Whereas `executeQuery` returns a `ResultSet` object containing the results of the query sent to the DBMS, the return value for `executeUpdate` is an `int` that indicates how many rows of a table were updated. For instance, the following code shows the return value of `executeUpdate` being assigned to the variable *n* :

```
updateSales.setInt(1, 50);
updateSales.setString(2, "Espresso");
int n = updateSales.executeUpdate();
// n = 1 because one row had a change in it
```

The table `COFFEES` was updated by having the value `50` replace the value in the column `SALES` in the row for `Espresso`. That update affected one row in the table, so *n* is equal to 1.

When the method `executeUpdate` is used to execute a DDL statement, such as in creating a table, it returns the `int` `0`. Consequently, in the following code fragment, which executes the DDL statement used to create the table `COFFEES`, *n* will be assigned a value of `0`:

```
int n = executeUpdate(createTableCoffees); // n = 0
```

Note that when the return value for `executeUpdate` is 0, it can mean one of two things: (1) the statement executed was an update statement that affected zero rows, or (2) the statement executed was a DDL statement.

## 2.10  Using Joins

Sometimes you need to use two or more tables to get the data you want. For example, suppose the proprietor of The Coffee Break wants a list of the coffees he buys from Acme, Inc. This involves information in the `COFFEES` table as well as the yet-to-be-created SUPPLIERS table. This is a case where a *join* is needed. A join is a database operation that relates two or more tables by means of values that they share in common. In our example database, the tables COFFEES and SUPPLIERS both have the column SUP_ID, which can be used to join them.

Before we go any further, we need to create the table SUPPLIERS and populate it with values.

The code below creates the table SUPPLIERS:

```
String createSUPPLIERS = "create table SUPPLIERS (SUP_ID INTEGER, " +
    "SUP_NAME VARCHAR(40), STREET VARCHAR(40), CITY VARCHAR(20), " +
    "STATE CHAR(2), ZIP CHAR(5))";
stmt.executeUpdate(createSUPPLIERS);
```

The following code inserts rows for three suppliers into SUPPLIERS:

```
stmt.executeUpdate("insert into SUPPLIERS values (101, " +
    "'Acme, Inc.', '99 Market Street', 'Groundsville', " +
    "'CA', '95199'");
stmt.executeUpdate("Insert into SUPPLIERS values (49," +
    " 'Superior Coffee', '1 Party Place', 'Mendocino', 'CA', " +
    "'95460'");
stmt.executeUpdate("Insert into SUPPLIERS values (150, " +
    "'The High Ground', '100 Coffee Lane', 'Meadows', 'CA', '93966'");
```

The following code selects the whole table and lets us see what the table SUPPLIERS looks like:

```
ResultSet rs = stmt.executeQuery("select * from SUPPLIERS");
```

The result set will look similar to this:

| SUP_ID | SUP_NAME | STREET | CITY | STATE | ZIP |
|--------|----------|--------|------|-------|-----|
| 101 | Acme, Inc. | 99 Market Street | Groundsville | CA | 95199 |
| 49 | Superior Coffee | 1 Party Place | Mendocino | CA | 95460 |
| 150 | The High Ground | 100 Coffee Lane | Meadows | CA | 93966 |

Now that we have the tables COFFEES and SUPPLIERS, we can proceed with the scenario where the owner wants to get a list of the coffees he buys from a particular supplier. The names of the suppliers are in the table SUPPLIERS, and the names of the coffees are in the table COFFEES. Since both tables have the column SUP_ID, this column can be used in a join. It follows that you need some way to distinguish which SUP_ID column you are referring to. This is done by preceding the column name with the table name, as in "COFFEES.SUP_ID" to indicate that you mean the column SUP_ID in the table COFFEES. The following code, in which *stmt* is a Statement object, will select the coffees bought from Acme, Inc.:

```
String query = "SELECT COFFEES.COF_NAME " +
               "FROM COFFEES, SUPPLIERS " +
               "WHERE SUPPLIERS.SUP_NAME LIKE 'Acme, Inc.' and " +
               "SUPPLIERS.SUP_ID = COFFEES.SUP_ID";

ResultSet rs = stmt.executeQuery(query);
System.out.println("Coffees bought from Acme, Inc.: ");
while (rs.next()) {
    String coffeeName = getString("COF_NAME");
    System.out.println("     " + coffeeName);
}
```

This will produce the following output:

```
Coffees bought from Acme, Inc.:
      Colombian
      Colombian_Decaf
```

## 2.11 Using Transactions

There are times when you do not want one statement to take effect unless another one also succeeds. For example, when the proprietor of The Coffee Break updates the amount of coffee sold each week, he will also want to update the total amount sold to date. However, he will not want to update one without also updating the other; otherwise, the data will be inconsistent. The way to be sure that either both actions occur or neither action occurs is to use a *transaction*. A transaction is a set of one or more statements that are executed together as a unit, so either all of the statements are executed, or none of the statements is executed.

### 2.11.1   Disabling Auto-commit Mode

When a connection is created, it is in auto-commit mode. This means that each individual SQL statement is treated as a transaction and will be automatically committed right after it is executed. (To be more precise, the default is for an SQL statement to be committed when it is *completed*, not when it is *executed*. A statement is completed when all of its result sets and update counts have been retrieved. In almost all cases, however, a statement is completed, and therefore committed, right after it is executed.)

The way to allow two or more statements to be grouped into a transaction is to disable auto-commit mode. This is demonstrated in the following line of code, where *con* is an active connection:

```
con.setAutoCommit(false);
```

### 2.11.2   Committing a Transaction

Once auto-commit mode is disabled, no SQL statements will be committed until you call the method `commit` explicitly. All statements executed after the previous call to the method `commit` will be included in the current transaction and will be committed together as a unit. The following code, in which *con* is an active connection, illustrates a transaction:

```
con.setAutoCommit(false);
PreparedStatement updateSales = con.prepareStatement(
        "UPDATE COFFEES SET SALES = ? WHERE COF_NAME LIKE ?");
updateSales.setInt(1, 50);
updateSales.setString(2, "Colombian");
updateSales.executeUpdate();
PreparedStatement updateTotal = con.prepareStatement(
    "UPDATE COFFEES SET TOTAL = TOTAL + ? WHERE COF_NAME LIKE ?");
updateTotal.setInt(1, 50);
updateTotal.setString(2, "Colombian");
updateTotal.executeUpdate();
con.commit();
con.setAutoCommit(true);
```

In this example, auto-commit mode is disabled for the connection *con*, which means that the two prepared statements *updateSales* and *updateTotal* will be committed together when the method `commit` is called. Whenever the `commit` method is called (either automatically when auto-commit mode is enabled or explicitly when it is disabled), all changes resulting from statements in the transaction will be made permanent. In this case, that means that the `SALES` and `TOTAL` columns for Colombian coffee have been changed to 50 (if `TOTAL` had been 0 previously) and will retain this value until they are changed with another update statement. "Sample Code 6" on page 78 illustrates a similar kind of transaction but uses a `for` loop to supply values to the `setXXX` methods for *updateSales* and *updateTotal*.

The final line of the previous example enables auto-commit mode, which means that each statement will once again be committed automatically when it is completed. You will then be back to the default state where you do not have to call the method `commit` yourself. It is advisable to disable auto-commit mode only while you want to be in transaction mode. This way, database locks are not unnecessarily held for multiple statements, thereby increasing the likelihood of conflicts with other users.

### 2.11.3   Using Transactions to Preserve Data Integrity

In addition to grouping statements together for execution as a unit, transactions can help to preserve the integrity of the data in a table. For instance, suppose that an employee was supposed to enter new coffee prices in the table `COFFEES` but delayed doing it for a few days. In the meantime, prices rose, and today the owner is in the process of entering the higher prices. The employee finally gets around to entering the now outdated prices at the same time that the owner is trying to update the table. After inserting the outdated prices, the employee realizes that they are no longer valid and calls the `Connection` method `rollback` to undo their effects. (The method `rollback` aborts a transaction and restores values to what they were before the attempted update.) At the same time, the owner is executing a `SELECT` statement and printing out the new prices. In this situation, it is possible that the owner will print a price that was later rolled back to its previous value, making the printed price incorrect.

This kind of situation can be avoided by using transactions. If a DBMS supports transactions, and almost all of them do, it will provide some level of protection against conflicts that can arise when two users access data at the same time.

To avoid conflicts during a transaction, a DBMS will use *locks*, mechanisms for blocking access by others to the data that is being accessed by the transaction. (Note that in auto-commit mode, where each statement is a transaction, locks are held for only one statement.) Once a lock is set, it will remain in force until the transaction is committed or rolled back. For example, a DBMS could lock a row of a table until updates to it have been committed. The effect of this lock would be to prevent a user from getting a *dirty read*, that is, reading a value before it is made permanent. (Accessing an updated value that has not been committed is considered a dirty read because it is possible for that value to be rolled back to its previous value. If you read a value that is later rolled back, you will have read an invalid value.)

How locks are set is determined by what is called a *transaction isolation level*, which can range from not supporting transactions at all to supporting transactions that enforce very strict access rules.

One example of a transaction isolation level is TRANSACTION_READ_COMMITTED, which will not allow a value to be accessed until after it has been committed. In other words, if the transaction isolation level is set to TRANSACTION_READ_COMMITTED, the DBMS will not allow dirty reads to occur. The interface Connection includes five values which represent the transaction isolation levels you can use in JDBC. These are defined in "Connection Fields" starting on page 161.

Normally, you do not need to do anything about the transaction isolation level; you can just use the default one for your DBMS. JDBC allows you to find out what transaction isolation level your DBMS is set to (using the Connection method getTransactionIsolation) and also allows you to set it to another level (using the Connection method setTransactionIsolation). Keep in mind, however, that even though JDBC allows you to set a transaction isolation level, doing so will have no effect unless the driver and DBMS you are using support it. For those who need more information, the overview of the interface Connection, starting on page 143, explains transactions and transaction isolation levels in more detail.

### 2.11.4   When to Call the Method rollback

As mentioned earlier, calling the method rollback aborts a transaction and returns any values that were modified to their previous values. If you are trying to execute one or more statements in a transaction and get an SQLException, you should call the method rollback to abort the transaction and start the transaction all over again. That is the only way to be sure of what has been committed and what has not been committed. Catching an SQLException tells you that something is wrong, but it does not tell you what was or was not committed. Since you cannot count on the fact that nothing was committed, calling the method rollback is the only way to be sure.

"Sample Code 6" on page 78 demonstrates a transaction and includes a `catch` block that invokes the method `rollback`. In this particular situation, it is not really necessary to call `rollback`, and we do it mainly to illustrate how it is done. If the application continued and used the results of the transaction, however, it would be necessary to include a call to `rollback` in the `catch` block in order to protect against using possibly incorrect data.

## 2.12   Stored Procedures

A stored procedure is a group of SQL statements that form a logical unit and perform a particular task. Stored procedures are used to encapsulate a set of operations or queries to execute on a database server. For example, operations on an employee database (hire, fire, promote, lookup) could be coded as stored procedures executed by application code. Stored procedures can be compiled and executed with different parameters and results, and they may have any combination of input, output, and input/output parameters.

Stored procedures are supported by most DBMSs, but there is a fair amount of variation in their syntax and capabilities. For this reason, we will show you a simple example of what a stored procedure looks like and how it is invoked from JDBC, but this sample is not intended to be run.

### 2.12.1   SQL Statements for Creating a Stored Procedure

This section looks at a very simple stored procedure that has no parameters. Even though most stored procedures do something more complex than this example, it serves to illustrate some basic points about them. As previously stated, the syntax for defining a stored procedure is different for each DBMS. For example, some use `begin . . .` end or other keywords to indicate the beginning and ending of the procedure definition. In some DBMSs, the following SQL statement creates a stored procedure:

```
create procedure SHOW_SUPPLIERS
as
select SUPPLIERS.SUP_NAME, COFFEES.COF_NAME
from SUPPLIERS, COFFEES
where SUPPLIERS.SUP_ID = COFFEES.SUP_ID
order by SUP_NAME
```

The following code puts the SQL statement into a string and assigns it to the variable *createProcedure*, which we will use later:

```
String createProcedure = "create procedure SHOW_SUPPLIERS " +
                "as " +
                "select SUPPLIERS.SUP_NAME, COFFEES.COF_NAME " +
                "from SUPPLIERS, COFFEES " +
                "where SUPPLIERS.SUP_ID = COFFEES.SUP_ID " +
                "order by SUP_NAME";
```

The following code fragment uses the Connection object *con* to create a Statement object, which is used to send the SQL statement creating the stored procedure to the database:

```
Statement stmt = con.createStatement();
stmt.executeUpdate(createProcedure);
```

The procedure SHOW_SUPPLIERS will be compiled and then stored in the database as a database object that can be called, similar to the way you would call a method.

### 2.12.2  Calling a Stored Procedure from JDBC

JDBC allows you to call a database stored procedure from a Java program. The first step is to create a CallableStatement object. As with Statement and Prepared-Statement objects, this is done with an open Connection object. A CallableState-ment object contains a *call* to a stored procedure; it does not contain the stored procedure itself. The first line of code below creates a call to the stored procedure SHOW_SUPPLIERS using the connection *con*. The part that is enclosed in curly braces is the escape syntax for stored procedures. When the driver encounters "{call SHOW_SUPPLIERS}", it will translate this escape syntax into the native SQL used by the database to call the stored procedure named SHOW_SUPPLIERS.

```
CallableStatement cs = con.prepareCall("{call SHOW_SUPPLIERS}");
ResultSet rs = cs.executeQuery();
```

The ResultSet *rs* will be similar to the following:

| SUP_NAME | COF_NAME |
| --- | --- |
| Acme, Inc. | Colombian |
| Acme, Inc. | Colombian_Decaf |
| Superior Coffee | French_Roast |
| Superior Coffee | French_Roast_Decaf |
| The High Ground | Espresso |

Note that the method used to execute `cs` is `executeQuery` because `cs` calls a stored procedure that contains one query and thus produces one result set. If the procedure had contained one update or one DDL statement, the method `execute-Update` would have been the one to use. It is sometimes the case, however, that a stored procedure contains more than one SQL statement, in which case it will produce more than one result set, more than one update count, or some combination of result sets and update counts. In this case, where there are multiple results, the method `execute` should be used to execute the `CallableStatement`. The section "Using the Method execute" on page 348 explains how to use this method and retrieve all results.

The class `CallableStatement` is a subclass of `PreparedStatement`, so a `CallableStatement` object can take input parameters just as a `PreparedStatement` object can. In addition, a `CallableStatement` object can take output parameters or parameters that are for both input and output. Check "CallableStatement Overview" on page 129 and "SQL Statement with INOUT Parameters" on page 388 for examples and more detailed information.

## 2.13 Creating Complete JDBC Applications

Up to this point, you have seen only code fragments. Later in this chapter you will see sample programs that are complete applications you can run.

The first sample code creates the table COFFEES; the second one inserts values into the table and prints the results of a query. The third application creates the table SUPPLIERS, and the fourth populates it with values. After you have run this code, you can try a query that is a join between the tables COFFEES and SUPPLIERS, as in the fifth code example. The sixth code sample is an application that demonstrates a transaction and also shows how to set placeholder parameters in a PreparedStatement object using a for loop.

Because they are complete applications, they include some elements of the Java programming language we have not shown before in the code fragments. We will explain these elements briefly here, but if you need more explanation, you should refer to one of the many books on Java. We especially recommend *The Java™ Tutorial,* by MaryCampione and Kathy Walrath, and *The Java™ Language Specification,* by James Gosling, Bill Joy, and Guy Steele. Both books are published by Addison-Wesley.

### 2.13.1   Putting Code in a Class Definition

In Java, any code you want to execute must be inside a class definition. You type the class definition in a file and give the file the name of the class with .java appended to it. So if you have a class named MySQLStatement, its definition should be in a file named MySQLStatement.java.

### 2.13.2   Importing Classes to Make Them Visible

The first thing to do is to import the packages or classes you will be using in the new class. The classes in our examples all use the java.sql package (the JDBC API), which is made available when the following line of code precedes the class definition:

```
import java.sql.*;
```

The star (*) indicates that all of the classes in the package java.sql are to be imported. Importing a class makes it visible and means that you do not have to write out the fully qualified name when you use a method or field from that class. If you do not include "import java.sql.*;" in your code, you will have to write "java.sql." plus the class name in front of all the JDBC fields or methods you use every time you use them. Note that you can import individual classes selectively rather than a whole package. Java does not require that you import classes or packages, but doing so makes writing code a lot more convenient.

Any lines importing classes appear at the top of all the code samples, as they must if they are going to make the imported classes visible to the class being defined. The actual class definition follows any lines that import classes.

### 2.13.3  Using the `main` Method

If a class is to be executed, it must contain a `static` `public` `main` method. This method comes right after the line declaring the class and invokes the other methods in the class. The keyword `static` indicates that this method operates on a class level rather than on individual instances of a class. The keyword `public` means that members of any class can access this method. Since we are not just defining classes to be used by other classes but instead want to run them, the example applications in this chapter all include a `main` method. Chapter 3 has an example of a class that is used by another class rather than running by itself; this class, in "Sample Code 10 and 11" on page 94, does not have a `main` method.

### 2.13.4  Using `try` and `catch` Blocks

Something else all the sample applications include is `try` and `catch` blocks. These are the Java programming language's mechanism for handling exceptions. Java requires that when a method throws an exception, there be some mechanism to handle it. Generally a `catch` block will catch the exception and specify what happens (which you may choose to be nothing). In the sample code, we use two `try` blocks and two `catch` blocks. The first `try` block contains the method `Class.forName`, from the `java.lang` package. This method throws a `ClassNotFoundException`, so the `catch` block immediately following it deals with that exception. The second `try` block contains JDBC methods, which all throw `SQLExceptions`, so one `catch` block at the end of the application can handle all of the rest of the exceptions that might be thrown because they will all be `SQLException` objects.

### 2.13.5  Retrieving Exceptions

JDBC lets you see the warnings and exceptions generated by your DBMS and by the Java compiler. To see exceptions, you can have a `catch` block print them out. For example, the following two `catch` blocks from the sample code print out a message explaining the exception:

```
try {
    // Code that could generate an exception goes here.
    // If an exception is generated, the catch block below
    // will print out information about it.
} catch(SQLException ex) {
    System.err.println("SQLException: " + ex.getMessage());
}
```

```
try {
    Class.forName("myDriverClassName");
} catch(java.lang.ClassNotFoundException e) {
    System.err.print("ClassNotFoundException: ");
    System.err.println(e.getMessage());
}
```

If you were to run CreateCOFFEES.java twice, you would get an error message similar to this:

```
SQLException: There is already an object named 'COFFEES' in the da-
tabase.
Severity 16, State 1, Line 1
```

This example illustrates printing out the message component of an SQLException object, which is sufficient for most situations.

There are actually three components, however, and to be complete, you can print them all out. The following code fragment shows a catch block that is complete in two ways. First, it prints out all three parts of an SQLException object: the message (a string that describes the error), the SQL state (a string identifying the error according to the X/Open SQLState conventions), and the vendor error code (a number that is the driver vendor's error code number). The SQLException object *ex* is caught, and its three components are accessed with the methods get-Message, getSQLState, and getErrorCode.

The second way the following catch block is complete is that it gets all of the exceptions that might have been thrown. If there is a second exception, it will be chained to *ex*, so ex.getNextException is called to see if there is another exception. If there is, the while loop continues and prints out the next exception's message, SQLState, and vendor error code. This continues until there are no more exceptions.

```
try {
    // Code that could generate an exception goes here.
    // If an exception is generated, the catch block below
    // will print out information about it.
} catch(SQLException ex) {
    System.out.println("\n--- SQLException caught ---\n");
    while (ex != null) {
```

```
            System.out.println("Message:     " + ex.getMessage ());
            System.out.println("SQLState:    " + ex.getSQLState ());
            System.out.println("ErrorCode:   " + ex.getErrorCode ());
            ex = ex.getNextException();
            System.out.println("");
        }
    }
```

If you were to substitute the catch block above into Sample Code 1 (Create-Coffees) and run it after the table COFFEES had already been created, you would get the following printout:

```
--- SQLException caught ---

Message:  There is already an object named 'COFFEES' in the
database.
Severity 16, State 1, Line 1
SQLState: 42501
ErrorCode:   2714
```

SQLState is a code defined in X/Open and ANSI–92 that identifies the exception. Two examples of SQLState code numbers and their meanings follow:

```
08001 - No suitable driver
HY011 - Operation invalid at this time
```

The vendor error code is specific to each driver, so you need to check your driver documentation for a list of error codes and what they mean.

### 2.13.6  Retrieving Warnings

SQLWarning objects are a subclass of SQLException that deal with database access warnings. Warnings do not stop the execution of an application, as exceptions do; they simply alert the user that something did not happen as planned. For example, a warning might let you know that a privilege you attempted to revoke was not revoked. Or a warning might tell you that an error occurred during a requested disconnection.

A warning can be reported on a Connection object, a Statement object (including PreparedStatement and CallableStatement objects), or a ResultSet object. Each of these classes has a getWarnings method, which you must invoke in order to see the first warning reported on the calling object. If getWarning returns a warning, you can call the SQLWarning method getNextWarning on it to get any additional warnings. Executing a statement automatically clears the warnings from a previous statement, so they do not build up. This means, however, that if you want to retrieve warnings reported on a statement, you must do so before you execute another statement. You can get more information on warnings in the chapter "SQLWarning" on page 337.

The following code fragment illustrates how to get complete information about any warnings reported on the Statement object *stmt* and also on the ResultSet object *rs*:

```
Statement stmt = con.createStatement();
ResultSet rs = stmt.executeQuery("select COF_NAME from COFFEES");
while (rs.next()) {
    String coffeeName = rs.getString("COF_NAME");
    System.out.println("Coffees available at the Coffee Break:  ");
    System.out.println("     " + coffeeName);
    SQLWarning warning = stmt.getWarnings();
    if (warning != null) {
        System.out.println("\n---Warning---\n");
        while (warning != null) {
            System.out.println("Message: " + warning.getMessage());
            System.out.println("SQLState: " + warning.getSQLState());
            System.out.print("Vendor error code: ");
            System.out.println(warning.getErrorCode());
            System.out.println("");
            warning = warning.getNextWarning();
        }
    }
    SQLWarning warn = rs.getWarnings();
    if (warn != null) {
        System.out.println("\n---Warning---\n");
        while (warn != null) {
            System.out.println("Message: " + warn.getMessage());
            System.out.println("SQLState: " + warn.getSQLState());
            System.out.print("Vendor error code: ");
```

```
            System.out.println(warn.getErrorCode());
            System.out.println("");
            warn = warn.getNextWarning();
        }
    }
}
```

Warnings are actually rather uncommon. Of those that are reported, by far the most common warning is a `DataTruncation` warning, a subclass of `SQLWarning`. All `DataTruncation` objects have an SQLState of `01004`, indicating that there was a problem with reading or writing data. `DataTruncation` methods let you find out in which column or parameter data was truncated, whether the truncation was on a read or write operation, how many bytes should have been transferred, and how many bytes were actually transferred. See "DataTruncation" on page 247 if you want more information.

## 2.14  Running the Sample Applications

You are now ready to actually try out some sample code. The directory `book.html` contains complete, runnable applications that illustrate concepts presented in this chapter and the next. You can download this sample code from the JDBC web site located at:

```
http://www.javasoft.com/products/jdbc/book.html
```

Before you can run one of these applications, you will need to edit the file by substituting the appropriate information for the following variables:

*url*—the JDBC URL; parts one and two are supplied by your driver, and the third part specifies your data source

*myLogin*—your login name or user name

*myPassword*—your password for the DBMS

*myDriver.ClassName*—the class name supplied with your driver

The first example application is the class `CreateCoffees`, which is in a file named `CreateCoffees.java`. Below are instructions for running `CreateCoffees.java` on the three major platforms.

The first line in the instructions below compiles the code in the file Create-Coffees.java. If the compilation is successful, it will produce a file named CreateCoffees.class, which contains the bytecodes translated from the file CreateCoffees.java. These bytecodes will be interpreted by the Java Virtual Machine, which is what makes it possible for Java code to run on any machine with a Java Virtual Machine installed on it.

The second line of code is what actually makes the code run. Note that you use the name of the class, CreateCoffees, *not* the name of the file, Create-Coffees.class.

### UNIX

```
javac CreateCoffees.java
java CreateCoffees
```

### Windows 95/NT

```
javac CreateCoffees.java
java CreateCoffees
```

### MacOS

Drag the CreateCoffees.java file icon onto the Java Compiler icon
Double-click the CreateCoffees.class file icon

## 2.15  Sample Code

As stated previously, you will find the .java files for these applications on the JDBC web page at the following URL:

```
http://www.javasoft.com/products/jdbc/book.html
```

Much of this code should look familiar because the code samples incorporate JDBC code fragments used in earlier examples.

### 2.15.1  Sample Code 1 and 2

Sample Code 1 is `CreateCoffees.java`, and Sample Code 2 is `InsertCoffees.java`. After you have created the table `COFFEES` with Sample Code 1, you can use Sample Code 2 to populate it with values.

You create the table `COFFEES` by simply running the application `CreateCoffees.java`, (the first sample code below), following the steps previously described in "Running the Sample Applications" on page 67. `CreateCoffees.java` uses standard SQL data types and will work for most DBMSs.

It is possible that your DBMS uses nonstandard names for data types or that it uses its own types that are specific to it. Because of this possibility, we have provided an application, called `SQLTypesCreate.java`, that will discover the local type names for you and then use them to create your table. You will find this application and its explanation starting on page 117, but do not feel that you need to understand it before you can run it. Even though it contains some features that are not explained until later, running it is quite easy, as you will see.

Before running `SQLTypesCreate.java`, you will need to modify it by substituting the appropriate URL, login name, password, and driver class name, as is true with all of the sample code. Then, on Solaris and Windows platforms, run the application by typing the following two lines at the command line:

```
javac SQLTypesCreate.java
java SQLTypesCreate
```

On a Macintosh platform, you drag the `SQLTypesCreate.java` icon onto the Java compiler icon and then double-click the `SQLTypesCreate.class` file icon.

The application will prompt you for the table name, column names, and column types. You just type the following after the appropriate prompts:

```
COFFEES
COF_NAME
VARCHAR
32
SUP_ID
INTEGER
PRICE
FLOAT
SALES
```

```
INTEGER
TOTAL
INTEGER
```

The output from SQLTypesCreate is printed after the application. This output shows what you will see on the screen when you run the application, and it also includes the responses you need to type (the responses just listed) in order to create the table we use in later applications.

After you have created the table COFFEES, you are ready to run InsertCoffees.java, which inserts values into COFFEES, sends a select statement, retrieves the results of the query, and prints out the results. If you ran CreateCoffees.java and got no results after running InsertCoffees.java, your DBMS probably did not create the table COFFEES. Try creating the table again by running SQLTypesCreate.java and then run InsertCoffees.java again.

The file CreateCoffees.java follows:

```java
import java.sql.*;

public class CreateCoffees {

    public static void main(String args[]) {

        String url = "jdbc:mySubprotocol:myDataSource";
        Connection con;
        String createString;
        createString = "create table COFFEES " +
                       "(COF_NAME VARCHAR(32), " +
                       "SUP_ID INTEGER, " +
                       "PRICE FLOAT, " +
                       "SALES INTEGER, " +
                       "TOTAL INTEGER)";
        Statement stmt;

        try {
            Class.forName("myDriver.ClassName");
```

```
        } catch(java.lang.ClassNotFoundException e) {
            System.err.print("ClassNotFoundException: ");
            System.err.println(e.getMessage());
        }

        try {
            con = DriverManager.getConnection(url,
                                "myLogin", "myPassword");

            stmt = con.createStatement();
            stmt.executeUpdate(createString);

            stmt.close();
            con.close();

        } catch(SQLException ex) {
            System.err.println("SQLException: " + ex.getMessage());
        }
    }
}
```

The file `InsertCoffees.java` follows:

```
import java.sql.*;

public class InsertCoffees {

    public static void main(String args[]) {

        String url = "jdbc:mySubprotocol:myDataSource";
        Connection con;
        Statement stmt;
        String query = "select COF_NAME, PRICE from COFFEES";

        try {
            Class.forName("myDriver.ClassName");
```

```java
    } catch(java.lang.ClassNotFoundException e) {
        System.err.print("ClassNotFoundException: ");
        System.err.println(e.getMessage());
    }

    try {

        con = DriverManager.getConnection(url,
                            "myLogin", "myPassword");

        stmt = con.createStatement();

        stmt.executeUpdate("insert into COFFEES " +
            "values('Colombian', 101, 7.99, 0, 0)");

        stmt.executeUpdate("insert into COFFEES " +
            "values('French_Roast', 49, 8.99, 0, 0)");

        stmt.executeUpdate("insert into COFFEES " +
            "values('Espresso', 150, 9.99, 0, 0)");

        stmt.executeUpdate("insert into COFFEES " +
            "values('Colombian_Decaf', 101, 8.99, 0, 0)");

        stmt.executeUpdate("insert into COFFEES " +
            "values('French_Roast_Decaf', 49, 9.99, 0, 0)");

        ResultSet rs = stmt.executeQuery(query);

        System.out.println("Coffee Break Coffees and Prices:");
        while (rs.next()) {
            String s = rs.getString("COF_NAME");
            float f = rs.getFloat("PRICE");
            System.out.println(s + "    " + f);
        }

        stmt.close();
        con.close();
```

```
        } catch(SQLException ex) {
            System.err.println("SQLException: " + ex.getMessage());
        }
    }
}
```

The printout for `InsertCoffees.java` looks like this:

➥ Coffee Break Coffees and Prices:
➥ Colombian    7.99
➥ French_Roast    8.99
➥ Espresso    9.99
➥ Colombian_Decaf    8.99
➥ French_Roast_Decaf    9.99

## 2.15.2 Sample Code 3 and 4

Sample Code 3 is `CreateSuppliers.java`, and Sample Code 4 is `InsertSuppliers.java`. These applications are similar to Sample Code 1 and 2 except that `CreateSuppliers.java` creates the table SUPPLIERS, and `InsertSuppliers.java` populates the table SUPPLIERS.

If you needed to use the generic application `SQLTypesCreate` to create the table COFFEES, you will also need to use it to create the table SUPPLIERS. Follow the same directions, using the following responses:

SUPPLIERS
SUP_NAME
VARCHAR
40
STREET
VARCHAR
40
CITY
VARCHAR
20
STATE

```
CHAR
2
ZIP
CHAR
5
```

Here is the file CreateSuppliers.java:

```java
import java.sql.*;

public class CreateSuppliers {

    public static void main(String args[]) {

        String url = "jdbc:mySubprotocol:myDataSource";
        Connection con;
        String createString;
        createString = "create table SUPPLIERS " +
                    "(SUP_ID INTEGER, " +
                    "SUP_NAME VARCHAR(40), " +
                    "STREET VARCHAR(40), " +
                    "CITY VARCHAR(20), " +
                    "STATE CHAR(2), ZIP CHAR(5))";

        Statement stmt;

        try {
            Class.forName("myDriver.ClassName");

        } catch(java.lang.ClassNotFoundException e) {
            System.err.print("ClassNotFoundException: ");
            System.err.println(e.getMessage());
        }

        try {
            con = DriverManager.getConnection(url,
                            "myLogin", "myPassword");
```

```
        stmt = con.createStatement();
        stmt.executeUpdate(createString);

        stmt.close();
        con.close();

    } catch(SQLException ex) {
        System.err.println("SQLException: " + ex.getMessage());
    }

  }

}
```

The following code, found in the file InsertSuppliers.java, inserts values into the table SUPPLIERS, queries for the name and supplier identification number for each of the suppliers, and prints out the results.

```
import java.sql.*;

public class InsertSuppliers {

    public static void main(String args[]) {

        String url = "jdbc:mySubprotocol:myDataSource";
        Connection con;
        Statement stmt;
        String query = "select SUP_NAME, SUP_ID from SUPPLIERS";

        try {
            Class.forName("myDriver.ClassName");

        } catch(java.lang.ClassNotFoundException e) {
            System.err.print("ClassNotFoundException: ");
            System.err.println(e.getMessage());
        }
```

```java
    try {
        con = DriverManager.getConnection(url,
                            "myLogin", "myPassword");

        stmt = con.createStatement();

        stmt.executeUpdate("insert into SUPPLIERS " +
            "values(49, 'Superior Coffee', '1 Party Place', " +
            "'Mendocino', 'CA', '95460')");

        stmt.executeUpdate("insert into SUPPLIERS " +
            "values(101, 'Acme, Inc.', '99 Market Street', " +
            "'Groundsville', 'CA', '95199')");

        stmt.executeUpdate("insert into SUPPLIERS " +
            "values(150, 'The High Ground', '100 Coffee Lane', " +
            "'Meadows', 'CA', '93966')");

        ResultSet rs = stmt.executeQuery(query);

        System.out.println("Suppliers and their ID Numbers:");
        while (rs.next()) {
            String s = rs.getString("SUP_NAME");
            int n = rs.getInt("SUP_ID");
            System.out.println(s + "    " + n);
        }

        stmt.close();
        con.close();

    } catch(SQLException ex) {
        System.err.println("SQLException: " + ex.getMessage());
    }
}
}
```

The printout for InsertSuppliers.java follows:

➥ Suppliers and their ID Numbers:
➥ Superior Coffee   49
➥ Acme, Inc.   101
➥ The High Ground   150

### 2.15.3  Sample Code 5

Sample Code 5 is the file Join.java. This application does a simple join between the tables COFFEES and SUPPLIERS. It should look familiar because it incorrporates an example used previously into a runnable program. Here is the file Join.java:

```java
import java.sql.*;

public class Join {

    public static void main(String args[]) {

        String url = "jdbc:mySubprotocol:myDataSource";
        Connection con;
        String query = "select SUPPLIERS.SUP_NAME, COFFEES.COF_NAME " +
                    "from COFFEES, SUPPLIERS " +
                    "where SUPPLIERS.SUP_NAME like 'Acme, Inc.' and " +
                    "SUPPLIERS.SUP_ID = COFFEES.SUP_ID";
        Statement stmt;

        try {
            Class.forName("myDriver.ClassName");

        } catch(java.lang.ClassNotFoundException e) {
            System.err.print("ClassNotFoundException: ");
            System.err.println(e.getMessage());
        }

        try {
            con = DriverManager.getConnection (url,
                                "myLogin", "myPassword");

            stmt = con.createStatement();
```

```
            ResultSet rs = stmt.executeQuery(query);
            System.out.println("Supplier, Coffee:");
            while (rs.next()) {
                String supName = rs.getString(1);
                String cofName = rs.getString(2);
                System.out.println("     " + supName + ", " + cofName);
            }

            stmt.close();
            con.close();

        } catch(SQLException ex) {
            System.err.print("SQLException: ");
            System.err.println(ex.getMessage());
        }
    }
}
```

The output of Join.java looks like this:

```
➡ Supplier, Coffee:
➡     Acme, Inc., Colombian
➡     Acme, Inc., Colombian_Decaf
```

### 2.15.4  Sample Code 6

Sample Code 6 is the file TransactionPairs.java. This application uses two PreparedStatement objects, one to update the SALES column and one to update the TOTAL column. The values for the input parameters are set using a for loop that iterates through an array. Refer back to "Using a Loop to Set Values" on page 52 for a more thorough explanation.

In TransactionPairs.java there are five transactions, each occurring in one iteration through the for loop. In each iteration, the values for the input parameters are set, the two prepared statements are executed, and the method commit is called. Thus, each iteration constitutes a transaction, ensuring that neither *updateTotal* nor *updateSales* will be committed unless the other is committed.

This code invokes the method con.rollback in a catch block, which is explained in the section "When to Call the Method rollback" on page 58. Because of that, we initialized the Connection object *con* to null. Then in the catch block, we tested to see if *con* is still null. If it is, a connection was never even established, and the exception being caught is a result of that failure. In other words, *con* was not assigned a value in the following statement: con = DriverManager.getConnection(url, "myLogin", "myPassword"). Consequently, it is not necessary to call the method rollback because nothing was committed. If *con* had not originally been set to null, the Java compiler would have complained that *con* might not have been initialized.

Here is TransactionPairs.java:

```java
import java.sql.*;

public class TransactionPairs {

    public static void main(String args[]) {

        String url = "jdbc:mySubprotocol:myDataSource";
        Connection con = null;
        Statement stmt;
        PreparedStatement updateSales;
        PreparedStatement updateTotal;
        String updateString = "update COFFEES " +
                    "set SALES = ? where COF_NAME like ?";

        String updateStatement = "update COFFEES " +
                "set TOTAL = TOTAL + ? where COF_NAME like ?";
        String query = "select COF_NAME, SALES, TOTAL from COFFEES";

        try {
            Class.forName("myDriver.ClassName");

        } catch(java.lang.ClassNotFoundException e) {
            System.err.print("ClassNotFoundException: ");
            System.err.println(e.getMessage());
        }
```

```
try {

    con = DriverManager.getConnection(url,
                        "myLogin", "myPassword");

    updateSales = con.prepareStatement(updateString);
    updateTotal = con.prepareStatement(updateStatement);
    int [] salesForWeek = {175, 150, 60, 155, 90};
    String [] coffees = {"Colombian", "French_Roast",
                    "Espresso", "Colombian_Decaf",
                    "French_Roast_Decaf"};
    int len = coffees.length;
    con.setAutoCommit(false);
    for (int i = 0; i < len; i++) {
        updateSales.setInt(1, salesForWeek[i]);
        updateSales.setString(2, coffees[i]);
        updateSales.executeUpdate();

        updateTotal.setInt(1, salesForWeek[i]);
        updateTotal.setString(2, coffees[i]);
        updateTotal.executeUpdate();
        con.commit();
    }

    con.setAutoCommit(true);

    updateSales.close();
    updateTotal.close();

    stmt = con.createStatement();
    ResultSet rs = stmt.executeQuery(query);

    while (rs.next()) {
        String c = rs.getString("COF_NAME");
        int s = rs.getInt("SALES");
        int t = rs.getInt("TOTAL");
        System.out.println(c + "      " + s + "      " + t);
    }
```

```
        stmt.close();
        con.close();

    } catch(SQLException ex) {
        System.err.println("SQLException: " + ex.getMessage());
        if (con != null) {
            try {
                System.err.print("Transaction is being ");
                System.err.println("rolled back");
                con.rollback();
            } catch(SQLException excep) {
                System.err.print("SQLException: ");
                System.err.println(excep.getMessage());
            }
        }
    }
}
```

When the initial values for SALES and TOTAL are 0, the output looks like this:

```
➡ Colombian          175        175
➡ French_Roast          150        150
➡ Espresso         60      60
➡ Colombian_Decaf        155        155
➡ French_Roast_Decaf        90         90
```

If you were to run TransactionPairs a second time, the printout would be:

```
➡ Colombian          175        350
➡ French_Roast          150        300
➡ Espresso         60     120
➡ Colombian_Decaf        155        310
➡ French_Roast_Decaf        90        180
```

## 2.16  Creating an Applet from an Application

Suppose that the owner of The Coffee Break wants to display his current coffee prices in an applet on his web page. He can be sure of always displaying the most current price by having the applet get the price directly from his database.

In order to do this, he needs to create two files of code, one with applet code, and one with HTML code. The applet code contains the JDBC code that would appear in a regular application plus additional code for running the applet and displaying the results of the database query. In our example, the applet code is in the file OutputApplet.java. To display our applet in an HTML page, the file OutputApplet.html tells the browser what to display and where to display it.

The rest of this section will tell you about various elements found in applet code that are not present in standalone application code. Some of these elements involve advanced aspects of the Java programming language. We will give you some rationale and some basic explanation, but explaining them fully is beyond the scope of this book. For purposes of this sample applet, you only need to grasp the general idea, so don't worry if you don't understand everything. You can use the applet code as a template, substituting your own queries for the one in the applet.

### 2.16.1  Writing Applet Code

To begin with, applets will import classes not used by standalone applications. Our applet imports two classes that are special to applets: the class Applet, which is part of the java.applet package, and the class Graphics, which is part of the java.awt package. This applet also imports the general-purpose class java.util.Vector so that we have access to an array-like container whose size can be modified. This code uses Vector objects to store query results so that they can be displayed later.

All applets extend the Applet class; that is, they are subclasses of Applet. Therefore, every applet definition must contain the words extends Applet, as shown here:

```
public class MyAppletName extends Applet {
  . . .
}
```

In our applet example, this line also includes the words implements Runnable, so it looks like this:

```
public class OutputApplet extends Applet implements Runnable {
  . . .
}
```

Runnable is an interface that makes it possible to run more than one *thread* at a time. A thread is a sequential flow of control, and it is possible for a program to be multithreaded, that is, to have many threads doing different things concurrently. (We introduced this concept in "Java Is Multithreaded" on page 24.) The class OutputApplet implements Runnable by defining the method run, Runnable's only method. In our example the run method contains the JDBC code for opening a connection, executing a query, and getting the results from the result set. Since database connections can be slow, and can sometimes take several seconds, it is generally a good idea to structure an applet so that it can handle the database work in a separate thread.

Similar to a standalone application, which must have a main method, an applet must implement at least one init, start, or paint method. Our example applet defines a start method and a paint method. Every time start is invoked, it creates a new thread (named *worker*) to re-evaluate the database query. Every time paint is invoked, it displays either the query results or a string describing the current status of the applet.

As stated previously, the run method defined in OutputApplet contains the JDBC code. When the thread *worker* invokes the method start, the run method is called automatically, and it executes the JDBC code in the thread *worker*. The code in run is very similar to the code you have seen in our other sample code with three exceptions. First, it uses the class Vector to store the results of the query. Second, it does not print out the results but rather adds them to the Vector *results* for display later. Third, it likewise does not print out exceptions and instead records error messages for later display.

Applets have various ways of drawing, or displaying, their content. This applet, a very simple one that has only text, uses the method drawString (part of the Graphics class) to display its text. The method drawString takes three arguments: (1) the string to be displayed, (2) the x coordinate, indicating the horizontal starting point for displaying the string, and (3) the y coordinate, indicating the vertical starting point for displaying the string (which is below the text).

The method paint is what actually displays something on the screen, and in OutputApplet.java, it is defined to contain calls to the method drawString. The main thing drawString displays is the contents of the Vector *results* (the stored query results). When there are no query results to display, drawString will display the current contents of the String *message*. This string will be "Initializing" to begin with. It gets set to "Connecting to database" when the method start is called, and the method setError sets it to an error message when an exception is caught. Thus, if the database connection takes much time, the person viewing this applet will see the message "Connecting to database" because that will be the contents of *message* at that time. (The method `paint` is called by AWT when it wants the applet to display its current state on the screen.)

The last two methods defined in the class `OutputApplet`, `setError` and `setResults` are private, which means that they can be used only by `OutputApplet`. These methods both invoke the method `repaint`, which clears the screen and calls `paint`. So if `setResults` calls `repaint`, the query results will be displayed, and if `setError` calls `repaint`, an error message will be displayed.

A final point to be made is that all the methods defined in `OutputApplet` except `run` are *synchronized*. The keyword `synchronized` indicates that while a method is accessing an object, other `synchronized` methods are blocked from accessing that object. The method `run` is not declared `synchronized` so that the applet can still paint itself on the screen while the database connection is in progress. If the database access methods were `synchronized`, they would prevent the applet from being repainted while they are executing, and that could result in delays with no accompanying status message.

To summarize, in an applet, it is good programming practice to do some things you would not need to do in a standalone application:

1. Put your JDBC code in a separate thread

2. Display status messages on the screen during during any delays, such as when a database connection is taking a long time

3. Display error messages on the screen instead of printing them to `System.out` or `System.err`.

### 2.16.2  Running an Applet

Before running our sample applet, you need to compile the file `OutputApplet.java`. This creates the file `OutputApplet.class`, which is referenced by the file `OutputApplet.html`.

The easiest way to run an applet is to use the appletviewer, which is included as part of the JDK. Simply follow the instructions below for your platform to compile and run `OutputApplet.java`:

### UNIX

```
javac OutputApplet.java
appletviewer OutputApplet.html
```

**Windows 95/NT**

```
javac OutputApplet.java
appletviewer OutputApplet.html
```

**MacOS**

Drag the `OutputApplet.java` file icon onto the Java Compiler icon
Drag the `OutputApplet.html` file icon onto the appletviewer icon

Applets loaded over the network are subject to various security restrictions. Although this can seem bothersome at times, it is absolutely necessary for network security, and security is one of the major advantages of programming with Java. An applet cannot make network connections except to the host it came from unless the browser allows it. Whether one is able to treat locally installed applets as "trusted" also depends on the security restrictions imposed by the browser. An applet cannot ordinarily read or write files on the host that is executing it, and it cannot load libraries or define native methods.

Applets can usually make network connections to the host they came from, so they can work very well on intranets.

The JDBC–ODBC Bridge driver is a somewhat special case. It can be used quite successfully for intranet access, but it requires that ODBC, the bridge, the bridge native library, and JDBC be installed on every client. With this configuration, intranet access works from Java applications and from trusted applets. However, since the bridge requires special client configuration, it is not practical to run applets on the Internet with the JDBC–ODBC Bridge driver. Note that this is a limitation of the JDBC–ODBC Bridge, not of JDBC. With a pure Java JDBC driver, you do not need any special configuration to run applets on the Internet.

### 2.16.3 Sample Code 7 and 8

Sample Code 7 is `OutputApplet.java`, and Sample Code 8 is `OutputApplet.html`. The sample code in this section is a demonstration JDBC applet. It displays some simple standard output from the table `COFFEES`.

The contents of `OutputApplet.java` are printed first, and the contents of the file `OutputApplet.html` follow.

Here is `OutputApplet.java`:

```java
import java.applet.Applet;
import java.awt.Graphics;
import java.util.Vector;
import java.sql.*;

public class OutputApplet extends Applet implements Runnable {
    private Thread worker;
    private Vector queryResults;
    private String message = "Initializing";
    public synchronized void start() {
        // Every time "start" is called, we create a worker thread to
        // re-evaluate the database query.
        if (worker == null) {
            message = "Connecting to database";
            worker = new Thread(this);
            worker.start();
        }
    }

    public void run() {
        String url = "jdbc:mySubprotocol:myDataSource";
        String query = "select COF_NAME, PRICE from COFFEES";

        try {
            Class.forName("myDriver.ClassName");
        } catch(Exception ex) {
            setError("Can't find Database driver class: " + ex);
            return;
        }

        try {
            Vector results = new Vector();
            Connection con = DriverManager.getConnection(url,
                        "myLogin", "myPassword");
            Statement stmt = con.createStatement();
            ResultSet rs = stmt.executeQuery(query);
            while (rs.next()) {
                String s = rs.getString("COF_NAME");
                float f = rs.getFloat("PRICE");
```

```
                String text = s + "      " + f;
                results.addElement(text);
            }

            stmt.close();
            con.close();

            setResults(results);

        } catch(SQLException ex) {
            setError("SQLException: " + ex);
        }
    }

    public synchronized void paint(Graphics g) {
        // If there are no results available, display the current
        // message.
        if (queryResults == null) {
            g.drawString(message, 5, 50);
            return;
        }

        // Display the results.
        g.drawString("Prices of coffee per pound:   ", 5, 10);
        int y = 30;
        java.util.Enumeration enum = queryResults.elements();
        while (enum.hasMoreElements()) {
            String text = (String)enum.nextElement();
            g.drawString(text, 5, y);
            y = y + 15;
        }
    }

    private synchronized void setError(String mess) {
        queryResults = null;
        message = mess;
        worker = null;
        // And ask AWT to repaint this applet.
```

```
        repaint();
    }

    private synchronized void setResults(Vector results) {
        queryResults = results;
        worker = null;
        // And ask AWT to repaint this applet.
        repaint();
    }
}
```

What follows is the html file that places our applet on the HTML page.

```
<HTML>
<HEAD>
<TITLE> Query Output </TITLE>
</HEAD>
<BODY>
<CENTER>
Output from query select NAME, PRICE from COFFEES
<BR>
<APPLET CODEBASE=. CODE="OutputApplet.class" WIDTH=350 HEIGHT=200>
</CENTER>
</APPLET>
</BODY>
</HTML>
```

# Metadata Tutorial

$T$HIS chapter shows you how to use the two metadata classes, ResultSetMetaData and DatabaseMetaData. ResultSetMetaData provides information about a particular ResultSet object, and DatabaseMetaData provides information about a database or a database management system (DBMS). If you write programs that use advanced, nonstandard database features or programs that dynamically discover database tables, you will need to use metadata. If you do not write such programs, you can skip this chapter.

The reference chapters "ResultSetMetaData" starting on page 319 and "DatabaseMetaData" starting on page 163 give basic information about these two interfaces, and we recommend that you familiarize yourself with them before going through this chapter. The emphasis here is on example code that puts together metadata methods in programs that illustrate their usefulness. We assume that readers of this chapter are familiar with the material in the preceding chapter, "Basic Tutorial."

## 3.1  Getting Information about a Result Set

When you send a SELECT statement using JDBC, you get back a ResultSet object containing the data that satisfied your criteria. You can get information about this ResultSet object by creating a ResultSetMetaData object and invoking ResultSetMetaData methods on it. The following code, in which the variable *con* is a Connection object, demonstrates this:

```
Statement stmt = con.createStatement();
ResultSet rs = stmt.executeQuery("select * from COFFEES");
ResultSetMetaData rsmd = rs.getMetaData();
```

The ResultSetMetaData object *rsmd* contains all the metadata information about the ResultSet *rs*, and you can now use *rsmd* to invoke ResultSetMetaData methods to access this information. Except for the method getColumnCount, which gives the total number of columns in the result set, all of these methods return information about an individual column in *rs*.

### 3.1.1    Using the Method getColumnCount

Probably the most frequently used ResultSetMetaData method is getColumnCount. As just stated, this method tells you how many columns the result set has.

```
ResultSet rs = stmt.executeQuery("select * from COFFEES");
ResultSetMetaData rsmd = rs.getMetaData();
int numberOfColumns = rsmd.getColumnCount();
```

Since the query selected all of the columns in COFFEES, which has five columns, the variable *numberOfColumns* is assigned the value 5. This number is most often used in a for loop to iterate through the columns in a result set row, as in the code fragment below:

```
while (rs.next()) {
    for (int i = 1; i<= numberOfColumns; i++) {
        String s = rs.getString(i);
        System.out.println("Column " + i + ":   " + s);
        System.out.println("");
    }
}
```

Note that the ResultSet method used to retrieve all of the column values in this example is getString. This is the easiest way to retrieve values when you do not know the type for each column. "Using the Method getString" starting on page 46 explained this in more detail.

### 3.1.2    Sample Code 9

Sample Code 9 is the file SQLStatement.java. Because this code uses the methods getColumnCount and getString, as just described, it can be used as a template for simple queries. The query it currently contains is the example of a join used in "Basic Tutorial." It prints out the coffee names supplied by Acme, Inc. You can simply substitute another SELECT statement, and the results of that query will be printed out for you.

SQLStatement.java looks like this:

```java
import java.sql.*;

public class SQLStatement  {

    public static void main(String args[]) {

        String url = "jdbc:mySubprotocol:myDataSource";
        Connection con;
        String query = "select SUPPLIERS.SUP_NAME, COFFEES.COF_NAME " +
                       "from COFFEES, SUPPLIERS " +
                       "where SUPPLIERS.SUP_NAME like 'Acme, Inc.' and " +
                       "SUPPLIERS.SUP_ID = COFFEES.SUP_ID";
        Statement stmt;

        try {
            Class.forName("myDriver.ClassName");

        } catch(java.lang.ClassNotFoundException e) {
            System.err.print("ClassNotFoundException: ");
            System.err.println(e.getMessage());
        }

        try {
            con = DriverManager.getConnection(url,
                                "myLogin", "myPassword");

            stmt = con.createStatement();

            ResultSet rs = stmt.executeQuery(query);
            ResultSetMetaData rsmd = rs.getMetaData();
            int numberOfColumns = rsmd.getColumnCount();
            int rowCount = 1;
            while (rs.next()) {
                System.out.println("Row " + rowCount + ":  ");
                for (int i = 1; i <= numberOfColumns; i++) {
```

```
                System.out.print("   Column " + i + ":  ");
                System.out.println(rs.getString(i));
            }
            System.out.println("");
            rowCount++;
        }
        stmt.close();
        con.close();

    } catch(SQLException ex) {
        System.err.print("SQLException: ");
        System.err.println(ex.getMessage());
    }
  }
}
```

Running this application with its current query produces this printout:

```
➡ Row 1:
➡     Column 1:   Acme, Inc.
➡     Column 2:   Colombian
➡
➡ Row 2:
➡     Column 1:   Acme, Inc.
➡     Column 2:   Colombian_Decaf
```

### 3.1.3    Using Other ResultSetMetaData Methods

Let's suppose that the select statement that generated the ResultSet *rs* was in a stored procedure and that we do not know how many columns *rs* has or what the column names are. We can call the ResultSetMetaData methods getColumnCount and getColumnLabel on the object *rsmd* to find out how many columns *rs* has and what string is recommended as the label for each of the columns.

The following code fragment, which prints the column names on one line and then the contents of each row on succeeding lines, illustrates using the methods getColumnCount and getColumnLabel. You can see this code as used in a complete application in "Sample Code 10 and 11" starting on page 94.

```
Statement stmt = con.createStatement();
ResultSet rs = stmt.executeQuery(query);
ResultSetMetaData rsmd = rs.getMetaData();
int numberOfColumns = rsmd.getColumnCount();
for (int i = 1; i<=numberOfColumns; i++) {
    if (i > 1) { System.out.print(", "); }
    String columnName = rsmd.getColumnLabel(i);
    System.out.print(columnName);
}
System.out.println("");
while (rs.next ()) {
    for (int i=1; i<=numberOfColumns; i++) {
        if (i > 1) { System.out.print(", "); }
        String columnValue = rs.getString(i);
        System.out.print(columnValue);
    }
    System.out.println("");
}
stmt.close();
```

If this code fragment were run in a complete Java application, the output would look similar to this:

```
➥ COF_NAME,  SUP_ID,  PRICE,  SALES,  TOTAL
➥ Colombian,  101,  7.99,  175,  350
➥ French_Roast,  49,  8.99,  150,  300
➥ Espresso,  150,  9.99,  60,  120
➥ Colombian_Decaf,  101,  8.99,  155,  310
➥ French_Roast_Decaf,  49,  10.75,  90,  180
```

### 3.1.4   Getting Column Type Information

Two `ResultSetMetaData` methods provide information about the type of a result set column: `getColumnType` and `getColumnTypeName`. The method `getColumnType` tells you the JDBC type (the generic SQL type) for values stored in a specified column. It returns the JDBC type as an `int`; you can refer to the class `java.sql.Types` on page 376 to see which JDBC type that number represents. For example, the following code fragment gets the JDBC type for the second column in the `ResultSet` *rs*:

```
int jdbcType = rs.getColumnType(2);
```

If the second column stores values that have JDBC type INTEGER, *jdbcType* will be assigned the integer 4, which is java.sql.Types.INTEGER. Note that the recommended programming style is to use the JDBC type name rather than its integer value.

The method getColumnTypeName returns the name used by the DBMS for that JDBC type. "Getting Information about DBMS Types" starting on page 106 looks at the DatabaseMetaData method getTypeInfo, which gives information about the types used by a DBMS.

### 3.1.5    Sample Code 10 and 11

Sample Code 10 is the file PrintColumnTypes.java, and Sample Code 11 is the file PrintColumns.java. The following code defines the class PrintColumnTypes. This class consists of one method, printColTypes, that prints out statements with the return values of the two methods getColumnType and getColumnTypeName. The method printColTypes, shown next, is called in the class PrintColumns, which is explained after the following code. Here is PrintColumnTypes.java:

```java
import java.sql.*;

public class PrintColumnTypes  {
    public static void printColTypes(ResultSetMetaData rsmd)
                                            throws SQLException {
        int columns = rsmd.getColumnCount();
        for (int i = 1; i <= columns; i++) {
            int jdbcType = rsmd.getColumnType(i);
            String name = rsmd.getColumnTypeName(i);
            System.out.print("Column " + i + " is JDBC type " + jdbcType);
            System.out.println(", which the DBMS calls " + name);
        }
    }
}
```

The class PrintColumnTypes does not contain a main method, so it cannot be executed by itself. It can be called by an application that does contain a main method, however, as is done in the application in the file PrintColumns.java, shown later.

As must be done in any JDBC application, `PrintColumns.java` loads the driver and establishes a connection with the DBMS. Next it creates the `ResultSet` object *rs* by executing a query and then creates the `ResultSetMetaData` object *rsmd* by calling the method `getMetaData` on *rs*. The `ResultSetMetaData` object *rsmd* is then used several times to get information about the `ResultSet` *rs*.

The method `printColTypes` (in the class `PrintColumnTypes`, shown above) uses *rsmd* three times. First it uses *rsmd* to call the method `getColumnCount`. The results of this method are used in a `for` loop that iterates through the columns in the `ResultSet` *rs*. Next `printColTypes` invokes the methods `getColumnType` and `getColumnTypeName` on *rsmd*. As just mentioned, `printColTypes` uses the results of these two methods to print out a statement for each column in *rs*, giving the JDBC type code number for that column and also the local DBMS name for that data type. The printout for `printColTypes` is the first part of the output for the application `PrintColumns`, shown later, and it is also shown here for convenience. This printout represents what will be returned by most DBMSs:

```
➡ Column 1 is JDBC type 12, which the DBMS calls VARCHAR
➡ Column 2 is JDBC type 4, which the DBMS calls INTEGER
➡ Column 3 is JDBC type 8, which the DBMS calls DOUBLE PRECISION
➡ Column 4 is JDBC type 4, which the DBMS calls INTEGER
➡ Column 5 is JDBC type 4, which the DBMS calls INTEGER
➡
```

After passing *rsmd* to the method `printColTypes`, the application uses *rsmd* two more times. Like `printColTypes`, it invokes `getColumnCount` on *rsmd* in order to use it to iterate through the columns in *rs*. Then it calls the method `getColumn-Name` on *rsmd* to print out the column names in *rs*.

Finally, the application `PrintColumns` prints out the values in each row of *rs*. The query that produced *rs* was `select * from COFFEES`, so all of the values in the table `COFFEES` are printed. The printout follows the code in the file `PrintColumns.java`, which is shown next:

```
import java.sql.*;

class PrintColumns  {

    public static void main(String args[]) {

        String url = "jdbc:mySubprotocol:myDataSource";
```

```
Connection con;
String query = "select * from COFFEES";
Statement stmt;

try {
   Class.forName("myDriver.ClassName");

} catch(java.lang.ClassNotFoundException e) {
   System.err.print("ClassNotFoundException: ");
   System.err.println(e.getMessage());
}

try {
   con = DriverManager.getConnection(url,
                        "myLogin", "myPassword");

   stmt = con.createStatement();

   ResultSet rs = stmt.executeQuery(query);
   ResultSetMetaData rsmd = rs.getMetaData();

   PrintColumnTypes.printColTypes(rsmd);
   System.out.println("");

   int numberOfColumns = rsmd.getColumnCount();

   for (int i = 1; i <= numberOfColumns; i++) {
      if (i > 1) System.out.print(",  ");
      String columnName = rsmd.getColumnName(i);
      System.out.print(columnName);
   }
   System.out.println("");

   while (rs.next()) {
      for (int i = 1; i <= numberOfColumns; i++) {
         if (i > 1) System.out.print(",  ");
         String columnValue = rs.getString(i);
         System.out.print(columnValue);
      }
```

```
            System.out.println("");
        }

        stmt.close();
        con.close();
    } catch(SQLException ex) {
        System.err.print("SQLException: ");
        System.err.println(ex.getMessage());
    }
  }
}
```

The output of this code will be similar to the following, with the values in the PRICE, SALES, and TOTAL columns varying according to what has been entered:

```
➡ Column 1 is JDBC type 12, which the DBMS calls VARCHAR
➡ Column 2 is JDBC type 4, which the DBMS calls INTEGER
➡ Column 3 is JDBC type 6, which the DBMS calls FLOAT
➡ Column 4 is JDBC type 4, which the DBMS calls INTEGER
➡ Column 5 is JDBC type 4, which the DBMS calls INTEGER
➡
➡ COF_NAME,  SUP_ID,  PRICE,  SALES,   TOTAL
➡ Colombian,  101,  7.99,  175,   350
➡ French_Roast,  49,  8.99,  150,   300
➡ Espresso,  150,  9.99,  60,   120
➡ Colombian_Decaf,  101,  8.99,  155,   310
➡ French_Roast_Decaf,  49,  9.99,  90,   180
```

### 3.1.6   Sample Code 12

Sample Code 12 is the file RSMetaDataMethods.java. In addition to using the method getColumnCount, this code sample illustrates using the following Result-SetMetaData methods:

```
getTableName
getColumnTypeName
isCaseSensitive
isWritable
```

These methods do what their names suggest. The method `getTableName` returns the name of the table from which this result set column was derived. The method `getColumnTypeName` returns the type name used by this particular DBMS for values stored in this result set column. The method `isCaseSensitive` returns `true` if a value stored in this column is case sensitive and `false` otherwise. The method `isWritable` returns `true` if it is possible for a write operation on a value stored in this column to succeed; otherwise it returns `false`.

The results of these methods are printed out for each column of the `ResultSet` *rs.* All of the results from the query `SELECT * FROM COFFEES` are also printed out so that you can see the values to which the column information refers.

The following is the file `RSMetaDataMethods.java`:

```java
import java.sql.*;

public class RSMetaDataMethods {

    public static void main(String args[]) {

        String url = "jdbc:mySubprotocol:myDataSource";
        Connection con;
        Statement stmt;

        try {
            Class.forName("myDriver.ClassName");

        } catch(java.lang.ClassNotFoundException e) {
            System.err.print("ClassNotFoundException: ");
            System.err.println(e.getMessage());
        }

        try {
            con = DriverManager.getConnection(url,
                            "myLogin", "myPassword");

            stmt = con.createStatement();

            ResultSet rs = stmt.executeQuery("select * from COFFEES");
            ResultSetMetaData rsmd = rs.getMetaData();
```

```
        int numberOfColumns = rsmd.getColumnCount();
        for (int i = 1; i <= numberOfColumns; i++) {
            String colName = rsmd.getColumnName(i);
            String tableName = rsmd.getTableName(i);
            String name = rsmd.getColumnTypeName(i);
            boolean caseSen = rsmd.isCaseSensitive(i);
            boolean w = rsmd.isWritable(i);
            System.out.println("Information for column " + colName);
            System.out.println("    Column is in table " + tableName);
            System.out.println("    DBMS name for type is " + name);
            System.out.println("    Is case sensitive:  " + caseSen);
            System.out.println("    Is possibly writable:  " + w);
            System.out.println("");
        }

        while (rs.next()) {
            for (int i = 1; i<=numberOfColumns; i++) {
                String s = rs.getString(i);
                System.out.print(s + "  ");
            }
            System.out.println("");
        }

        stmt.close();
        con.close();

    } catch(SQLException ex) {
        System.err.println("SQLException: " + ex.getMessage());
    }
  }
}
```

Here is the output of RSMetaDataMethods.java for one DBMS:

```
➥ Information for column COF_NAME
➥     Column is in table COFFEES
➥     DBMS name for type is VARCHAR
➥     Is case sensitive:  true
➥     Is possibly writable:  true
➥
```

➡ Information for column SUP_ID
➡     Column is in table COFFEES
➡     DBMS name for type is INTEGER
➡     Is case sensitive:  false
➡     Is possibly writable:  true
➡
➡ Information for column PRICE
➡     Column is in table COFFEES
➡     DBMS name for type is DOUBLE PRECISION
➡     Is case sensitive:  false
➡     Is possibly writable:  true
➡
➡ Information for column SALES
➡     Column is in table COFFEES
➡     DBMS name for type is INTEGER
➡     Is case sensitive:  false
➡     Is possibly writable:  true
➡
➡ Information for column TOTAL
➡     Column is in table COFFEES
➡     DBMS name for type is INTEGER
➡     Is case sensitive:  false
➡     Is possibly writable:  true
➡
➡ Colombian  101  7.99  175  350
➡ French_Roast  49  8.99  150  300
➡ Espresso  150  9.99  60  220
➡ Colombian_Decaf  101  8.99  155  310
➡ French_Roast_Decaf  49  10.75  90  180

### 3.1.7   Getting Other Information

Several ResultSetMetaData methods give you information relevant to numeric types:

isAutoIncrement
isCurrency
isSigned
getPrecision
getScale

These methods have names that are largely self-explanatory. (*Precision* is the total number of digits, and *scale* is the number of digits to the right of the decimal point.)

The method `isNullable` tells you whether you can use `null` as a value for a specified column, and `getColumnDisplaySize` gives you the limit for how many characters normally fit in a specified column.

## 3.2    Getting Information about a Database or Database System

The interface `DatabaseMetaData` has more than 130 methods for getting information about a database or DBMS. See "DatabaseMetaData" starting on page 163 for an overview of this class and an explanation of each method.

Once you have an open connection with a DBMS, you can create a `DatabaseMetaData` object that contains information about that database system. Using the `Connection` object *con*, the following line of code creates the `DatabaseMetaData` object *dbmd*:

```
DatabaseMetaData dbmd = con.getMetaData():
```

### 3.2.1    Categories of `DatabaseMetaData` Methods

`DatabaseMetaData` methods can be organized into roughly four major categories based on the types of their return values. The first three categories return a single value; the fourth category returns a result set with one to eighteen columns.

### 3.2.2    Methods that Return a `String`

The smallest category returns a `String` object. Some of these methods get information about the DBMS as a whole, such as the URL for the DBMS, the user name, the product name, the product version, the driver name, and the driver version. Others return information such as the character used to escape wildcard characters, the term the DBMS uses for *schema,* the term the DBMS uses for *catalog,* and the term the DBMS uses for *procedure.* Some methods return a `String` object which is a comma-separated list. These methods give you lists of SQL keywords, numeric functions, string functions, system functions, and time/date functions.

As an example of this category, let us look at the method `getSearchStringEscape`. For some of the `DatabaseMetaData` methods, you can supply a search string pattern as a parameter. If you wanted to use a table name such as Emp_Info as a search string parameter, you would need to indicate that the underscore character (_) was part of the name and not a wildcard character. To do this, you would need to precede the underscore with the driver's escape character. The method get-SearchStringEscape will tell you what that escape character is for your driver. This is demonstrated in the following code fragment:

```
Connection con = DriverManager.getConnection (url,
                         "myLogin", "myPassword");
DatabaseMetaData dbmd = con.getMetaData();
String escape = dbmd.getSearchStringEscape();
System.out.print("The search string escape for this ");
System.out.println("driver is " + escape);
con.close();
```

When this code fragment is put into a complete Java application and run, the output looks like this:

➥ The search string escape for this driver is \

Now we know that we need to use a backslash (\) as the escape character, as in "Emp\_Info."

The method getSQLKeywords returns a String that is a comma-separated list of the keywords used by the DBMS that are not also SQL92 keywords. The code fragment that follows will produce the output that follows it:

```
Connection con = DriverManager.getConnection (url,
                         "myLogin", "myPassword");
DatabaseMetaData dbmd = con.getMetaData();
String dbmsKeywords = dbmd.getSQLKeywords();
System.out.print("The keywords used by this DBMS that ");
System.out.println("are not also SQL92 keywords:   ");
System.out.println(dbmsKeywords);
con.close();
```

➥ The keywords used by this DBMS that are not also SQL92 keywords: (this output has been changed to break at commas)
➥ arith_overflow,break,browse,bulk,char_convert,checkpoint,
➥ clustered,commit,compute,confirm,controlrow,data_pgs,
➥ database,dbcc,disk,dummy,dump,endtran,errlvl,

➡ errorexit,exit,fillfactor,
➡ holdlock,identity_insert,if,kill,lineno,load,mirror,mirrorexit,
➡ noholdlock,nonclustered,numeric_truncation,
➡ offsets,once,over,perm,permanent,plan,print,proc,processexit,
➡ raiserror,read,readtext,
➡ reconfigure,replace,reserved_pgs,return,role,rowcnt,
➡ rowcount,rule,save,setuser,shared,shutdown,some,
➡ statistics,stripe,syb_identity,syb_restree,
➡ syb_terminate,temp,textsize,tran,trigger,truncate,
➡ tsequal,used_pgs,user_option,waitfor,while,writetext

If you are writing a driver for a DBMS, one of the things you need to do is to determine which scalar functions are supported by that DBMS so that you can either implement those functions or map them to the proper DBMS syntax. ("Support Scalar Functions" starting on page 404 in Appendix A explains more about this.) Calling the method getStringFunctions will give you a list of the string functions the DBMS supports, as in the following code fragment:

```
DatabaseMetaData dbmd = con.getMetaData();
String stringFunctions = dbmd.getStringFunctions();
System.out.println("The string functions supported by this DBMS:");
System.out.println(stringFunctions);
```

The output for this particular DBMS looks like this:

➡ The string functions supported by this DBMS:
(this output has been changed to break at commas)
➡ ASCII,CHAR,CONCAT,
➡ DIFFERENCE,LCASE,LEFT,LENGTH,LTRIM,REPEAT,RIGHT,RTRIM,
➡ SOUNDEX,SPACE,SUBSTRING,UCASE

### 3.2.3   Methods that Return an `int`

The next category of DatabaseMetaData methods returns an int, which is usually a limit of some sort that applies to the target DBMS with the current driver. These methods generally have the form getMaxXXX where XXX is what is being limited. You can find out the maximum number of characters allowed for a statement or for names; names include user name and names of tables, columns, cursors, schemas, catalogs, and procedures. You can also get the limit on the number of tables you can include in a SELECT statement, or the maximum number of columns you can have in a table, an index, a SELECT statement, a GROUP BY clause, or an ORDER BY clause.

Other methods tell you how many connections you can have at one time, how many statements you can have active at the same time, and how long an index can be.

The code fragment below finds out how long a column name may be:

```
DatabaseMetaData dbmd = con.getMetaData();
int len = dbmd.getMaxColumnNameLength();
String columnName = "AnExtraordinarilyLongColumnName";
if(columnName.length() > len) {
    System.out.print("The maximum number of characters allowed ");
    System.out.println("in a column name:   " + len);
    System.out.println(columnName + " has " + columnName.length());
}
```

The output for one DBMS is shown below:

```
➥ The maximum number of characters allowed in a column name:   30
➥ AnExtraordinarilyLongColumnName has 31
```

### 3.2.4    Methods that Return a `boolean`

The category with the largest number of methods is the category that returns a `boolean`, that is, either `true` or `false`. The majority of these have the form `supportsXXX`, where XXX is a capability that the DBMS supports or does not support. In all, there are more than seventy methods that return a `boolean`. Looking at "DatabaseMetaData Interface Definition" starting on page 166 will give you an overview of the methods in this category.

### 3.2.5    Methods that Return a `ResultSet` Object

The fourth category is the most complex. These methods return `ResultSet` objects that can be as simple as one column for each row returned or as complex as eighteen columns for each row returned. In the sample code following this, we will show you examples of using these methods and the results they return.

### 3.2.6    Sample Code 13

Sample Code 13 is the file `TableTypes.java`. This application depends on the method `getTableTypes`, which is a good example of a `DatabaseMetaData` method that returns a simple `ResultSet` object. Each row in the result set has only one col-

umn, which indicates one of the types of tables available in the DBMS. The method
getDatabaseProductName is an example of a method that returns a String object.
Here is the file TableTypes.java, which demonstrates the use of these two methods:

```java
import java.sql.*;

public class TableTypes  {

    public static void main(String args[]) {

        String url = "jdbc:mySubprotocol:myDataSource";
        Connection con;

        try {
            Class.forName("myDriver.ClassName");

        } catch(java.lang.ClassNotFoundException e) {
            System.err.print("ClassNotFoundException: ");
            System.err.println(e.getMessage());
        }

        try {
            con = DriverManager.getConnection(url,
                              "myLogin", "myPassword");

            DatabaseMetaData dbmd = con.getMetaData();
            String dbmsName = dbmd.getDatabaseProductName();
            ResultSet rs = dbmd.getTableTypes();
            System.out.print("The following types of tables are ");
            System.out.println("available in " + dbmsName + ":  ");

            while (rs.next()) {
                String tableType = rs.getString("TABLE_TYPE");
                System.out.println("    " + tableType);
            }

            rs.close();
            con.close();
```

```
    } catch(SQLException ex) {
        System.err.print("SQLException: ");
        System.err.println(ex.getMessage());
    }
  }
}
```

The output from one driver and DBMS looks like this:

➥ The following types of tables are available in SQL Server:
➥    SYSTEM TABLE
➥    TABLE
➥    VIEW

### 3.2.7    Getting Information about DBMS Types

The method getTypeInfo, which returns one of the more complex ResultSet objects, tells you which SQL types a DBMS uses. If, for example, you want to create a table but are not sure about which types are available, you can get the information you need by calling getTypeInfo. This method tells you not only what data types the database uses but, as its name suggests, also gives information about them. This information includes the type's name as used by the DBMS; its type from the class java.sql.Types; what character, if any, is used before and after a quoted literal; what parameters, if any, are used in a create statement using this type; whether the type is nullable, case sensitive, or searchable; and so on.

The method getTypeInfo returns a ResultSet object with each row representing information about one type available in the DBMS. Each of these rows has eighteen columns giving information about that data type (two of which are currently not used).

### 3.2.8    Sample Code 14

Sample Code 14 is the file TypeInfo.java. This application prints out five of the result set columns produced by the DatabaseMetaData method getTypeInfo. These columns are TYPE_NAME, DATA_TYPE, CREATE_PARAMS, NULLABLE, and CASE_SENSITIVE.

```java
import java.sql.*;

public class TypeInfo {

    public static void main(String args[]) {

        String url = "jdbc:mySubprotocol:myDataSource";
        Connection con;
        DatabaseMetaData dbmd;

        try {
            Class.forName("myDriver.ClassName");

        } catch(java.lang.ClassNotFoundException e) {
            System.err.print("ClassNotFoundException: ");
            System.err.println(e.getMessage());
        }

        try {
            con = DriverManager.getConnection(url,
                              "myLogin", "myPassword");

            dbmd = con.getMetaData();

            ResultSet rs = dbmd.getTypeInfo();
            while (rs.next()) {
                String typeName = rs.getString("TYPE_NAME");
                short dataType = rs.getShort("DATA_TYPE");
                String createParams = rs.getString("CREATE_PARAMS");
                int nullable = rs.getInt("NULLABLE");
                boolean caseSensitive = rs.getBoolean("CASE_SENSITIVE");
                System.out.println("DBMS type " + typeName + ":");
                System.out.println("    java.sql.Types: " + dataType);
                System.out.print("    parameters used to create: ");
                System.out.println(createParams);
                System.out.println("    nullable?: " + nullable);
                System.out.print("    case sensitive?: ");
```

```
                System.out.println(caseSensitive);
                System.out.println("");
            }

        con.close();

    } catch(SQLException ex) {
        System.err.println("SQLException: " + ex.getMessage());
    }
  }
}
```

If you run this code, you will get back results that show all the types available with your particular database system; the types available will vary from one DBMS to another. The value in the column DATA_TYPE, printed after "java.sql.Types:" in the output that follows, gives a number representing the JDBC type (the generic SQL type) to which the DBMS type corresponds. You can find this number and the name of the JDBC type it represents in the class java.sql.Types, on page 376.

Note that a type may be listed more than once, which means that it corresponds to more than one JDBC type. In that case, the one listed first is the preferred type, and that is the one you should use.

The following is just part of the printout for the particular DBMS we are using to give you an idea of what it looks like:

```
➡ DBMS type bit:
➡       java.sql.Types:   -7
➡       parameters used to create: null
➡       nullable?:   0
➡       case sensitive?:   false
➡
➡ DBMS type tinyint:
➡       java.sql.Types:   -6
➡       parameters used to create: null
➡       nullable?:   1
➡       case sensitive?:   false
➡
➡ DBMS type image:
➡       java.sql.Types:   -4
➡       parameters used to create: null
```

```
➡        nullable?:  1
➡        case sensitive?:  false
➡
➡ DBMS type varchar:
➡        java.sql.Types:  12
➡        parameters used to create: max length
➡        nullable?:  1
➡        case sensitive?:  true
➡
```

Let's examine what this printout means by looking in detail at two of the types listed. First let's look at the type varchar line by line.

```
➡ DBMS type varchar:
```

This indicates that varchar is one of the DBMS types you can use for values in this database.

```
➡        java.sql.Types:  12
```

This column indicates that this type corresponds most closely to java.sql.Types.VARCHAR, which is indicated by the number 12. ("Types Class Definition" starting on page 376 lists the constants used to identify SQL types.)

```
➡        parameters used to create: max length
```

This column indicates that when this type is used in a CREATE TABLE statement, it must include a parameter indicating the maximum length, as shown in the following example, where the maximum length is set to 32 characters:

```
CREATE TABLE COFFEES
(COF_NAME VARCHAR(32),
 . . .
 . . . )
```

```
➡        nullable?:  1
```

The number 1 indicates that NULL values are allowed for this type. 0 means that nulls are not allowed for this type, and 2 means that it is not known whether NULL is allowed. (The explanation for the method getTypeInfo lists the possible values for the column "NULLABLE," and the section "DatabaseMetaData Fields" starting on page 236 gives the numbers that correspond to these possible values.)

➡    case sensitive?:  true

This indicates that in this database system, the type varchar is case sensitive, which means that a value stored in a column of this type is case sensitive.

Now let's look at the entry for image:

```
➡ DBMS type image:
➡        java.sql.Types:  -4
➡        parameters used to create: null
➡        nullable?:  1
➡        case sensitive?:  false
```

This entry indicates that the DBMS has the type image and that it corresponds to java.sql.Types.LONGVARBINARY, which has the value -4. The other information given is that no parameters are used in the creation of the type image, it may be a null, and it is not case sensitive.

### 3.2.9    Getting Information about Primary and Foreign Keys

The methods that return information about primary and foreign keys are further examples of DatabaseMetaData methods that return ResultSet objects. These methods are getPrimaryKeys, getImportedKeys, getExportedKeys, and getCross-Reference. We will give examples using two of them to illustrate how they work in general.

If you specify a primary key in your statement creating a table, the DBMS will keep track of that primary key in a metadata table. The JDBC method getPrimaryKeys will return information stored in the DBMS about that primary key. The following create table statements demonstrate how to define a primary key:

```
create table COFFEES
(COF_NAME VARCHAR(32) NOT NULL,
SUP_ID INTEGER,
PRICE FLOAT,
SALES INTEGER,
TOTAL INTEGER,
primary key(COF_NAME))
```

```
create table SUPPLIERS
(SUP_ID INTEGER NOT NULL,
SUP_NAME VARCHAR(40),
STREET VARCHAR(40),
CITY VARCHAR(20),
STATE CHAR(2),
ZIP CHAR(5),
primary key(SUP_ID))
```

### 3.2.10  Sample Code 15

Sample Code 15 is the file `PrimaryKeysSuppliers.java`. If you have defined your tables specifying the primary keys, as illustrated, you can call the method `getPrimaryKeys` to get a description of the primary key columns in a table. For example, the following application defines a primary key in its `CREATE TABLE` statement and then prints out information about that primary key.

```
import java.sql.*;

public class PrimaryKeysSuppliers  {

    public static void main(String args[]) {

        String url = "jdbc:mySubprotocol:myDataSource";
        Connection con;
        String createString = "create table SUPPLIERSPK " +
                        "(SUP_ID INTEGER NOT NULL, " +
                        "SUP_NAME VARCHAR(40), " +
                        "STREET VARCHAR(40), " +
                        "CITY VARCHAR(20), " +
                        "STATE CHAR(2), " +
                        "ZIP CHAR(5), " +
                        "primary key(SUP_ID))";
        Statement stmt;

        try {
            Class.forName("myDriver.ClassName");
```

```java
        } catch(java.lang.ClassNotFoundException e) {
            System.err.print("ClassNotFoundException: ");
            System.err.println(e.getMessage());
        }

        try {
            con = DriverManager.getConnection(url,
                                "myLogin", "myPassword");

            stmt = con.createStatement();
            stmt.executeUpdate(createString);

            DatabaseMetaData dbmd = con.getMetaData();

            ResultSet rs = dbmd.getPrimaryKeys(
                                            null, null, "SUPPLIERSPK");
            while (rs.next()) {
                String name = rs.getString("TABLE_NAME");
                String columnName = rs.getString("COLUMN_NAME");
                String keySeq = rs.getString("KEY_SEQ");
                String pkName = rs.getString("PK_NAME");
                System.out.println("table name :  " + name);
                System.out.println("column name:  " + columnName);
                System.out.println("sequence in key:  " + keySeq);
                System.out.println("primary key name:  " + pkName);
                System.out.println("");
            }

            rs.close();
            con.close();

        } catch(SQLException ex) {
            System.err.print("SQLException: ");
            System.err.println(ex.getMessage());
        }
    }
}
```

The output for this DBMS looks like this:

```
➡ table name :   SUPPLIERSPK
➡ column name:   SUP_ID
➡ sequence in key:  1
➡ primary key name:  null
➡
```

Note that primary keys, and therefore also foreign keys, can be more than one column. (Recall that a primary key uniquely identifies a row in a table, and it may take more than one column to do that. In fact, it is possible that all of the columns in a row could be included in the primary key.) If the primary key consists of multiple columns, the method getPrimaryKeys (as well as getExportedKeys, getImportedKeys, and getCrossReference) will describe each of them. The value in the column KEY_SEQ indicates which column is being described. For example, if there are two columns that constitute the primary key, a value of 2 in the KEY_SEQ column refers to the second column of the primary key. In the output above, the value in KEY_SEQ is 1, so this row of the result set is describing the first column in the primary key for the table SUPPLIERS. Of course, in this particular case, there is only one column serving as the primary key.

Defining a foreign key is similar to defining a primary key, except that you also need to give the name of the table that it references. In other words, a foreign key is a column in one table that also occurs in another table, and in the other table that column is the primary key. In our tables COFFEES and SUPPLIERS, the column SUP_ID is the primary key in SUPPLIERS and the foreign key in COFFEES. Now we will once again create the COFFEES table, this time including a declaration of its foreign key and the table it references (the table in which that column is the primary key):

```
create table COFFEESFK
(COF_NAME VARCHAR(32) NOT NULL,
SUP_ID INTEGER,
PRICE FLOAT,
SALES INTEGER,
TOTAL INTEGER,
primary key(COF_NAME),
foreign key(SUP_ID) references SUPPLIERSPK)
```

### 3.2.11  Sample Code 16

Sample Code 16 is the file `ForeignKeysCoffees.java`. The method `getImported-Keys` tells you about the foreign keys imported into a table. In the table `COFFEES`, `SUP_ID` is an imported key, and it references the table `SUPPLIERS`, where `SUP_ID` is the primary key. Note that you must have created the table `SUPPLIERSPK` before you run `ForeignKeysCoffees`. This table is created in `PrimaryKeysSuppliers`, so if you run the code samples in order, you will have no problem. If you have not created `SUPPLIERSPK`, you will get an exception when you run `ForeignKeysCoffees` because the table it creates, `COFFEESFK`, refers to `SUPPLIERSPK`.

A call to `getImportedKeys(null, null, COFFEESFK)` gets a description of the column `SUP_ID`. A call to `getExportedKeys(null, null, SUPPLIERSPK)` will also get a description of the column `SUP_ID`. You can think of the column `SUP_ID` as being imported into `COFFEESFK` and exported from `SUPPLIERSPK`.

The following code sample illustrates using `getImportedKeys`:

```
import java.sql.*;

public class ForeignKeysCoffees  {

    public static void main(String args[]) {

        String url = "jdbc:mySubprotocol:myDataSource";
        Connection con;
        String createString = "create table COFFEESFK " +
                    "(COF_NAME VARCHAR(32) NOT NULL, " +
                    "SUP_ID INTEGER, " +
                    "PRICE FLOAT, " +
                    "SALES INTEGER, " +
                    "TOTAL INTEGER, " +
                    "primary key(COF_NAME), " +
                    "foreign key(SUP_ID) references SUPPLIERSPK)";
        Statement stmt;

        try {
            Class.forName("myDriver.ClassName");
```

```
} catch(java.lang.ClassNotFoundException e) {
    System.err.print("ClassNotFoundException: ");
    System.err.println(e.getMessage());
}

try {
    con = DriverManager.getConnection(url,
                        "myLogin", "myPassword");

    stmt = con.createStatement();
    stmt.executeUpdate(createString);

    DatabaseMetaData dbmd = con.getMetaData();

    ResultSet rs = dbmd.getImportedKeys(null, null, "COFFEESFK");
    while (rs.next()) {
        String pkTable = rs.getString("PKTABLE_NAME");
        String pkColName = rs.getString("PKCOLUMN_NAME");
        String fkTable = rs.getString("FKTABLE_NAME");
        String fkColName = rs.getString("FKCOLUMN_NAME");
        short updateRule = rs.getShort("UPDATE_RULE");
        short deleteRule = rs.getShort("DELETE_RULE");
        System.out.print("primary key table name :  ");
        System.out.println(pkTable);
        System.out.print("primary key column name :  ");
        System.out.println(pkColName);
        System.out.print("foreign key table name :  ");
        System.out.println(fkTable);
        System.out.print("foreign key column name :  ");
        System.out.println(fkColName);
        System.out.println("update rule:  " + updateRule);
        System.out.println("delete rule:  " + deleteRule);
        System.out.println("");
    }

    rs.close();
    stmt.close();
    con.close();
```

```
        } catch(SQLException ex) {
            System.err.print("SQLException: ");
            System.err.println(ex.getMessage());
        }
    }
}
```

The output on the DBMS we are using looks like this:

```
➡ primary key table name :   SUPPLIERSPK
➡ primary key column name :   SUP_ID
➡ foreign key table name :   COFFEESFK
➡ foreign key column name :   SUP_ID
➡ update rule:   1
➡ delete rule:   1
```

The explanation in the reference section for the method `getImportedKeys` tells you that there are five possible values for the columns `UPDATE_RULE` and `DELETE_RULE`: `importedKeyNoAction`, `importedKeyCascade`, `importedKeySetNull`, `importedKeySetDefault`, and `importedKeyRestrict`. The value `1`, returned for both the update rule and the delete rule, is `importedKeyRestrict`, which means that the column `SUP_ID` in table `SUPPLIERSPK` may not be updated or deleted because it has been imported to another table (in this case the table `COFFEESFK`). For example, if you try to delete the table `SUPPLIERSPK`, you will get an exception telling you that you cannot delete `SUPPLIERSPK` because another table references it. You can find an explanation for the possible return values in the section "DatabaseMetaData Fields" starting on page 236.

## 3.3    A Generic Application

DBMSs generally use standard SQL types. But if you want to write a generic application that works for all DBMSs, you can do so with the help of methods from `ResultSetMetaData` and `DatabaseMetaData`. The following sample code, `SQLTypesCreate.java`, is an example of this. It creates a table by prompting the user for the necessary input (table name, column name(s), and column type(s)) and then incrementally constructing a `CREATE TABLE` statement that works for the particular DBMS with which it is being run.

The key method in this application is the `DatabaseMetaData` method `get-TypeInfo`, which is used to ascertain what types a DBMS uses and how these relate to the JDBC SQL types. The method `getTypeInfo` was explained in detail in the section "Getting Information about DBMS Types" starting on page 106.

We include this code because it is an example of a generic application, but even more importantly, because we want to make it possible for all readers to create the tables `COFFEES` and `SUPPLIERS`, no matter what data types their DBMSs may use.

### 3.3.1 Sample Code 17 and 18

Sample Code 17 is the file `DataType.java`, and Sample Code 18 is the file `SQL-TypesCreate.java`. The first step in writing this application is to build an array based on the JDBC SQL types. We chose to make this array, which we call `typeArray`, an array of classes. Each class object represents a type and includes the four values needed for each type: the JDBC SQL type code number, the JDBC SQL type name, the local DBMS name, and the parameters, if there are any, that must be included in the `CREATE TABLE` statement.

We opted to use an array of classes because classes offer data encapsulation. The class we defined, `DataTypes`, has five fields, one for each of the four values just mentioned plus a boolean to indicate whether any fields still need to be given values. It has one constructor that takes a JDBC SQL type code and a JDBC SQL type name, which are used to initialize instances of `DataType`. The local DBMS name and parameters are initially set to `null`. The fields are private, so they can be accessed only through the public methods defined in this class. There are `get` methods to retrieve the values for each of the fields, but there is only one `set` method. This method, called `setLocalTypeAndParams`, sets the values for `local-Type` and `param`, the two values that may vary from one DBMS to another. It also sets the variable *needsSetting* to `false` so that the status can be tested to prevent setting the values for `localType` and `param` again. (The method `getTypeInfo` may return more than one entry for the local type, and the first one is the one that should be used. Setting *needsSetting* to `false` guarantees that no subsequent entries can replace the first entry.) The two fields `code` and `SQLType` are constants defined in `java.sql.Types`, and their values can be set only at initialization.

Here is the definition for the class `DataType`, contained in the file `DataType.java`:

```java
public class DataType {

    private int code;
    private String SQLType;
    private String localType = null;
    private String params = null;
    private boolean needsSetting = true;

    public DataType(int code, String SQLType) {
        this.code = code;
        this.SQLType = SQLType;

    }

    public boolean needsToBeSet() {
        return needsSetting;
    }

    public int getCode() {
        return code;
    }

    public String getSQLType() {
        return SQLType;
    }

    public String getLocalType() {
        return localType;
    }

    public String getParams() {
        return params;
    }
```

```
    public void setLocalTypeAndParams(String local, String p) {
        if (needsSetting) {
            localType = local;
            params = p;
            needsSetting = false;
        }
    }
}
```

Our array, `typeArray`, is initialized with instances of the class `DataType`. Each instance is created with an SQL type code and the corresponding SQL type name (both constants from the class `java.sql.Types`) plus two fields initialized with `null`. We will set the values for these null fields from the information returned by the method `getTypeInfo`.

The rest of the application gets input from the user to build a CREATE TABLE statement. To get user input, we defined the method `getInput`, which prints the prompt it is given and returns what the user types in response.

Whenever the user is asked to supply the type for a column name, a list of the SQL types from which to choose is printed on the screen. Type names are included in the list only if the DBMS has an equivalent type. This is tested by calling the method `needsToBeSet` on each instance of `DataType`. If the return value is `false`, indicating that a local DBMS type has been set for this particular SQL data type, then this data type is printed as part of the list presented to the user.

The application `SQLTypesCreate.java` looks like this:

```
import java.sql.*;

public class SQLTypesCreate {

    public static void main(String [] args) {
        String url = "jdbc:mySubprotocol:myDataSource";
        Connection con;
        Statement stmt;

        try {
            Class.forName("myDriver.ClassName");
```

```
    } catch(java.lang.ClassNotFoundException e) {
        System.err.print("ClassNotFoundException: ");
        System.err.println(e.getMessage());
    }

    try {
        con = DriverManager.getConnection(url,
                            "myLogin", "myPassword");
        stmt = con.createStatement();
        String tableName;
        String columnName;
        String sqlType;

    // create an array of class DataType initialized with
    // the SQL code, the SQL type name, and two null entries
    // for the local type name and the creation parameter(s)

    DataType [] typeArray = {
        new DataType(java.sql.Types.BIT, "BIT"),
        new DataType(java.sql.Types.TINYINT, "TINYINT"),
        new DataType(java.sql.Types.SMALLINT, "SMALLINT"),
        new DataType(java.sql.Types.INTEGER, "INTEGER"),
        new DataType(java.sql.Types.BIGINT, "BIGINT"),
        new DataType(java.sql.Types.FLOAT, "FLOAT"),
        new DataType(java.sql.Types.REAL, "REAL"),
        new DataType(java.sql.Types.DOUBLE, "DOUBLE"),
        new DataType(java.sql.Types.NUMERIC, "NUMERIC"),
        new DataType(java.sql.Types.DECIMAL, "DECIMAL"),
        new DataType(java.sql.Types.CHAR, "CHAR"),
        new DataType(java.sql.Types.VARCHAR, "VARCHAR"),
        new DataType(java.sql.Types.LONGVARCHAR, "LONGVARCHAR"),
        new DataType(java.sql.Types.DATE, "DATE"),
        new DataType(java.sql.Types.TIME,"TIME"),
        new DataType(java.sql.Types.TIMESTAMP, "TIMESTAMP"),
        new DataType(java.sql.Types.BINARY, "BINARY"),
        new DataType(java.sql.Types.VARBINARY, "VARBINARY"),
        new DataType(java.sql.Types.LONGVARBINARY, "LONGVARBINARY"),
        new DataType(java.sql.Types.NULL, "NULL"),
        new DataType(java.sql.Types.OTHER, "OTHER"),
    };
```

```
DatabaseMetaData dbmd = con.getMetaData();
ResultSet rs = dbmd.getTypeInfo();
while (rs.next()) {
    int codeNumber = rs.getInt("DATA_TYPE");
    String dbmsName = rs.getString("TYPE_NAME");
    String createParams = rs.getString("CREATE_PARAMS");

    // find entry that matches the SQL code,
    // and if local type and params are not already set,
    // set them
    for (int i = 0; i < typeArray.length; i++) {
        if (typeArray[i].getCode() == codeNumber) {
            typeArray[i].setLocalTypeAndParams(
                            dbmsName, createParams);

        }
    }
}

String tableNamePrompt = "Enter the table name " +
                    "and hit Return: ";
tableName = getInput(tableNamePrompt);
String createTableString = "create table " +
                    tableName + " (";

String commaAndSpace = ", ";
boolean firstTime = true;
while (true){
    System.out.println("");
    String columnNamePrompt = "Enter a column name " +
            "(or nothing when finished) \nand hit Return: ";
    columnName = getInput(columnNamePrompt);
    if (firstTime) {
        if (columnName.length() == 0) {
            System.out.print("Need at least one column;");
            System.out.println(" please try again");
            continue;
        } else {
            createTableString += columnName + " ";
```

```
            firstTime = false;
        }
    } else if (columnName.length() == 0) {
            break;
    } else {
        createTableString += commaAndSpace
            + columnName + " ";
    }

    // print only the JDBC SQL types for which there
    // is a corresponding DBMS type
    System.out.println("");
    System.out.println("LIST OF TYPES YOU MAY USE:  ");
    for (int i = 0; i < typeArray.length; i++) {
        if (! typeArray[i].needsToBeSet()) {
            System.out.println(typeArray[i].getSQLType());
        }
    }
    System.out.println("");

    // prompt the user and use the responses to construct a
    // CREATE TABLE statement
    int index;
    while (true) {
        String typePrompt = "Enter a column type " +
                "from the list and hit Return:  ";
        sqlType = getInput(typePrompt);
        for (index = 0; index < typeArray.length; index++) {
            if (typeArray[index].getSQLType().
                                equalsIgnoreCase(sqlType)){
                break;
            }
        }

        if (index < typeArray.length) { // there was a match
            break;
        }
```

```
                    System.out.println("");
                    System.out.print(sqlType + " does not match ");
                    System.out.println("available types.");
                    System.out.println("");
                }

                String params;
                String localTypeName;
                params = typeArray[index].getParams();
                localTypeName = typeArray[index].getLocalType();
                String paramString;
                if (params != null) {
                    String parameterPrompt = "Enter " + params + ":  ";
                    paramString = "(" + getInput(parameterPrompt) + ")";
                } else {
                    paramString = "";
                }
                createTableString += localTypeName + paramString;
            }

            createTableString += ")";
            System.out.println("");
            System.out.print("Your CREATE TABLE statement as ");
            System.out.println("sent to your DBMS:  ");
            System.out.println(createTableString);
            System.out.println("");

            stmt.executeUpdate(createTableString);

            stmt.close();
            con.close();

        } catch(SQLException ex) {
            System.err.println("SQLException: " + ex.getMessage());
        }
    }

    public static String getInput(String prompt) throws SQLException {
```

```
        System.out.print(prompt);
        System.out.flush();

        try {
            java.io.BufferedReader bin;
            bin = new java.io.BufferedReader(
                    new java.io.InputStreamReader(System.in));

            String result = bin.readLine();
            return result;

        } catch(java.io.IOException ex) {
            System.out.println("Caught java.io.IOException:");
            System.out.println(ex.getMessage());
            return "";
        }
    }
}
```

The following example is what you will see when you run SQLTypesCreate. This printout has our responses included in bold type.

```
➥ Enter the table name and hit Return: COFFEES
➥
➥ Enter a column name (or nothing when finished)
➥ and hit Return: COF_NAME
➥
➥ LIST OF TYPES YOU MAY USE:
➥ BIT
➥ TINYINT
➥ SMALLINT
➥ INTEGER
➥ FLOAT
➥ REAL
➥ NUMERIC
➥ DECIMAL
➥ CHAR
➥ VARCHAR
➥ LONGVARCHAR
➥ BINARY
➥ VARBINARY
```

➡ LONGVARBINARY
➡ NULL
➡
➡ Enter a column type from the list and hit Return:    **VARCHAR**
➡ Enter max length:    **32**
➡
➡ Enter a column name (or nothing when finished)
➡ and hit Return: **SUP_ID**
➡
➡ LIST OF TYPES YOU MAY USE:
(types omitted)
➡
➡ Enter a column type from the list and hit Return:    **INTEGER**
➡
➡ Enter a column name (or nothing when finished)
➡ and hit Return: **PRICE**
➡
➡ LIST OF TYPES YOU MAY USE:
(types omitted)
➡
➡ Enter a column type from the list and hit Return:    **FLOAT**
➡
➡ Enter a column name (or nothing when finished)
➡ and hit Return: **SALES**
➡
➡ LIST OF TYPES YOU MAY USE:
(types omitted)
➡
➡ Enter a column type from the list and hit Return:    **INTEGER**
➡
➡ Enter a column name (or nothing when finished)
➡ and hit Return: **TOTAL**
➡
➡ LIST OF TYPES YOU MAY USE:
(types omitted)
➡
➡ Enter a column type from the list and hit Return:    **INTEGER**
➡
➡ Enter a column name (or nothing when finished) and hit Return:
➡
➡ Your CREATE TABLE statement as sent to your DBMS:
➡ create table COFFEES (COF_NAME varchar(32), SUP_ID int, PRICE
   real, SALES int, TOTAL int)

# Part Two

Part Two contains the reference chapters, a chapter on mapping Java and SQL types, and two appendices. The reference chapters are arranged alphabetically for easy lookup. For reading about JDBC classes and interfaces, however, we recommend the following order:

1. Connection   (Chapter 5)

2. Statement   (Chapter 17)

3. ResultSet   (Chapter 13)

4. PreparedStatement   (Chapter 12)

5. CallableStatement   (Chapter 4)

The order in which other chapters are read does not matter as much, but we suggest reading about the exception classes in the order SQLException, SQLWarning, and DataTruncation, and reading about the time/date classes in the order Date, Time, and Timestamp.

Each reference chapter starts out with an overview of the class or interface. The second part of each chapter is the class or interface definition, which lists the methods and fields, if there are any, in a logical order. The explanations of the methods and fields, which follow, are arranged alphabetically to make looking them up easier.

127

# CHAPTER 4

# CallableStatement

## 4.1 CallableStatement Overview

A CallableStatement object provides a way to call stored procedures in a standard way for all RDBMSs. A stored procedure is stored in a database; the *call* to the stored procedure is what a CallableStatement object contains. This call is written in an escape syntax that may take one of two forms: one form with a result parameter, and the other without one. (See "SQL Escape Syntax in Statement Objects" on page 345 for complete information on escape syntax.) A result parameter, a kind of OUT parameter, is the return value for the stored procedure. Both forms may have a variable number of parameters used for input (IN parameters), output (OUT parameters), or both (INOUT parameters). A question mark serves as a placeholder for a parameter.

The syntax for invoking a stored procedure in JDBC is shown here. Note that the square brackets indicate that what is between them is optional; they are not themselves part of the syntax.

```
{call procedure_name[(?, ?, ...)]}
```

The syntax for a procedure that returns a result parameter is:

```
{? = call procedure_name[(?, ?, ...)]}
```

The syntax for a stored procedure with no parameters would look like this:

```
{call procedure_name}
```

Normally, anyone creating a `CallableStatement` object would already know that the DBMS being used supports stored procedures and what those procedures are. If one needed to check, however, various `DatabaseMetaData` methods will supply such information. For instance, the method `supportsStoredProcedures` will return `true` if the DBMS supports stored procedure calls, and the method `getProcedures` will return a description of the stored procedures available. See "DatabaseMetaData" on page 163 for more information.

`CallableStatement` inherits `Statement` methods, which deal with SQL statements in general, and it also inherits `PreparedStatement` methods, which deal with IN parameters. All of the methods defined in `CallableStatement` deal with OUT parameters or the output aspect of INOUT parameters: registering the JDBC types of the OUT parameters, retrieving values from them, or checking whether a returned value was JDBC `NULL`. Whereas the `getXXX` methods defined in `ResultSet` retrieve values from a result set, the `getXXX` methods in `CallableStatement` retrieve values from the OUT parameters and/or return value of a stored procedure.

### 4.1.1    Creating a `CallableStatement` Object

`CallableStatement` objects are created with the `Connection` method `prepareCall`. The following example, in which *con* is an active JDBC `Connection` object, creates an instance of `CallableStatement`:

```
CallableStatement cstmt = con.prepareCall(
                          "{call getTestData(?, ?)}");
```

The variable *cstmt* contains a call to the stored procedure `getTestData`, which has two argument parameters and no result parameter. Whether the ? placeholders are IN, OUT, or INOUT parameters depends on the stored procedure `getTestData`.

### 4.1.2    IN Parameters

Passing in any IN parameter values to a `CallableStatement` object is done using the `setXXX` methods inherited from `PreparedStatement`. The type of the value being passed in determines which `setXXX` method to use (`setFloat` to pass in a `float` value, `setBoolean` to pass in a `boolean`, and so on). See the section "Passing IN Parameters" on page 278 for an example of using IN parameters. Of the programs that use parameters, the vast majority use only IN parameters.

### 4.1.3    OUT Parameters

If the stored procedure returns OUT parameters, the JDBC type of each OUT parameter must be registered before the `CallableStatement` object can be executed. This is necessary because some DBMSs require the SQL type (which the JDBC type represents), not because JDBC requires it. JDBC types, a set of generic SQL type identifiers that represent the most commonly used SQL types, are explained fully in the chapter "Mapping SQL and Java Types" on page 379.

Registering the JDBC type is done with the method `registerOutParameter`. Then after the statement has been executed, `CallableStatement`'s getXXX methods can be used to retrieve OUT parameter values. The correct `CallableStatement.getXXX` method to use is the Java type that corresponds to the JDBC type registered for that parameter. (The standard mapping from JDBC types to Java types is shown in Table 21.1 on page 393.) In other words, `registerOutParameter` uses a JDBC type (so that it matches the data type that the database will return), and getXXX casts this to a Java type.

To illustrate, the following code registers the OUT parameters, executes the stored procedure called by *cstmt*, and then retrieves the values returned in the OUT parameters. The method `getByte` retrieves a Java byte from the first OUT parameter, and `getBigDecimal` retrieves a java.math.BigDecimal object (with three digits after the decimal point) from the second OUT parameter. The method `executeQuery` is used to execute *cstmt* because the stored procedure that it calls returns a result set.

```
CallableStatement cstmt = con.prepareCall(
                                "{call getTestData(?, ?)}");
cstmt.registerOutParameter(1, java.sql.Types.TINYINT);
cstmt.registerOutParameter(2, java.sql.Types.DECIMAL, 3);
ResultSet rs = cstmt.executeQuery();
// . . . retrieve result set values with rs.getXXX methods
byte x = cstmt.getByte(1);
java.math.BigDecimal n = cstmt.getBigDecimal(2, 3);
```

Unlike `ResultSet`, `CallableStatement` does not provide a special mechanism for retrieving large OUT values incrementally.

### 4.1.4    Numbering of Parameters

When a method takes an `int` specifying which parameter to act upon (`setXXX`, `getXXX`, and `registerOutParameter`), that `int` refers to ? placeholder parameters only, with numbering starting at one. The parameter number does not refer to literal parameters that might be supplied to a stored procedure call. For example, the following code fragment illustrates a stored procedure call with one literal parameter and one ? parameter:

```
CallableStatement cstmt = con.prepareCall(
                                "{call getTestData(25, ?)}");
cstmt.registerOutParameter(1, java.sql.Types.TINYINT);
```

In this code, the first argument to `registerOutParameter`, the int 1, refers to the first ? parameter (and in this case, the only ? parameter). It does not refer to the literal 25, which is the first parameter to the stored procedure.

### 4.1.5    INOUT Parameters

A parameter that supplies input as well as accepts output (an INOUT parameter) requires a call to the appropriate `setXXX` method (inherited from `PreparedStatement`) in addition to a call to the method `registerOutParameter`. The `setXXX` method sets a parameter's value as an input parameter, and the method `registerOutParameter` registers its JDBC type as an output parameter. The `setXXX` method provides a Java value that the driver converts to a JDBC value before sending it to the database. The JDBC type of this IN value and the JDBC type supplied to the method `registerOutParameter` should be the same. Then to retrieve the output value, a corresponding `getXXX` method is used. For example, a parameter whose Java type is byte should use the method `setByte` to assign the input value, should supply a `TINYINT` as the JDBC type to `registerOutParameter`, and should use `getByte` to retrieve the output value. ("Mapping SQL and Java Types" on page 379 contains tables of type mappings.)

The following example assumes that there is a stored procedure `reviseTotal` whose only parameter is an INOUT parameter. The method `setByte` sets the parameter to 25, which the driver will send to the database as a JDBC `TINYINT`. Next `registerOutParameter` registers the parameter as a JDBC `TINYINT`. After the stored procedure is executed, a new JDBC `TINYINT` value is returned, and the method `getByte` will retrieve this new value as a Java byte. Since the stored procedure called in this example returns an update count, the method `executeUpdate` is used.

```
CallableStatement cstmt = con.prepareCall(
                                    "{call reviseTotal(?)}");
cstmt.setByte(1, 25);
cstmt.registerOutParameter(1, java.sql.Types.TINYINT);
cstmt.executeUpdate();
byte x = cstmt.getByte(1);
```

### 4.1.6   Retrieve OUT Parameters after Results

Because of limitations imposed by some DBMSs, it is recommended that for maximum portability, all of the results in a `ResultSet` object generated by the execution of a `CallableStatement` object should be retrieved before OUT parameters are retrieved. When all values have been retrieved from a result set, the method `ResultSet.next` will return `false`.

If a `CallableStatement` object returns multiple `ResultSet` objects (which is possible only if it is executed with a call to the method `execute`), all of the results should be retrieved before OUT parameters are retrieved. In this case, to be sure that all results have been accessed, the `Statement` methods `getResultSet`, `getUpdateCount`, and `getMoreResults` need to be called until there are no more results. When all results have been exhausted, the method `getMoreResults` returns `false`, and the method `getUpdateCount` returns -1. See "Using the Method execute" on page 348 for more information.

After all values have been retrieved from `ResultSet` objects (using `ResultSet.getXXX` methods), and after it has been determined that there are no more update counts, values from OUT parameters can be retrieved (using `CallableStatement.getXXX` methods).

### 4.1.7   Retrieving NULL Values as OUT Parameters

The value returned to an OUT parameter may be JDBC `NULL`. When this happens, the JDBC `NULL` value will be converted so that the value returned by a `getXXX` method will be `null`, `0`, or `false`, depending on the `getXXX` method type. As with `ResultSet` objects, the only way to know if a value of `0` or `false` was originally JDBC `NULL` is to test it with the method `wasNull`, which returns `true` if the last value

read by a getXXX method was JDBC NULL, and false otherwise. The ResultSet
section "NULL Result Values" on page 302 contains more information.

## 4.2    CallableStatement Definition

```
package java.sql;
public interface CallableStatement extends PreparedStatement {
    void registerOutParameter(int parameterIndex, int jdbcType)
                                                    throws SQLException;
    boolean wasNull() throws SQLException;
    boolean getBoolean(int parameterIndex) throws SQLException;
    byte getByte(int parameterIndex) throws SQLException;
    short getShort(int parameterIndex) throws SQLException;
    int getInt(int parameterIndex) throws SQLException;
    long getLong(int parameterIndex) throws SQLException;
    float getFloat(int parameterIndex) throws SQLException;
    double getDouble(int parameterIndex) throws SQLException;
    java.math.BigDecimal getBigDecimal(int parameterIndex)
                                                    throws SQLException;
    String getString(int parameterIndex) throws SQLException;
    byte[] getBytes(int parameterIndex) throws SQLException;
    java.sql.Date getDate(int parameterIndex) throws SQLException;
    java.sql.Time getTime(int parameterIndex) throws SQLException;
    java.sql.Timestamp getTimestamp(int parameterIndex)
                                                    throws SQLException;
    //-------------------------------------------------------------
    //                      Advanced features:
    //-------------------------------------------------------------
    Object getObject(int parameterIndex) throws SQLException;
}
```

## 4.3    CallableStatement Methods

The following methods are inherited from Statement:

| | | |
|---|---|---|
| cancel | getMoreResults | setCursorName |
| clearWarnings | getQueryTimeout | setEscapeProcessing |
| close | getResultSet | setMaxFieldSize |
| getMaxFieldSize | getUpdateCount | setMaxRows |
| getMaxRows | getWarnings | setQueryTimeout |

The following methods are inherited from `PreparedStatement`:

| | | |
|---|---|---|
| clearParameters | setByte | setObject |
| execute | setBytes | setShort |
| executeQuery | setDate | setString |
| executeUpdate | setDouble | setTime |
| setAsciiStream | setFloat | setTimestamp |
| setBigDecimal | setInt | setUnicodeStream |
| setBinaryStream | setLong | |
| setBoolean | setNull | |

## getBigDecimal

```
java.math.BigDecimal getBigDecimal(int parameterIndex, int scale)
                                          throws SQLException
```

Gets the value of a JDBC `Numeric` parameter as a `java.math.BigDecimal` object with *scale* digits to the right of the decimal point.

**PARAMETERS:**

*parameterIndex*    1 indicates the first parameter, 2 the second, and so on.

*scale*    the number of digits to the right of the decimal point.

**RETURNS:**

the parameter value as a `java.math.BigDecimal` object. If the value is SQL NULL, the result is `null`.

**EXAMPLE:**

```
java.math.BigDecimal n = cstmt.getBigDecimal(2, 6);
// gets the second OUT parameter as a java.math.BigDecimal object
// with 6 digits to the right of the decimal point
```

## getBoolean

```
boolean getBoolean(int parameterIndex) throws SQLException
```

Gets the value of a JDBC `BIT` parameter as a Java `boolean`.

**PARAMETERS:**

*parameterIndex*    1 indicates the first parameter, 2 the second, and so on.

**RETURNS:**

the parameter value as a Java `boolean`. If the value is SQL `NULL`, the result is `false`.

**EXAMPLE:**
```
boolean b = cstmt.getBoolean(1);
// gets the first OUT parameter as a Java boolean
```

## getByte

```
byte getByte(int parameterIndex) throws SQLException
```

Gets the value of a JDBC `TINYINT` parameter as a Java `byte`.

**PARAMETERS:**

*parameterIndex*          1 indicates the first parameter, 2 the second, and so on.

**RETURNS:**

the parameter value as a Java `byte`. If the value is SQL `NULL`, the result is 0.

**EXAMPLE:**
```
byte q = cstmt.getByte(2); // gets the second OUT parameter as a byte
```

## getBytes

```
byte[] getBytes(int parameterIndex) throws SQLException
```

Gets the value of a JDBC `BINARY`, `VARBINARY`, or `LONGVARBINARY` parameter as a Java `byte[]`.

**PARAMETERS:**

*parameterIndex*          1 indicates the first parameter, 2 the second, and so on.

**RETURNS:**

the parameter value as a Java `byte[]`. If the value is SQL `NULL`, the result is `null`.

**EXAMPLE:**
```
byte [] q = cstmt.getBytes(1);
// gets the first OUT parameter as an array of bytes
```

## getDate

```
java.sql.Date getDate(int parameterIndex) throws SQLException
```

Gets the value of a JDBC DATE parameter as a java.sql.Date object.

**PARAMETERS:**
*parameterIndex*        1 indicates the first parameter, 2 the second, and so on.

**RETURNS:**
the parameter value as a java.sql.Date object. If the value is SQL NULL, the result is null.

**EXAMPLE:**
```
Date d = cstmt.getDate(3);
// gets the third OUT parameter as a java.sql.Date object
```

## getDouble

```
double getDouble(int parameterIndex) throws SQLException
```

Gets the value of a JDBC DOUBLE or JDBC FLOAT parameter as a Java double.

**PARAMETERS:**
*parameterIndex*        1 indicates the first parameter, 2 the second, and so on.

**RETURNS:**
the parameter value as a Java double. If the value is SQL NULL, the result is 0.

**EXAMPLE:**
```
double d = cstmt.getDouble(2);
// gets the second OUT parameter as a double
```

## getFloat

```
float getFloat(int parameterIndex) throws SQLException
```

Gets the value of a JDBC FLOAT parameter as a Java float.

**PARAMETERS:**
*parameterIndex*        1 indicates the first parameter, 2 the second, and so on.

**RETURNS:**
the parameter value as a Java float. If the value is SQL NULL, the result is 0.

**EXAMPLE:**
```
float f = cstmt.getFloat(1);
// gets the first OUT parameter as a float
```

## getInt

```
int getInt(int parameterIndex) throws SQLException
```

Gets the value of a JDBC INTEGER parameter as a Java int.

**PARAMETERS:**
*parameterIndex*        1 indicates the first parameter, 2 the second, and so on.

**RETURNS:**
the parameter value as a Java int. If the value is SQL NULL, the result is 0.

**EXAMPLE:**
```
int x = cstmt.getInt(2); // gets the second OUT parameter as an int
```

## getLong

```
long getLong(int parameterIndex) throws SQLException
```

Gets the value of a JDBC BIGINT parameter as a Java long.

**PARAMETERS:**
*parameterIndex*        1 indicates the first parameter, 2 the second, and so on.

**RETURNS:**
the parameter value as a Java long. If the value is SQL NULL, the result is 0.

**EXAMPLE:**
```
long x = cstmt.getLong(2); // gets the second OUT parameter as a long
```

## getObject

```
Object getObject(int parameterIndex) throws SQLException
```

Gets the value of parameter *parameterIndex* as a Java object.

This method returns a Java object whose type corresponds to the JDBC type that was registered for this parameter using the method `registerOutParameter`. By registering the target JDBC type as `java.sql.Types.OTHER`, this method may be used to read database-specific abstract data types. This is discussed in detail in "Dynamic Data Access" on page 391.

**PARAMETERS:**
*parameterIndex*        1 indicates the first parameter, 2 the second, and so on.

**RETURNS:**
a `java.lang.Object` object holding the OUT parameter value.

**EXAMPLE:**
```
Object obj = cstmt.getObject(2);
// gets the second OUT parameter as the type that was registered for
// this parameter
```
The following example demonstrates using an object after it has been retrieved:
```
if (obj instanceOf Wombat) {
    Wombat w = (Wombat)obj;
    w.burrow();
}
```

**SEE:**
`java.sql.Types`
"JDBC Types Mapped to Java Object Types" on page 395.


## getShort

```
short getShort(int parameterIndex) throws SQLException
```

Gets the value of a JDBC SMALLINT parameter as a Java short.

**PARAMETERS:**
*parameterIndex*        1 indicates the first parameter, 2 the second, and so on.

**RETURNS:**
the parameter value as a Java short. If the value is SQL NULL, the result is 0.

**EXAMPLE:**
```
short s = cstmt.getShort(1);
// gets the first OUT parameter as a short
```

## getString

String **getString**(int *parameterIndex*) throws SQLException

Gets the value of a JDBC CHAR, VARCHAR, or LONGVARCHAR parameter as a Java String.

For the fixed-length type JDBC CHAR, the String object returned will have exactly the same value the JDBC CHAR value had in the database, including any padding added by the database.

**PARAMETERS:**
*parameterIndex*          1 indicates the first parameter, 2 the second, and so on.

**RETURNS:**
the parameter value as a String object. If the value is SQL NULL, the result is null.

**EXAMPLE:**
String s = cstmt.getString(2);
// gets the second OUT parameter as a String object

## getTime

java.sql.Time **getTime**(int *parameterIndex*) throws SQLException

Gets the value of a JDBC TIME parameter as a java.sql.Time object.

**PARAMETERS:**
*parameterIndex*          1 indicates the first parameter, 2 the second, and so on.

**RETURNS:**
the parameter value as a java.sql.Time object. If the value is SQL NULL, the result is null.

**EXAMPLE:**
Time t = cstmt.getTime(4);
// gets the fourth OUT parameter as a java.sql.Time object

## getTimestamp

java.sql.Timestamp **getTimestamp**(int *parameterIndex*)
                                        throws SQLException;

Gets the value of a JDBC TIMESTAMP parameter as a java.sql.Timestamp object.

**PARAMETERS:**

parameterIndex        1 indicates the first parameter, 2 the second, and so on.

**RETURNS:**

the parameter value as a java.sql.Timestamp object. If the value is SQL NULL, the result is null.

**EXAMPLE:**
```
Timestamp ts = cstmt.getTimestamp(2);
// gets the second OUT parameter as a java.sql.Timestamp object
```

## egisterOutParameter

```
oid registerOutParameter (int parameterIndex, int jdbcType)
                                               throws SQLException
```

Registers the OUT parameter in ordinal position *parameterIndex* to the JDBC type *jdbcType*. All OUT parameters must be registered before a stored procedure is executed.

The JDBC type specified by *jdbcType* for an OUT parameter determines the Java type that must be used in the method getXXX to read the value of that parameter. See "JDBC Types Mapped to Java Types" on page 393.

If the JDBC type expected to be returned to this output parameter is specific to this particular database, *jdbcType* should be java.sql.Types.OTHER. The method CallableStatement.getObject will retrieve the value.

**PARAMETERS:**

parameterIndex        1 indicates the first parameter, 2 the second, and so on.

jdbcType              the JDBC type code defined by java.sql.Types. If the
                      parameter is of type NUMERIC or DECIMAL, the version of
                      registerOutParameter that accepts a scale value
                      should be used.

**EXAMPLE:**
```
cstmt.registerOutParameter(3, Types.TIMESTAMP);
// registers the third parameter to be of type JDBC TIMESTAMP
```

**SEE:**
```
java.sql.Types
```

## registerOutParameter

```
void registerOutParameter (int parameterIndex, int jdbcType,
                                    int scale)throws SQLException
```

Registers the parameter in ordinal position *parameterIndex* to be of JDBC type *jdbcType*. This method must be called before executing a stored procedure.

The JDBC type specified by *jdbcType* for an OUT parameter determines the Java type that must be used in the method getXXX to read the value of that parameter. See "JDBC Types Mapped to Java Types" on page 393.

This version of registerOutParameter should be used when the parameter is of JDBC type NUMERIC or DECIMAL.

**PARAMETERS:**

| | |
|---|---|
| *parameterIndex* | 1 indicates the first parameter, 2 the second, and so on. |
| *jdbcType* | the JDBC type code defined by java.sql.Types. |
| *scale* | the desired number of digits to the right of the decimal point. It must be greater than or equal to zero. |

**EXAMPLE:**
```
cstmt.registerOutParameter(3, Types.NUMERIC, 4);
// registers the third parameter to be of type NUMERIC with
// 4 digits after the decimal point
```

**SEE:**
```
java.sql.Types
```

## wasNull

```
boolean wasNull() throws SQLException
```

Indicates whether or not the last OUT parameter read had the value SQL NULL. Note that this method should be called only after calling the method getXXX; otherwise, there is no value to use in determining whether it is null or not.

**RETURNS:**
true if the last parameter read was SQL NULL; false otherwise.

**EXAMPLE:**
```
String s = cstmt.getString(2);
boolean b = cstmt.wasNull(); // b is true if s is SQL NULL
```

CHAPTER **5**

# Connection

## 5.1   Connection Overview

**A** Connection object represents a connection with a database. A connection session includes the SQL statements that are executed and the results that are returned over that connection. A single application can have one or more connections with a single database, or it can have connections with many different databases.

A user can get information about a Connection object's database by invoking the Connection.getMetaData method. This method returns a DatabaseMetaData object that contains information about the database's tables, the SQL grammar it supports, its stored procedures, the capabilities of this connection, and so on. Readers who want more information can check "DatabaseMetaData" on page 163.

### 5.1.1   Opening a Connection

The standard way to establish a connection with a database is to call the method DriverManager.getConnection. This method takes a string containing a URL. The DriverManager class, referred to as the JDBC management layer, attempts to locate a driver than can connect to the database represented by that URL. The DriverManager class maintains a list of registered Driver classes, and when the method getConnection is called, it checks with each driver in the list until it finds one that can connect to the database specified in the URL. The Driver method connect uses this URL to actually establish the connection.

A user can bypass the JDBC management layer and call Driver methods directly. This could be useful in the rare case that two drivers can connect to a database and the user wants to explicitly select a particular driver. Normally, however, it is much easier to just let the `DriverManager` class handle opening a connection. The chapters "Driver" on page 257 and "DriverManager" on page 263 give more detailed information.

The following code exemplifies opening a connection to a database located at the URL `jdbc:odbc:wombat` with a user ID of `oboy` and `12Java` as the password :

```
String url = "jdbc:odbc:wombat";
Connection con = DriverManager.getConnection(url, "oboy", "12Java");
```

### 5.1.2   URLs in General Use

Since URLs often cause some confusion, we will first give a brief explanation of URLs in general and then go on to a discussion of JDBC URLs.

A URL (Uniform Resource Locator) gives information for locating a resource on the Internet. It can be thought of as an address.

The first part of a URL specifies the protocol used to access information, and it is always followed by a colon. Some common protocols are `ftp`, which specifies "file transfer protocol," and `http`, which specifies "hypertext transfer protocol." If the protocol is `file`, it indicates that the resource is in a local file system rather than on the Internet. (Underlining in the examples below is used to indicate the part being described; it is not part of the URL.)

```
ftp://javasoft.com/docs/JDK-1_apidocs.zip
http://java.sun.com/products/JDK/CurrentRelease
file:/home/haroldw/docs/tutorial.html
```

The rest of a URL, everything after the first colon, gives information about where the data source is located. If the protocol is `file`, the rest of the URL is the path to a file. For the protocols `ftp` and `http`, the rest of the URL identifies the host and may optionally give a path to a more specific site. For example, here is the URL for the JavaSoft home page. This URL identifies only the host:

```
http://www.javasoft.com
```

By navigating from this home page, you can go to many other pages, one of which is the JDBC home page. The URL for the JDBC home page is more specific and looks like this:

```
http://www.javasoft.com/products/jdbc
```

### 5.1.3   JDBC URLs

A JDBC URL provides a way of identifying a database so that the appropriate driver will recognize it and establish a connection with it. Driver writers are the ones who actually determine what the JDBC URL that identifies their particular driver will be. Users do not need to worry about how to form a JDBC URL; they simply use the URL supplied with the drivers they are using. JDBC's role is to recommend some conventions for driver writers to follow in structuring their JDBC URLs.

Since JDBC URLs are used with various kinds of drivers, the conventions are of necessity very flexible. First, they allow different drivers to use different schemes for naming databases. The odbc subprotocol, for example, lets the URL contain attribute values (but does not require them).

Second, JDBC URLs allow driver writers to encode all necessary connection information within them. This makes it possible, for example, for an applet that wants to talk to a given database to open the database connection without requiring the user to do any system administration chores.

Third, JDBC URLs allow a level of indirection. This means that the JDBC URL may refer to a logical host or database name that is dynamically translated to the actual name by a network naming system. This allows system administrators to avoid specifying particular hosts as part of the JDBC name. There are a number of different network name services (such as DNS, NIS, and DCE), and there is no restriction about which ones can be used.

The standard syntax for JDBC URLs is shown here. It has three parts, which are separated by colons:

```
jdbc:<subprotocol>:<subname>
```

The three parts of a JDBC URL are broken down as follows:

1. jdbc—the protocol. The protocol in a JDBC URL is always jdbc.

2. <subprotocol>—the name of the driver or the name of a database connectivity mechanism, which may be supported by one or more drivers. A prominent example of a subprotocol name is odbc, which has been reserved for URLs that specify ODBC–style data source names. For example, to access a database through a JDBC–ODBC bridge, one might use a URL such as the following:

```
jdbc:odbc:fred
```

In this example, the subprotocol is odbc, and the subname fred is a local ODBC data source.

If one wants to use a network name service (so that the database name in the JDBC URL does not have to be its actual name), the naming service can be the subprotocol. So, for example, one might have a URL like:

```
jdbc:dcenaming:accounts-payable
```

In this example, the URL specifies that the local DCE naming service should resolve the database name accounts-payable into a more specific name that can be used to connect to the real database.

3. <subname>—a way to identify the database. The subname can vary, depending on the subprotocol, and it can have a subsubname with any internal syntax the driver writer chooses. The point of a subname is to give enough information to locate the database. In the previous example, fred is enough because ODBC provides the remainder of the information. A database on a remote server requires more information, however. If the database is to be accessed over the Internet, for example, the network address should be included in the JDBC URL as part of the subname and should follow the standard URL naming convention of

```
//hostname:port/subsubname
```

Supposing that dbnet is a protocol for connecting to a host on the Internet, a JDBC URL might look like this:

```
jdbc:dbnet://wombat:356/fred
```

### 5.1.4   The odbc Subprotocol

The subprotocol odbc is a special case. It has been reserved for URLs that specify ODBC-style data source names and has the special feature of allowing any number of attribute values to be specified after the subname (the data source name). The full syntax for the odbc subprotocol is:

```
jdbc:odbc:<data-source-name>[;<attribute-name>=<attribute-value>]*
```

Thus all of the following are valid jdbc:odbc names:

```
jdbc:odbc:qeor7
jdbc:odbc:wombat
jdbc:odbc:wombat;CacheSize=20;ExtensionCase=LOWER
jdbc:odbc:qeora;UID=kgh;PWD=fooey
```

### 5.1.5    Registering Subprotocols

A driver developer can reserve a name to be used as the subprotocol in a JDBC URL. When the `DriverManager` class presents this name to its list of registered drivers, the driver for which this name is reserved should recognize it and establish a connection to the database it identifies. For example, "odbc" is reserved for the JDBC–ODBC Bridge. If there were, for another example, a Miracle Corporation, it might want to register "miracle" as the subprotocol for the JDBC driver that connects to its Miracle DBMS so that no one else would use that name.

JavaSoft is acting as an informal registry for JDBC subprotocol names. To register a subprotocol name, send email to:

```
jdbc@wombat.eng.sun.com
```

### 5.1.6    Sending SQL Statements

Once a connection is established, it is used to pass SQL statements to its underlying database. JDBC does not put any restrictions on the kinds of SQL statements that can be sent; this provides a great deal of flexibility, allowing the use of database-specific statements or even non-SQL statements. It requires, however, that the user be responsible for making sure that the underlying database can process the SQL statements being sent and suffer the consequences if it cannot. For example, an application that tries to send a stored procedure call to a DBMS that does not support stored procedures will be unsuccessful and generate an exception. JDBC requires that a driver provide at least ANSI SQL-92 Entry Level capabilities in order to be designated JDBC Compliant. This means that users can count on at least this standard level of functionality.

JDBC provides three classes for sending SQL statements to the database, and three methods in the `Connection` interface create instances of these classes. These are the classes and the methods that create them:

1. Statement—created by the method createStatement. A Statement object is used for sending SQL statements with no parameters.

2. PreparedStatement—created by the method prepareStatement. A Prepared-Statement object is used for precompiled SQL statements. These can take one or more parameters as input arguments (IN parameters). PreparedStatement has a group of methods that set the value of IN parameters, which are sent to the database when the statement is executed. PreparedStatement extends Statement and therefore includes Statement methods. A PreparedStatement object has the potential to be more efficient than a Statement object because it has been precompiled and stored for future use. Therefore, a PreparedStatement object is sometimes used for an SQL statement that is executed many times in order to improve performance.

3. CallableStatement—created by the method prepareCall. CallableStatement objects are used to execute SQL stored procedures—a group of SQL statements that is called by name, much like invoking a function. A CallableStatement object inherits methods for handling IN parameters from PreparedStatement; it adds methods for handling OUT and INOUT parameters.

The following list gives a quick way to determine which Connection method is appropriate for creating different types of SQL statements:

- createStatement method is used for a simple SQL statement (no parameters)
- prepareStatement method is used for an SQL statement that is executed frequently
- prepareCall method is used for a call to a stored procedure

### 5.1.7   Transactions

A transaction consists of one or more statements that have been executed, completed, and then either committed or rolled back. When the method commit or rollback is called, the current transaction ends and another one begins.

A new connection is in auto-commit mode by default, meaning that when a statement is completed, the method commit will be called on that statement automatically. In this case, since each statement is committed individually, a transaction consists of only one statement. If auto-commit mode has been disabled, a transaction will not terminate until the method commit or rollback is called explicitly, so it will include all the statements that have been executed since the last invocation of either commit or rollback. In this second case, all the statements in the transaction are committed or rolled back as a group.

The beginning of a transaction requres no explicit call; it is implicitly initiated after disabling auto-commit mode or after calling the methods `commit` or `rollback`.

The method `commit` makes permanent any changes an SQL statement makes to a database, and it also releases any locks held by the transaction. The method `rollback` will discard those changes.

Sometimes a user doesn't want one change to take effect unless another one does also. This can be accomplished by disabling auto-commit and grouping both updates into one transaction. If both updates are successful, then the `commit` method is called, making the effects of both updates permanent; if one fails or both fail, then the `rollback` method is called, restoring the values that existed before the updates were executed.

Most JDBC drivers will support transactions. In order to be designated JDBC Compliant, a JDBC driver must support transactions.

### 5.1.8   Transaction Isolation Levels

If a DBMS supports transaction processing, it will have some way of managing potential conflicts that can arise when two transactions are operating on a database at the same time. A user can specify a transaction isolation level to indicate what level of care the DBMS should exercise in resolving potential conflicts. For example, what happens when one transaction changes a value and a second transaction reads that value before the change has been committed or rolled back? Should that be allowed, given that the changed value read by the second transaction will be invalid if the first transaction is rolled back? A JDBC user can instruct the DBMS to allow a value to be read before it has been committed ("dirty reads") with the following code, where *con* is the current connection:

```
con.setTransactionIsolation(TRANSACTION_READ_UNCOMMITTED);
```

The higher the transaction isolation level, the more care is taken to avoid conflicts. The `Connection` interface defines five levels, with the lowest specifying that transactions are not supported at all and the highest specifying that while one transaction is operating on a database, no other transactions may make any changes to the data read by that transaction. TRANSACTION_READ_UNCOMMITTED, used in the previous example, is one level up from the lowest level. Typically, the higher the level of isolation, the slower the application executes (due to increased locking overhead and decreased concurrency between users). The developer must balance the need for performance with the need for data consistency when making a decision about what isolation level to use. Of course, the level that can actually be supported depends on the capabilities of the underlying DBMS.

When a new `Connection` object is created, its transaction isolation level depends on the driver, but normally it is the default for the underlying database. A user may call the method `setIsolationLevel` to change the transaction isolation level, and the new level will be in effect for the rest of the connection session. To change the transaction isolation level for just one transaction, one needs to set it before executing any statements in the transaction and then to reset it after the transaction terminates. Changing the transaction isolation level during a transaction is not recommended, for it will trigger an immediate call to the method `commit`, causing any changes up to that point to be made permanent.

### 5.1.9   Using the Method `close` to Free DBMS Resources

It is recommended that programmers explicitly close connections and statements they have created when they are no longer needed.

A programmer writing code in Java and not using any outside resources does not need to worry about memory management. The garbage collector automatically removes objects when they are no longer being used and frees the memory they were using. When memory is running low, it will recycle discarded objects, making the memory they currently occupy available for quick reuse.

However, if an application uses external resources, as it does when it accesses a DBMS with JDBC, the garbage collector has no way of knowing the status of those resources. It will still recycle discarded objects, but if there is lots of free memory in the Java heap, it may garbage collect infrequently, even though the (small) amount of Java garbage is holding open large amounts of expensive database resources. Therefore, it is recommended that programmers explicitly close all connections and statements as soon as they are no longer needed, thereby freeing DBMS resources as early as possible. This applies especially to applications that are intended to work with different DBMSs because of variations from one DBMS to another.

## 5.2   `Connection` Interface Definition

```
package java.sql;
public interface Connection {
    Statement createStatement() throws SQLException;
    PreparedStatement prepareStatement(String sql)throws
                            SQLException;
```

```
    CallableStatement prepareCall(String sql) throws SQLException;
    String nativeSQL(String query) throws SQLException;
    void setAutoCommit(boolean enableAutoCommit) throws
                                    SQLException;
    boolean getAutoCommit() throws SQLException;
    void commit() throws SQLException;
    void rollback() throws SQL exception;
    void close() throws SQLException;
    boolean isClosed() throws SQLException;
//-----------------------------------------------------------------
//                  Advanced features:
//-----------------------------------------------------------------
    DatabaseMetaData getMetaData() throws SQLException;
    void setReadOnly(boolean readOnly) throws SQLException;
    boolean isReadOnly() throws SQLException;
    void setCatalog(String catalog) throws SQLException;
    String getCatalog() throws SQLException;
    int TRANSACTION_NONE            = 0;
    int TRANSACTION_READ_UNCOMMITTED = 1;
    int TRANSACTION_READ_COMMITTED   = 2;
    int TRANSACTION_REPEATABLE_READ  = 4;
    int TRANSACTION_SERIALIZABLE     = 8;
    void setTransactionIsolation(int level) throws SQLException;
    int getTransactionIsolation() throws SQLException;
    SQLWarning getWarnings() throws SQLException;
    void clearWarnings() throws SQLException;
}
```

## 5.3    Connection Methods

### clearWarnings

```
void clearWarnings() throws SQLException
```

Clears all warnings that have been reported by calls on this connection. After a call to the method clearWarnings, calls to the method getWarnings will return null until a new warning is reported for this connection.

**EXAMPLE:**
```
con.clearWarnings();
```

## close

```
void close() throws SQLException
```

Releases a `Connection` object's DBMS and JDBC resources immediately instead of waiting for them to be released automatically.

A connection is automatically closed when it is garbage collected; however, depending on this feature is not recommended. Certain fatal errors also result in a closed connection.

The recommended programming style is to explicitly close any `Connection` objects when they are no longer needed; this releases DBMS resources as soon as possible.

**EXAMPLE:**
```
con.close();
```

## commit

```
void commit() throws SQLException
```

Makes permanent all changes made to the database since the previous call to the method `commit` or `rollback` and releases any database locks currently held by this `Connection` object.

If a `Connection` object is in auto-commit mode, which is the default for new connections, then all its SQL statements will be executed and committed as individual transactions automatically. To execute and commit multiple statements as one transaction, auto-commit must be disabled (by calling `setAutoCommit(false)`) and the method `commit` must then be called explicitly.

**EXAMPLE:**
```
con.commit();
```

## createStatement

```
Statement createStatement() throws SQLException
```

SQL statements without parameters are normally executed using `State-`
`ment` objects. See the `Connection` method `prepareStatement` for information
about when it is more efficient to use a `PreparedStatement` object for a simple
SQL statement.

**RETURNS:**
a newly-created `Statement` object.

**EXAMPLE:**
```
Connection con = DriverManager.getConnection(url, "xyz", "");
Statement stmt = con.createStatement();
ResultSet rs = stmt.executeQuery("SELECT a, b, c FROM Table1");
```

## getAutoCommit

```
boolean getAutoCommit() throws SQLException
```

When a connection is in auto-commit mode, its SQL statements are committed automatically right after they are executed. This means that each statement is treated as a separate transaction and that any changes it produces are
either made permanent or discarded immediately. It also means that no locks
are retained in the underlying database. If the connection is not in auto-commit mode (the method `getAutoCommit` returns `false`), a transaction will
include all the SQL statements that have been executed since the last call to
the method `commit` or `rollback` and will not terminate until either the `commit`
or `rollback` method is called again. By default, a new connection is in auto-
commit mode.

**RETURNS:**
`true` if the connection is in auto-commit mode or `false` if it is not.

**EXAMPLE:**
```
boolean b = myConnection.getAutoCommit();
```

## getCatalog

```
String getCatalog() throws SQLException
```

The definition of a catalog name depends on the particular DBMS, but in
general, it is the outermost level of qualification for the name of a database

object. For example, a table can be referred to as "tableName," "database-Name.tableName," or "userName.databaseName.tableName." In this example, "userName.databaseName.tableName" is the fully qualified name, and "userName" is the catalog name. The fully qualified name can be expressed as "catalog.schema.tableName," where *catalog* is generally the user, and *schema* is generally the name of the database. For most databases, a new connection session begins in the database's default catalog, and in most cases, a user would not want to change it.

**RETURNS:**
a `String` object representing the `Connection` object's catalog name or `null` if there is none.

**EXAMPLE:**
```
String s = myConnection.getCatalog();
```

## getMetaData

```
DatabaseMetaData getMetaData() throws SQLException
```

Gets a `DatabaseMetaData` object containing information about the connection's database, including a description of the database's tables, its stored procedures, the SQL grammar the DBMS supports, and the capabilities of the connection. This object is used to access information about the database by calling `DatabaseMetaData` methods on it.

**RETURNS:**
a `DatabaseMetaData` object for this connection.

**EXAMPLE:**
```
DatabaseMetaData dbmd = myConnection.getMetaData();
```

**SEE:**
```
DatabaseMetaData
```

## getTransactionIsolation

```
int getTransactionIsolation() throws SQLException
```

The transaction isolation level of a newly created `Connection` object depends on the connection's driver. If the driver supports transaction isolation levels, it will be the default for the underlying database unless it has been changed. See "Transaction Isolation Levels" on page 149 for a discussion of transaction isolation levels.

**RETURNS:**
an `int` representing the connection's current transaction isolation mode. Valid values, in ascending order, are TRANSACTION_NONE, TRANSACTION_READ_UNCOMMITTED, TRANSACTION_READ_COMMITTED, TRANSACTION_REPEATABLE_READ, and TRANSACTION_SERIALIZABLE.

**EXAMPLE:**
```
int x = myConnection.getTransactionIsolation();
```

## getWarnings

```
SQLWarning getWarnings() throws SQLException
```

Gets the first warning reported by calls on this `Connection` object. Subsequent warnings will be chained to the first `SQLWarning`. This method does not clear warnings.

**RETURNS:**
the first `SQLWarning`; `null` if there have been no warnings reported or if the method `clearWarnings` has been called and there have been no subsequent warnings reported.

**EXAMPLE:**
```
SQLWarning w = con.getWarnings(); // get first warning
while(w != null) {
    System.out.println("Warning = " + w);
    w = w.getNextWarning();
    //get any warnings chained to the first one
}
```

**SEE:**
```
java.sql.SQLWarning
```

## isClosed

```
boolean isClosed() throws SQLException
```

Indicates whether the calling `Connection` object has been closed. A connection is closed if the method `close` has been called on it or if certain fatal errors have occurred.

**RETURNS:**
`true` if the connection is closed or `false` if it is still open.

**EXAMPLE:**
`boolean b = con.isClosed();`

## isReadOnly

`boolean isReadOnly() throws SQLException`

Being in read-only mode is a suggestion to the database that it can optimize performance by not worrying about write operations; it does not mean that the connection is prevented from writing to the database. It is expected that the default value for read-only is `false`; however, if a driver allows no updates to a database (the database is read-only), then a call to the method `isReadOnly` should return `true`.

**RETURNS:**
`true` if the connection is in read-only mode or `false` otherwise.

**EXAMPLE:**
`boolean b = con.isReadOnly();`

## nativeSQL

`String nativeSQL(String query) throws SQLException`

Translates *query* into the native query language of the underlying DBMS and returns it as a `String` object.

**PARAMETERS:**
*query*                    String containing an SQL statement.

**RETURNS:**
the native form of *query* as a Java `String` object.

**EXAMPLE:**
```
String query = "INSERT INTO Table1 (a, b, c)
                VALUES (10013, 'Washington', {d '1999-01-01'})";
```

```
String nativeForm = con.nativeSQL(query);
// The variable nativeForm contains a String object with query
// translated into the query language of the underlying database.
// For example, if the DBMS is Oracle, the variable nativeForm would
// contain a String object similar to the following:
//      "insert into Table1 (a, b, c)
//       values (10013, 'Washington', '01-JAN-99')"
// The escape syntax {d '1999-01-01'} signals the compiler to
// translate the date into native syntax.
```

**SEE:**
"SQL Escape Syntax in Statement Objects" on page 345

## prepareCall

```
CallableStatement prepareCall(String sql) throwsSQLException
```

An SQL stored procedure call statement is handled by creating a `Call-ableStatement` object for it. The `CallableStatement` object has methods for setting up its IN and OUT parameters, and it also provides methods for executing the stored procedure.

NOTE: This method is optimized for handling stored procedure call statements. Some drivers may send the call statement to the database when the method `prepareCall` creates a `CallableStatement`; others may wait until the `CallableStatement` object is executed. This has no direct effect on users; however, it does affect which methods throw certain `SQLExceptions`.

**PARAMETERS:**

*sql*
    an SQL statement that may contain one or more '?' parameter placeholders. Optimally, this should be a call to a stored procedure, but any SQL statement will be accepted.

**RETURNS:**
a new `CallableStatement` object containing the precompiled SQL statement.

**EXAMPLE:**
```
CallableStatement cstmt = con.prepareCall(
            "{call revisePrices(?, ?, ?)}");
```

## prepareStatement

PreparedStatement **prepareStatement**(String *sql*)throws SQLException

An SQL statement with or without IN parameters can be precompiled and stored in a PreparedStatement object. Expert programmers can use this object to efficiently execute a statement multiple times. PreparedStatement objects cannot contain SQL statements with OUT parameters; those require CallableStatement objects. See the method prepareCall.

NOTE: This method is optimized for handling parametric SQL statements that benefit from precompilation. If the driver supports precompilation, the method prepareStatement will send the statement to the database for precompilation. If the driver does not support precompilation, the statement may not be sent to the database until the PreparedStatement is executed. This has no direct effect on users; however, it does affect which methods throw certain SQLExceptions.

**PARAMETERS:**

*sql*                      An SQL statement that may contain one or more ? IN
                           parameter placeholders. It may not contain OUT or IN-
                           OUT parameter placeholders.

**RETURNS:**

a new precompiled PreparedStatement object containing the SQL statement supplied in *sql*.

**EXAMPLE:**
```
PreparedStatement pstmt = con.prepareStatement(
            "UPDATE Table1 SET a = ? WHERE key = ?");
```

## rollback

void **rollback**() throwsSQLException

Drops all changes made since the previous call to commit or rollback and releases any database locks currently held by the connection.

Note that when auto-commit is enabled (the default), the completion of each SQL statement will cause the commit method to be called automatically.

**EXAMPLE:**
```
con.rollback();
```

## setAutoCommit

```
void setAutoCommit(boolean enableAutoCommit) throws SQLException
```

Sets the connection's auto-commit mode to *enableAutoCommit*.

Newly created `Connection` objects are in auto-commit mode by default, which means that individual SQL statements are committed automatically when the statement is completed. To be able to group SQL statements into transactions and commit them or roll them back as a unit, auto-commit must be disabled by calling the method `setAutoCommit` with `false` as its argument. When auto-commit is disabled, the user must call either the `commit` or `rollback` method explicitly to end a transaction.

The commit occurs when the statement completes or the next execute occurs, whichever comes first. In the case of statements returning a `ResultSet` object, the statement completes when the last row of the result set has been retrieved or the `ResultSet` object has been closed. In advanced cases, a single statement may return multiple results as well as output parameter values. In this case, the commit may occur when all results and output parameter values have been retrieved, or the commit may occur after each result is retrieved.

**PARAMETERS:**

*enableAutoCommit*     either `true` to enable auto-commit mode or `false` to disable auto-commit mode.

**EXAMPLE:**
```
myConnection.setAutoCommit(false); // disables auto-commit mode
```

## setCatalog

```
void setCatalog(String catalog) throws SQLException
```

Sets the catalog name to *catalog*. The definition of a catalog name depends on the particular DBMS, but in general, it is the outermost level of qualification for the name of a database object. For example, a table can be referred to as "tableName," "databaseName.tableName," or "userName.databaseName.table-Name." In this example, "userName.databaseName.tableName" is the fully qualified name, and "userName" is the catalog name. The fully qualified name can be expressed as "catalog.schema.tableName," where *catalog* is generally the user, and *schema* is generally the name of the database.

A catalog name identifies a particular section of a database, so setting the catalog name selects a subspace of the `Connection` object's database to work in. Normally a user will work in the default catalog and will not use this method.

If the driver does not support catalogs, it will silently ignore this request.

**PARAMETERS:**

catalog                     a String object representing a catalog name.

**EXAMPLE:**
```
myConnection.setCatalog("userName");
```

## setReadOnly

```
void setReadOnly(boolean readOnly) throws SQLException
```

Sets the Connection object to read-only mode when *readOnly* is true and disables read-only mode when *readOnly* is false.

It is recommended that this method be called prior to execution of statements on a connection.

Note that read-only mode is only a hint to the driver to enable database optimizations; calling setReadOnly(true) does not necessarily cause writes to be prohibited.

**PARAMETERS:**

readOnly                    either true to enable read-only mode or false to disable read-only mode.

**EXAMPLE:**
```
myConnection.setReadOnly(true);
// enables read-only mode but does not prohibit writes
```

## setTransactionIsolation

```
void setTransactionIsolation(int level) throws SQLException
```

Sets the transaction isolation level of a connection object to *level* (if the underlying database supports setting transaction isolation values). The parameter *level* must be one of the TRANSACTION_* constants defined in the Connection interface.

This method generates an SQLException if the DBMS cannot support the isolation level requested and cannot substitute a higher level of isolation.

If this method is called while in the middle of a transaction, any changes up to that point will be committed.

**PARAMETERS:**

*level*                          one of TRANSACTION_READ_UNCOMMITTED, TRANS-
                                 ACTION_READ_COMMITTED, TRANSACTION_REPEATABLE-
                                 _READ, TRANSTRANSACTION_SERIALIZABLE. (TRANS-
                                 ACTION_NONE cannot be used because it specifies that
                                 transactions are not supported).

**EXAMPLE:**

```
myConnection.setTransactionIsolation(TRANSACTION_READ_COMMITTED);
//prohibits "dirty reads"
```

**SEE:**

"Connection Fields" below.

## 5.4   Connection Fields

The constant values defined in the Connection interface are used as parameters to the Connection method setTransactionIsolation. They are also the possible return values for the DatabaseMetaData method getDefaultTransactionIsolation, which returns the default transaction isolation level of the underlying database.

## TRANSACTION_NONE

```
public static final int TRANSACTION_NONE = 0
```

Transactions are not supported.

## TRANSACTION_READ_UNCOMMITTED

```
public static final int TRANSACTION_READ_UNCOMMITTED = 1
```

Specifies that "dirty reads," nonrepeatable reads, and phantom reads can occur. This level allows a row changed by one transaction to be read by another transaction before any changes in that row have been committed. If any of the changes are rolled back, the second transaction will have retrieved an invalid row.

## TRANSACTION_READ_COMMITTED

`public static final int TRANSACTION_READ_COMMITTED = 2`

Specifies that "dirty reads" are prevented; however, nonrepeatable reads and phantom reads can occur. In other words, this level only prohibits a transaction from reading a row with uncommitted changes in it.

## TRANSACTION_REPEATABLE_READ

`public static final int TRANSACTION_REPEATABLE_READ = 4`

Specifies that "dirty reads" and nonrepeatable reads are prevented; phantom reads can occur. This level prohibits a transaction from reading a row with uncommitted changes in it, and it also prohibits the situation where one transaction reads a row, a second transaction alters the row, and the first transaction rereads the row, getting different values the second time.

## TRANSACTION_SERIALIZABLE

`public static final int TRANSACTION_SERIALIZABLE = 8`

Specifies that "dirty reads," nonrepeatable reads, and phantom reads are all prevented. This level includes the prohibitions in `TRANSACTION_REPEATABLE_READ` and further prohibits the situation where one transaction reads all rows that satisfy a `WHERE` condition, a second transaction inserts a row that satisfies that `WHERE` condition, and the first transaction rereads for the same condition, retrieving the additional "phantom" row in the second read.

# CHAPTER 6

# DatabaseMetaData

## 6.1 **DatabaseMetaData** Overview

THE interface `java.sql.DatabaseMetaData` provides information about a database as a whole. One creates an instance of `DatabaseMetaData` and then uses that instance to call methods that retrieve information about a database. Another class, `ResultSetMetaData`, provides information about the columns in result sets.

Some of the `DatabaseMetaData` methods return a `ResultSet` object. All of the variables in `DatabaseMetaData`, which are by definition constants because they are in an interface, serve as possible values for columns in some of these `ResultSet` objects. For example, one of the columns in the `ResultSet` object returned by the method `getProcedures` is `PROCEDURE_TYPE`. There are three possible values for this column: `procedureResultUnknown`, `procedureNoResult`, and `procedureReturnsResult`. These three values, which describe the result returned by the procedure, are constants defined in `DatabaseMetaData`.

The `DatabaseMetaData` interface is used almost exclusively by driver and tool developers. A driver implements the `DatabaseMetaData` methods so that each method gives the appropriate response for its database. Tool developers will use the `DatabaseMetaData` methods to discover how their applications should deal with the underlying database. Users who simply send SQL statements to a database with which they are familiar can generally ignore this interface.

### 6.1.1 Creating a **DatabaseMetaData** Object

A `DatabaseMetaData` object is created with the `Connection` method `getMetaData`, as in the following code, where *con* is a `Connection` object:

```
DatabaseMetaData dbmd = con.getMetaData();
```

The variable *dbmd* contains a DatabaseMetaData object that can be used to get information about the database to which *con* is connected. This is done by calling a DatabaseMetaData method on *dbmd*, as in the following code fragment:

```
int n = dbmd.getMaxTableNameLength();
```

If the Connection object *con* is connected to a database called Human_Relations, the variable *n* indicates the maximum number of characters that can be used to name a table in Human_Relations.

### 6.1.2   ResultSet Objects as Return Values

Many of the DatabaseMetaData methods return lists of information in ResultSet objects. Data is retrieved from these ResultSet objects using the normal ResultSet.getXXX methods, such as getString and getInt. For example, the following code illustrates retrieving the values returned by the method getSchemas. This method returns a ResultSet object that has only one column, and that column stores a String object. Each row of the result set is the name of a schema that is available in this database.

```
ResultSet rs = dbms.getSchemas();
while (rs.next()) {
    String s = rs.getString(1);
    System.out.println("Schema name = " + s);
}
```

If a given form of data is not available, the getXXX methods should throw an SQLException.

Methods that are supposed to return a ResultSet object but fail to do so should also throw an SQLException. Any ResultSet object is a legal return value, including one that is empty.

### 6.1.3   String Patterns as Arguments

Some DatabaseMetaData methods take as an argument a String object that serves as a search pattern. These arguments all have "Pattern" as the last part of the variable name, such as in *schemaPattern*, *tableNamePattern*, *columnNamePattern*, and *procedureNamePattern*. Within one of these search patterns, an underscore (_) calls for a match of any single character, and a percent sign (%) calls for a match of zero or more characters. Supplying `null` signifies that this criterion should be ignored. If a database does not support a particular search criterion, the only value that can be supplied for that criterion is `null`. For example, if the method `getProcedures` were invoked with the following arguments, it would return information about procedures that are in any schema and whose names start with "REPLACE":

```
ResultSet rs = dbmd.getProcedures(null, null, "REPLACE%");
```

Thus, if there were procedures named `REPLACE_PRICE`, `REPLACEMENT_UPDATE`, and `REPLACE`, they would all be described in the `ResultSet` object *rs*; `REPLACING_NO_SALES` and `AUTOREPLACE`, however, would not be included.

Note that identifier name patterns are case-sensitive. What needs to be matched is the identifier name as it is stored in the database. Some databases, for example, store identifiers in their catalogs as all uppercase or all lowercase. This is true even if the identifier name was mixed case in the statement that created it. For example, consider the following statement:

```
CREATE TABLE newCars
(Model CHAR(10))
```

The table identifier `newCars` may be stored as `NEWCARS` in some databases; therefore, to access information about it using metadata methods, it may be necessary to use all uppercase characters in the search pattern.

The only sure way to make patterns database-independent is to discover the way identifiers are stored (with `DatabaseMetaData` methods), and then use the appropriate case in identifier name patterns.

`DatabaseMetaData` has several methods for determining whether identifier names are stored in the database as lowercase, mixed case, or uppercase:

- `storesLowerCaseIdentifiers`
- `storesLowerCaseQuotedIdentifiers`
- `storesMixedCaseIdentifiers`
- `storesMixedCaseQuotedIdentifiers`
- `storesUpperCaseIdentifiers`
- `storesUpperCaseQuotedIdentifiers`
- `supportsMixedCaseIdentifiers`
- `supportsMixedCaseQuotedIdentifiers`

If the methods with "QuotedIdentifiers" in their names return true, they allow nonalphanumeric characters if those characters are enclosed in quotation marks.

### 6.1.4    Pseudo Columns

Some of the variables in DatabaseMetaData (bestRowNotPseudo, bestRowPseudo, bestRowUnknown, versionColumnNotPseudo, versionColumnPseudo, and version-ColumnUnknown) indicate whether a column is a pseudo column. A pseudo column is a column that is generated by the database. A typical example is the ROWID column used by several database systems. This column contains identification numbers for rows in a result set. These identification numbers are not entered by the user; they are calculated by the database and stored in the pseudo column ROWID, which is not included as part of the result set returned to the user. Another example is a DBMS that for designated tables automatically increments identification numbers and assigns them as primary keys. The DBMS maintains a special pseudo column to keep track of the last number assigned. When a row is added to the table, the DBMS increments the last number in its pseudo column and assigns the new number to the appropriate column. In this case, the generated identification number is entered in a regular table column, whereas the number to increment is maintained in a pseudo column.

## 6.2    DatabaseMetaData Interface Definition

```
package java.sql;
public interface DatabaseMetaData {


//------------------------------------------------------------------
// First, a variety of minor information about the target database:
//------------------------------------------------------------------
    boolean allProceduresAreCallable() throws SQLException;
    boolean allTablesAreSelectable() throws SQLException;
    String getURL() throws SQLException;
    String getUserName() throws SQLException;
    boolean isReadOnly() throws SQLException;
    boolean nullsAreSortedHigh() throws SQLException;
    boolean nullsAreSortedLow() throws SQLException;
    boolean nullsAreSortedAtStart() throws SQLException;
```

```
    boolean nullsAreSortedAtEnd() throws SQLException;
    String getDatabaseProductName() throws SQLException;
    String getDatabaseProductVersion() throws SQLException;
    String getDriverName() throws SQLException;
    String getDriverVersion() throws SQLException;
    int getDriverMajorVersion();
    int getDriverMinorVersion();
    boolean usesLocalFiles() throws SQLException;
    boolean usesLocalFilePerTable() throws SQLException;
    boolean supportsMixedCaseIdentifiers() throws SQLException;
    boolean storesLowerCaseIdentifiers() throws SQLException;
    boolean storesUpperCaseIdentifiers() throws SQLException;
    boolean storesMixedCaseIdentifiers() throws SQLException;
    boolean supportsMixedCaseQuotedIdentifiers() throws SQLException;
    boolean storesUpperCaseQuotedIdentifiers() throws SQLException;
    boolean storesLowerCaseQuotedIdentifiers() throws SQLException;
    boolean storesMixedCaseQuotedIdentifiers() throws SQLException;
    String getIdentifierQuoteString() throws SQLException;
    String getSQLKeywords() throws SQLException;
    String getNumericFunctions() throws SQLException;
    String getStringFunctions() throws SQLException;
    String getSystemFunctions() throws SQLException;
    String getTimeDateFunctions() throws SQLException;
    String getSearchStringEscape() throws SQLException;
    String getExtraNameCharacters() throws SQLException;
    String getSchemaTerm() throws SQLException;
    String getProcedureTerm() throws SQLException;
    String getCatalogTerm() throws SQLException;
    boolean isCatalogAtStart() throws SQLException;
    String getCatalogSeparator() throws SQLException;
    int getDefaultTransactionIsolation() throws SQLException;

//-------------------------------------------------------------------
//        Functions describing which features are supported:
//-------------------------------------------------------------------
    boolean supportsAlterTableWithDropColumn() throws SQLException;
    boolean supportsColumnAliasing() throws SQLException;
    boolean nullPlusNonNullIsNull() throws SQLException;
```

```
boolean supportsConvert() throws SQLException;
boolean supportsConvert(int fromType, int toType)
                                          throws SQLException;
boolean supportsTableCorrelationNames() throws SQLException;
boolean supportsDifferentTableCorrelationNames()
                                          throws SQLException;
boolean supportsExpressionsInOrderBy() throws SQLException;
boolean supportsOrderByUnrelated() throws SQLException;
boolean supportsGroupBy() throws SQLException;
boolean supportsGroupByUnrelated() throws SQLException;
boolean supportsGroupByBeyondSelect() throws SQLException;
boolean supportsLikeEscapeClause() throws SQLException;
boolean supportsMultipleResultSets() throws SQLException;
boolean supportsMultipleTransactions() throws SQLException;
boolean supportsNonNullableColumns() throws SQLException;
boolean supportsMinimumSQLGrammar() throws SQLException;
boolean supportsCoreSQLGrammar() throws SQLException;
boolean supportsExtendedSQLGrammar() throws SQLException;
boolean supportsANSI92EntryLevelSQL() throws SQLException;
boolean supportsANSI92IntermediateSQL() throws SQLException;
boolean supportsANSI92FullSQL() throws SQLException;
boolean supportsIntegrityEnhancementFacility() throws SQLException;
boolean supportsOuterJoins() throws SQLException;
boolean supportsFullOuterJoins() throws SQLException;
boolean supportsLimitedOuterJoins() throws SQLException;
boolean supportsSchemasInDataManipulation() throws SQLException;
boolean supportsSchemasInProcedureCalls() throws SQLException;
boolean supportsSchemasInTableDefinitions() throws SQLException;
boolean supportsSchemasInIndexDefinitions() throws SQLException;
boolean supportsSchemasInPrivilegeDefinitions()
                                              throws SQLException;
boolean supportsCatalogsInDataManipulation() throws SQLException;
boolean supportsCatalogsInProcedureCalls() throws SQLException;
boolean supportsCatalogsInTableDefinitions() throws SQLException;
boolean supportsCatalogsInIndexDefinitions() throws SQLException;
boolean supportsCatalogsInPrivilegeDefinitions()
                                              throws SQLException;
boolean supportsPositionedDelete() throws SQLException;
boolean supportsPositionedUpdate() throws SQLException;
```

```
boolean supportsSelectForUpdate() throws SQLException;
boolean supportsStoredProcedures() throws SQLException;
boolean supportsSubqueriesInComparisons() throws SQLException;
boolean supportsSubqueriesInExists() throws SQLException;
boolean supportsSubqueriesInIns() throws SQLException;
boolean supportsSubqueriesInQuantifieds() throws SQLException;
boolean supportsCorrelatedSubqueries() throws SQLException;
boolean supportsUnion() throws SQLException;
boolean supportsUnionAll() throws SQLException;
boolean supportsOpenCursorsAcrossCommit() throws SQLException;
boolean supportsOpenCursorsAcrossRollback() throws SQLException;
boolean supportsOpenStatementsAcrossCommit() throws SQLException;
boolean supportsOpenStatementsAcrossRollback() throws SQLException;
boolean supportsTransactions() throws SQLException;
boolean supportsTransactionIsolationLevel(int level)
                                         throws SQLException;


//-------------------------------------------------------------------
//   The following group of methods exposes various limitations
//   based on the target database with the current driver.
//   Unless otherwise specified, a result of zero means there is no
//   limit or the limit is not known.
//-------------------------------------------------------------------
int getMaxBinaryLiteralLength() throws SQLException;
int getMaxCharLiteralLength() throws SQLException;
int getMaxColumnNameLength() throws SQLException;
int getMaxColumnsInGroupBy() throws SQLException;
int getMaxColumnsInIndex() throws SQLException;
int getMaxColumnsInOrderBy() throws SQLException;
int getMaxColumnsInSelect() throws SQLException;
int getMaxColumnsInTable() throws SQLException;
int getMaxConnections() throws SQLException;
int getMaxCursorNameLength() throws SQLException;
int getMaxIndexLength() throws SQLException;
int getMaxSchemaNameLength() throws SQLException;
int getMaxProcedureNameLength() throws SQLException;
int getMaxCatalogNameLength() throws SQLException;
int getMaxRowSize() throws SQLException;
boolean doesMaxRowSizeIncludeBlobs() throws SQLException;
```

```
    int getMaxStatementLength() throws SQLException;
    int getMaxStatements() throws SQLException;
    int getMaxTableNameLength() throws SQLException;
    int getMaxTablesInSelect() throws SQLException;
    int getMaxUserNameLength() throws SQLException;


//------------------------------------------------------------------
// Methods specifying whether you can have data definition statements
// as part of a transaction and what happens if you do:
//------------------------------------------------------------------
    boolean supportsDataDefinitionAndDataManipulationTransactions()
                                              throws SQLException;
    boolean supportsDataManipulationTransactionsOnly()
                                              throws SQLException;
    boolean dataDefinitionCausesTransactionCommit()throws SQLException;
    boolean dataDefinitionIgnoredInTransactions() throws SQLException;


//------------------------------------------------------------------
//     Methods that return ResultSet objects to describe
//     database objects:
//------------------------------------------------------------------
    ResultSet getProcedures(String catalog, String schemaPattern,
                String procedureNamePattern) throws SQLException;
    ResultSet getProcedureColumns(String catalog, String schemaPattern,
              String procedureNamePattern, String columnNamePattern)
                                              throws SQLException;
    ResultSet getTables(String catalog, String schemaPattern,
         String tableNamePattern, String types[]) throws SQLException;
    ResultSet getSchemas() throws SQLException;
    ResultSet getCatalogs() throws SQLException;
    ResultSet getTableTypes() throws SQLException;
    ResultSet getColumns(String catalog, String schemaPattern,
                String tableNamePattern, String columnNamePattern)
                                              throws SQLException;
    ResultSet getColumnPrivileges(String catalog, String schema,
         String table, String columnNamePattern) throws SQLException;
    ResultSet getTablePrivileges(String catalog, String schemaPattern,
              String tableNamePattern) throws SQLException;
    ResultSet getBestRowIdentifier(String catalog, String schema,
         String table, int scope, boolean nullable) throws SQLException;
```

```
ResultSet getVersionColumns(String catalog, String schema,
        String table) throws SQLException;
ResultSet getPrimaryKeys(String catalog, String schema,
        String table) throws SQLException;
ResultSet getImportedKeys(String catalog, String schema,
        String table) throws SQLException;
ResultSet getExportedKeys(String catalog, String schema,
        String table) throws SQLException;
ResultSet getCrossReference(String primaryCatalog,
            String primarySchema, String primaryTable,
            String foreignCatalog, String foreignSchema,
            String foreignTable) throws SQLException;
ResultSet getTypeInfo() throws SQLException;
ResultSet getIndexInfo(String catalog, String schema, String table,
        boolean unique, boolean approximate) throws SQLException;


//-------------------------------------------------------------------
//      Fields used as possible values returned by
//      DatabaseMetaData methods:
//-------------------------------------------------------------------
    // Possible values for getProcedureColumns
    public final static int procedureColumnUnknown = 0;
    public final static int procedureColumnIn = 1;
    public final static int procedureColumnInOut = 2;
    public final static int procedureColumnResult = 3;
    public final static int procedureColumnOut = 4;
    public final static int procedureColumnReturn = 5;
    public final static int procedureNoNulls = 0;
    public final static int procedureNullable = 1;
    public final static int procedureNullableUnknown = 2;

    // Possible values for getProcedures
    public final static int procedureResultUnknown = 0;
    public final static int procedureNoResult = 1;
    public final static int procedureReturnsResult = 2;

    // Possible values for getColumns
    public final static int columnNoNulls = 0;
```

```java
public final static int columnNullable = 1;
public final static int columnNullableUnknown = 2;

// Possible values for getBestRowIdentifier
public final static int bestRowTemporary = 0;
public final static int bestRowTransaction = 1;
public final static int bestRowSession = 2;
public final static int bestRowUnknown = 0;
public final static int bestRowNotPseudo = 1;
public final static int bestRowPseudo = 2;

// Possible values for getVersionColumns
public final static int versionColumnUnknown = 0;
public final static int versionColumnNotPseudo = 1;
public final static int versionColumnPseudo = 2;

// Possible values for getImportedKeys, getExportedKeys, and
// getCrossReference
public final static int importedKeyCascade = 0;
public final static int importedKeyRestrict = 1;
public final static int importedKeySetNull = 2;
public final static int importedKeyNoAction = 3;
public final static int importedKeySetDefault = 4;
public final static int importedKeyInitiallyDeferred  = 5;
public final static int importedKeyInitiallyImmediate = 6;
public final static int importedKeyNotDeferrable = 7;

// Possible values for getTypeInfo
public final static int typeNoNulls = 0;
public final static int typeNullable = 1;
public final static int typeNullableUnknown = 2;
public final static int typePredNone = 0;
public final static int typePredChar = 1;
public final static int typePredBasic = 2;
public final static int typeSearchable = 3;

// Possible values for getIndexInfo
public final static short tableIndexStatistic = 0;
public final static short tableIndexClustered = 1;
```

```
    public final static short tableIndexHashed = 2;
    public final static short tableIndexOther = 3;
}
```

## 6.3  DatabaseMetaData Methods

### allProceduresAreCallable

boolean **allProceduresAreCallable**() throws SQLException

Checks whether the current user has the required security rights to call all the procedures returned by the method getProcedures.

**RETURNS:**
true if so; false otherwise.

**EXAMPLE:**
```
DatabaseMetaData dbmd = myConnection.getMetaData();
boolean b = dbmd.allProceduresAreCallable();
```

### allTablesAreSelectable

boolean **allTablesAreSelectable**() throws SQLException

Checks whether the current user can use a SELECT statement with all of the tables returned by the method getTables.

**RETURNS:**
true if so; false otherwise.

**EXAMPLE:**
```
boolean b = dbmd.allTablesAreSelectable();
```

### dataDefinitionCausesTransactionCommit

boolean **dataDefinitionCausesTransactionCommit**()throws SQLException

Checks whether a data definition statement within a transaction forces the transaction to commit.

**RETURNS:**
true if so; `false` otherwise.

**EXAMPLE:**
```
boolean b = dbmd.dataDefinitionCausesTransactionCommit();
```

## dataDefinitionIgnoredInTransactions

```
boolean dataDefinitionIgnoredInTransactions() throws SQLException
```

Checks whether a data definition statement within a transaction is ignored.

**RETURNS:**
true if so; `false` otherwise.

**EXAMPLE:**
```
boolean b = dbmd.dataDefinitionIgnoredInTransactions();
```

## doesMaxRowSizeIncludeBlobs

```
boolean doesMaxRowSizeIncludeBlobs() throws SQLException
```

Checks whether the value returned by the method `getMaxRowSize` includes `LONGVARCHAR` and `LONGVARBINARY` blobs, that is, whether blobs are counted as part of the row size.

**RETURNS:**
true if so; `false` otherwise.

**EXAMPLE:**
```
boolean b = dbmd.doesMaxRowSizeIncludeBlobs();
```

## getBestRowIdentifier

```
ResultSet getBestRowIdentifier(String catalog, String schema,
        String table, int scope, boolean nullable) throws SQLException
```

Gets a description of a table's optimal set of columns that uniquely identifies a row. The descriptions are ordered by the column SCOPE.

**PARAMETERS:**

| | |
|---|---|
| *catalog* | a `String` object representing a catalog name; `""` retrieves those without a catalog; `null` indicates that the catalog name should be dropped from the selection criteria. |
| *schema* | a `String` object representing a schema name; `""` retrieves those without a schema; `null` indicates that the schema name should be dropped from the selection criteria. |
| *table* | a `String` object representing a table name. |
| *scope* | an `int` representing the scope of interest; one of `bestRowTemporary`, `bestRowTransaction`, or `bestRowSession`. |
| *nullable* | `true` to indicate that columns that are nullable may be included; `false` to exclude columns that can be null. |

**RETURNS:**

a `ResultSet` object, with each row being a description of a column that belongs to the optimal set of columns that uniquely identifies a row. This set may consist of one or more columns, and it may include pseudo columns.

Each column description has the following columns:

| | |
|---|---|
| 1. SCOPE | `short` indicating the actual scope of the result. The possible values are: |
| `bestRowTemporary` | —very temporary; valid only while using the row. |
| `bestRowTransaction` | —valid for the remainder of the current transaction. |
| `bestRowSession` | —valid for the remainder of the current session. |
| 2. COLUMN_NAME | `String` object giving the column name. |
| 3. DATA_TYPE | `short` indicating the generic SQL datatype from `java.sql.Types`. |
| 4. TYPE_NAME | `String` object giving the type name used by the data source. |
| 5. COLUMN_SIZE | `int` giving the precision. |
| 6. BUFFER_LENGTH | `int`. Not used. |
| 7. DECIMAL_DIGITS | `short` indicating the scale. |

| 8. PSEUDO_COLUMN | short indicating whether this is a pseudo column, such as an Oracle ROWID. |
|---|---|
| | The possible values are: |
| bestRowUnknown | —may or may not be a pseudo column. |
| bestRowNotPseudo | —is NOT a pseudo column. |
| bestRowPseudo | —is a pseudo column. |

**EXAMPLE:**
```
ResultSet rs = dbmd.getBestRowIdentifier(
                    "MYCATALOG", "MYSCHEMA", "TABLE1", 1, false);
```

## getCatalogs

```
ResultSet getCatalogs() throws SQLException
```

Gets the catalog names available in this database.
The results are ordered by catalog name.

**RETURNS:**
a ResultSet object, with each row representing a catalog name available in this database.

The ResultSet object has the following column:
1. TABLE_CAT             String object containing a catalog name.

**EXAMPLE:**
```
ResultSet rs = dbmd.getCatalogs();
```

## getCatalogSeparator

```
String getCatalogSeparator() throws SQLException
```

Gets the String object used to separate a catalog name and table name.

**RETURNS:**
a String object containing the separator string.

**EXAMPLE:**
```
String s = dbmd.getCatalogSeparator();
```

## getCatalogTerm

```
String getCatalogTerm() throws SQLException
```

Gets the database vendor's preferred term for catalog.

**RETURNS:**
a String object containing the vendor term for catalog.

**EXAMPLE:**
```
String s = dbmd.getCatalogTerm();
```

## getColumnPrivileges

```
ResultSet getColumnPrivileges(String catalog, String schema,
        String table, String columnNamePattern) throws SQLException
```

Gets a description of the access rights for a table's columns. Descriptions of privileges are returned only if all of the following are true: the catalog name of the column's table matches *catalog*, the schema name of the column's table matches *schema,* the column's table name matches *table*, and the column name matches *columnNamePattern*. The descriptions are ordered by the columns COLUMN_NAME and PRIVILEGE.

Note that getColumnPrivileges will return privileges that were set for the column and also those that were set for the table.

**PARAMETERS:**

| | |
|---|---|
| *catalog* | a String object representing a catalog name; "" retrieves column privileges in tables without a catalog; null indicates that the catalog name should be dropped from the selection criteria. |
| *schema* | a String object representing a schema name; "" retrieves column privileges in tables without a schema; null indicates that the schema name should be dropped from the selection criteria. |
| *table* | a String object representing a table name. |
| *columnNamePattern* | a String object representing a column name pattern. |

**RETURNS:**
a ResultSet object, with each row being a description of a column's privileges.

Each privilege description has the following columns:

| | |
|---|---|
| 1. TABLE_CAT | `String` object giving the table catalog, which may be `null`. |
| 2. TABLE_SCHEM | `String` object giving the table schema, which may be `null`. |
| 3. TABLE_NAME | `String` object giving the table name. |
| 4. COLUMN_NAME | `String` object giving the column name. |
| 5. GRANTOR | `String` object giving the grantor of access, which may be `null`. |
| 6. GRANTEE | `String` object giving the grantee of access. |
| 7. PRIVILEGE | `String` object naming the type of access (SELECT, INSERT, UPDATE, REFERENCES, and so on). |
| 8. IS_GRANTABLE | `String` object; "YES" indicates that the grantee is permitted to grant access to others, "NO" indicates that the grantee cannot grant access to others, and `null` indicates that it is unknown. |

**SEE:**
"String Patterns as Arguments" on page 164.

## getColumns

---

```
ResultSet getColumns(String catalog, String schemaPattern,
            String tableNamePattern, String columnNamePattern)
                                        throws SQLException
```

Gets a description of the table columns available in catalog *catalog*.

Descriptions of columns are returned only if the table schema name matches *schemaPattern*, the table name matches *tableNamePattern*, and the column name matches *columnNamePattern*. The descriptions are ordered by the columns TABLE_SCHEM, TABLE_NAME, and ORDINAL_POSITION.

**PARAMETERS:**

*catalog*       a `String` object representing a catalog name; "" retrieves columns for tables without a catalog; `null` indicates that the catalog name should be dropped from the selection criteria.

| | |
|---|---|
| *schemaPattern* | a String object representing a schema name pattern; "" retrieves columns for tables without a schema; null indicates that the schema name should be dropped from the selection criteria. |
| *tableNamePattern* | a String object representing a table name pattern. |
| *columnNamePattern* | a String object representing a column name pattern. |

**RETURNS:**

a ResultSet object, with each row being a description of a table column.

Each row in the ResultSet object has the following fields:

| | |
|---|---|
| 1. TABLE_CAT | String object giving the table catalog, which may be null. |
| 2. TABLE_SCHEM | String object giving the table schema, which may be null. |
| 3. TABLE_NAME | String object giving the table name. |
| 4. COLUMN_NAME | String object giving the column name. |
| 5. DATA_TYPE | short indicating the SQL type from java.sql.Types. |
| 6. TYPE_NAME | String object giving the local type name used by the data source. |
| 7. COLUMN_SIZE | int indicating the column size. For char or date types, this is the maximum number of characters; for numeric or decimal types, this is the precision. |
| 8. BUFFER_LENGTH | is not used. |
| 9. DECIMAL_DIGITS | int indicating the number of fractional digits. |
| 10. NUM_PREC_RADIX | int indicating the radix, which is typically either 10 or 2. |
| 11. NULLABLE | int indicating whether a column can be NULL. The possible values are: |
| columnNoNulls | —NULL values might not be allowed. |
| columnNullable | —NULL values are definitely allowed. |
| columnNullableUnknown | —Whether NULL values are allowed is unknown. |
| 12. REMARKS | String object containing an explanatory comment on the column; may be null. |
| 13. COLUMN_DEF | String object containing the default value for the column; may be null. |
| 14. SQL_DATA_TYPE | int; currently unused. |
| 15. SQL_DATETIME_SUB | int; currently unused. |
| 16. CHAR_OCTET_LENGTH | int indicating the maximum number of bytes in the column (for char types only). |

| 17. ORDINAL_POSITION | int indicating the index of the column in a table. The first column is 1, the second column is 2, and so on. |
| 18. IS_NULLABLE | String object; either "NO" indicating that the column definitely does not allow NULL values, "YES" indicating that the column might allow NULL values, or an empty string ("") indicating that nullability is unknown. |

**EXAMPLE:**
ResultSet rs = dbmd.getColumns(null, null, "EMPLOYEES", "%NAME");

**SEE:**
"String Patterns as Arguments" on page 164.


## getCrossReference

ResultSet **getCrossReference**(String *primaryCatalog*,
        String *primarySchema*, String *primaryTable*,
        String *foreignCatalog*, String *foreignSchema*,
        String *foreignTable*) throws SQLException


Describes how one table imports the keys of another table.

Gets a description of the foreign key columns in the table *foreignTable*. These foreign key columns reference the primary key columns of the table *primaryTable*. In other words, the foreign keys in *foreignTable* are the primary keys in *primaryTable*. The descriptions are ordered by the columns FKTABLE_CAT, FKTABLE_SCHEM, FKTABLE_NAME, and KEY_SEQ.

**PARAMETERS:**

| *primaryCatalog* | a String object representing the catalog name of the table that contains the primary key; "" retrieves those without a catalog; null indicates that the catalog name should be dropped from the selection criteria. |
| *primarySchema* | a String object representing the schema name of the table that contains the primary key; "" retrieves those without a schema; null indicates that the schema name should be dropped from the selection criteria. |

| | |
|---|---|
| *primaryTable* | a String object representing the name of the table that contains the primary key (the key exported to table *foreignTable*, where it becomes the foreign key). |
| *foreignCatalog* | a String object representing the catalog name of the table that contains the foreign key; "" retrieves those without a catalog; null indicates that the catalog name should be dropped from the selection criteria. |
| *foreignSchema* | a String object representing the schema name of the table that contains the foreign key; "" retrieves those without a schema; null indicates that the schema name should be dropped from the selection criteria. |
| *foreignTable* | a String object representing the name of the table that contains the foreign key (the primary key imported from table *primaryTable*). |

**RETURNS:**

a ResultSet object, with each row being a description of a foreign key column.

Each description has the following columns:

| | |
|---|---|
| 1. PKTABLE_CAT | String object giving the catalog of the primary key's table, which may be null. |
| 2. PKTABLE_SCHEM | String object giving the schema of the primary key's table, which may be null. |
| 3. PKTABLE_NAME | String object giving the table name of the primary key, which is *primaryTable*. |
| 4. PKCOLUMN_NAME | String object giving the column name of the primary key. |
| 5. FKTABLE_CAT | String object giving the catalog name (which may be null) of *foreignTable* (which may be null). |
| 6. FKTABLE_SCHEM | String object giving the schema name (which may be null) of *foreignTable* (which may be null). |
| 7. FKTABLE_NAME | String object giving the table name of the foreign key. |
| 8. FKCOLUMN_NAME | String object giving the column name of the foreign key. |
| 9. KEY_SEQ | short indicating the sequence number within the foreign key (useful if the foreign key consists of more than one column). |

| 10. UPDATE_RULE | short indicating what happens to the foreign key when the primary key is updated. The possible values are: |
| --- | --- |
| `importedKeyNoAction` | —if a primary key has been imported by another table, it cannot be updated. |
| `importedKeyCascade` | —if a primary key has been updated, change the foreign key to agree with it. |
| `importedKeySetNull` | —if a primary key has been updated, change the foreign key to `null`. |
| `importedKeySetDefault` | —if a primary key has been updated, change the foreign key to its default value. |
| `importedKeyRestrict` | —same as `importedKeyNoAction` (for ODBC 2.x compatibility). |
| 11. DELETE_RULE | short indicating what happens to the foreign key when the primary key is updated. The possible values are: |
| `importedKeyNoAction` | —if a primary key has been imported by another table, it cannot be deleted. |
| `importedKeyCascade` | —if a primary key has been deleted, delete rows that contain the foreign key. |
| `importedKeySetNull` | —if a primary key has been deleted, change the foreign key to `null`. |
| `importedKeySetDefault` | —if a primary key has been deleted, change the foreign key to its default value. |
| `importedKeyRestrict` | —same as `importedKeyNoAction` (for ODBC 2.x compatibility). |
| 12. FK_NAME | `String` object containing the name of the foreign key, which may be `null`. |
| 13. PK_NAME | `String` object containing the name of the primary key, which may be `null`. |
| 14. DEFERRABILITY | short indicating whether the evaluation of foreign key constraints can be deferred until commit. Possible values are: |
| `importedKeyInitiallyDeferred` | See SQL–92 for definition. |
| `importedKeyInitiallyImmediate` | See SQL–92 for definition. |
| `importedKeyNotDeferrable` | See SQL–92 for definition. |

**EXAMPLE:**

```
ResultSet rs = dbmd.getCrossReference("MYPRIMARYCATALOG",
    "MYPRIMARYSCHEMA", "MYPRIMARYTABLE","MYFOREIGNCATALOG",
    "MYFOREIGNSCHEMA", "MYFOREIGNTABLE");
```

## getDatabaseProductName

```
String getDatabaseProductName() throws SQLException
```

Gets the product name for this database.

**RETURNS:**
a String object representing the database product name.

**EXAMPLE:**
```
String s = dbmd.getDatabaseProductName();
```

## getDatabaseProductVersion

```
String getDatabaseProductVersion() throws SQLException
```

Gets the version for this database product.

**RETURNS:**
a String object representing the database version.

**EXAMPLE:**
```
String s = dbmd.getDatabaseProductVersion();
```

## getDefaultTransactionIsolation

```
int getDefaultTransactionIsolation() throws SQLException
```

Gets the database's default transaction isolation level. The values are the constants defined in java.sql.Connection.

**RETURNS:**
an int representing the default transaction isolation level. Possible values are TRANSACTION_NONE, TRANSACTION_READ_UNCOMMITTED, TRANSACTION_READ_COMMITTED, TRANSACTION_REPEATABLE_READ, and TRANSACTION_SERIALIZABLE.

**EXAMPLE:**
```
int level = dbmd.getDefaultTransactionIsolation();
```

**SEE:**
"Connection Fields" on page 161.

## getDriverMajorVersion

```
int getDriverMajorVersion()
```

Gets the JDBC driver's major version number.

**RETURNS:**
an int representing the JDBC driver's major version number.

**EXAMPLE:**
```
int n = dbmd.getDriverMajorVersion();
```

## getDriverMinorVersion

```
int getDriverMinorVersion()
```

Gets the JDBC driver's minor version number.

**RETURNS:**
an int representing the JDBC driver's minor version number.

**EXAMPLE:**
```
int n = dbmd.getDriverMinorVersion();
```

## getDriverName

```
String getDriverName() throws SQLException
```

Gets the name of this JDBC driver.

**RETURNS:**
a String object representing the JDBC driver name.

**EXAMPLE:**
```
String s = dbmd.getDriverName();
```

## getDriverVersion

```
String getDriverVersion() throws SQLException
```

Gets the version of this JDBC driver. This method combines the major and minor version numbers into a version string.

**RETURNS:**
a `String` object representing the JDBC driver version.

**EXAMPLE:**
```
String s = dbmd.getDriverVersion();
```

## getExportedKeys

```
ResultSet getExportedKeys(String catalog, String schema,
        String table) throws SQLException
```

Gets a description of the foreign key columns that reference the primary key columns in table *table* (the keys exported by table *table*). The descriptions are ordered by the columns FKTABLE_CAT, FKTABLE_SCHEM, FKTABLE_NAME, and KEY_SEQ.

**PARAMETERS:**

*catalog*        a `String` object representing a catalog name; "" retrieves those without a catalog; `null` indicates that the catalog name should be dropped from the selection criteria.

*schema*         a `String` object representing a schema name; "" retrieves those without a schema; `null` indicates that the schema name should be dropped from the selection criteria.

*table*          a `String` object representing the name of the table from which primary keys have been exported. These keys become foreign keys in the tables which import them.

**RETURNS:**
a `ResultSet` object, with each row being a description of a foreign key column.

Each description has the following columns:

1. PKTABLE_CAT        `String` object giving the catalog name of table *table*, which may be `null`.

2. PKTABLE_SCHEM      `String` object giving the schema name of table *table*, which may be `null`.

3. PKTABLE_NAME       `String` object giving the table name of table *table*.

| | |
|---|---|
| 4. PKCOLUMN_NAME | `String` object giving the column name of the primary key. |
| 5. FKTABLE_CAT | `String` object giving the table catalog name (which may be `null`) of the foreign key that was exported from table *table* (which may be `null`). |
| 6. FKTABLE_SCHEM | `String` object giving the table schema name (which may be `null`) of the foreign key that was exported from table *table* (which may be `null`). |
| 7. FKTABLE_NAME | `String` object giving the table name of the foreign key (the table to which the key was exported from table *table*). |
| 8. FKCOLUMN_NAME | `String` object giving the column name of the foreign key (the key that was exported from table *table*). |
| 9. KEY_SEQ | `short` indicating the sequence number within the foreign key (useful if the foreign key consists of more than one column). |
| 10. UPDATE_RULE | `short` indicating what happens to the foreign key when the primary key is updated. The possible values are: |
| `importedKeyNoAction` | —If a primary key has been imported by another table, it cannot be updated. |
| `importedKeyCascade` | —If a primary key has been updated, change the foreign key to agree with it. |
| `importedKeySetNull` | —If a primary key has been updated, change the foreign key to `null`. |
| `importedKeySetDefault` | —If a primary key has been updated, change the foreign key to its default value. |
| `importedKeyRestrict` | —This is the same as `importedKeyNoAction` (for ODBC 2.x compatibility). |
| 11. DELETE_RULE | `short` indicating what happens to the foreign key when the primary key is updated. The possible values are: |
| `importedKeyNoAction` | —If a primary key has been imported by another table, it cannot be deleted. |
| `importedKeyCascade` | —If a primary key has been deleted, delete rows that contain the foreign key. |
| `importedKeySetNull` | —If a primary key has been deleted, change the foreign key to `null`. |

| importedKeySetDefault | —If a primary key has been deleted, change the foreign key to its default value. |
| importedKeyRestrict | —This is the same as `importedKeyNoAction` (for ODBC 2.x compatibility). |
| 12. FK_NAME | `String` object containing the name of the foreign key, which may be `null`. |
| 13. PK_NAME | `String` object containing the name of the primary key, which may be `null`. |
| 14. DEFERRABILITY | `short` indicating whether the evaluation of foreign key constraints can be deferred until commit. |

Possible values are:

| `importedKeyInitiallyDeferred` | See SQL–92 for a definition. |
| `importedKeyInitiallyImmediate` | See SQL–92 for a definition. |
| `importedKeyNotDeferrable` | See SQL–92 for a definition. |

**EXAMPLE:**
```
ResultSet rs = dbmd.getExportedKeys(
                    "MYCATALOG", "MYSCHEMA", "TABLE1");
```

**SEE:**
```
getImportedKeys
```

## getExtraNameCharacters

```
String getExtraNameCharacters() throws SQLException
```

Gets the "extra" characters that can be used in unquoted identifier names (those beyond a-z, 0-9, and _). These characters are the ASCII special characters, such as @, %, etc., that can be used in names. Note that this method does not necessarily return the unicode characters of all the NLS characters accepted as identifier names.

**RETURNS:**
a `String` object containing the extra ASCII characters.

**EXAMPLE:**
```
String s = dbmd.getExtraNameCharacters();
```

## getIdentifierQuoteString

String **getIdentifierQuoteString**() throws SQLException

Gets the string used to quote SQL identifiers. This returns a space (" ") if identifier quoting isn't supported. A JDBC Compliant driver always uses a double quote character (").

**RETURNS:**
a String object representing the quoting string or a space if the database does not support quoting identifiers.

**EXAMPLE:**
String s = dbmd.getIdentifierQuoteString();

## getImportedKeys

ResultSet **getImportedKeys**(String *catalog*, String *schema*,
          String *table*) throws SQLException

Gets a description of the primary key columns that are referenced by the foreign key columns in table *table* (the primary keys imported by table *table*). The descriptions are ordered by the columns PKTABLE_CAT, PKTABLE_SCHEM, PKTABLE_NAME, and KEY_SEQ.

**PARAMETERS:**

| | |
|---|---|
| *catalog* | a String object representing a catalog name; "" retrieves those without a catalog; null indicates that the catalog name should be dropped from the selection criteria. |
| *schema* | a String object representing a schema name; "" retrieves those without a schema; null indicates that the schema name should be dropped from the selection criteria. |
| *table* | a String object representing the name of a table that has foreign keys. (It imports primary keys from another table.) |

**RETURNS:**
a ResultSet object, with each row being a description of a primary key column.

Each description has the following columns:

1. PKTABLE_CAT — `String` object giving the name of the catalog (which may be `null`) for the table containing the primary key being imported to table *table*.

2. PKTABLE_SCHEM — `String` object giving the name of the schema (which may be `null`) for the table containing the primary key being imported to table *table*.

3. PKTABLE_NAME — `String` object giving the table name of the primary key being imported to table *table*.

4. PKCOLUMN_NAME — `String` object giving the column name of the primary key being imported.

5. FKTABLE_CAT — `String` object giving the name of the catalog (which may be `null`) for table *table*, the table containing the foreign key.

6. FKTABLE_SCHEM — `String` object giving the name of the schema (which may be `null`) for table *table*, the table containing the foreign key.

7. FKTABLE_NAME — `String` object giving the name of table *table*, the table containing the foreign key.

8. FKCOLUMN_NAME — `String` object giving the column name of the foreign key.

9. KEY_SEQ — `short` indicating the sequence number within the foreign key (useful if the foreign key consists of more than one column).

10. UPDATE_RULE — `short` indicating what happens to the foreign key when the primary key is updated.

The possible values are:

`importedKeyNoAction` —If a primary key has been imported by another table, it cannot be updated.

`importedKeyCascade` —If a primary key has been updated, change the foreign key to agree with it.

`importedKeySetNull` —If a primary key has been updated, change the foreign key to `null`.

`importedKeySetDefault` —If a primary key has been updated, change the foreign key to its default value.

`importedKeyRestrict` —This is the same as `importedKeyNoAction` (for ODBC 2.x compatibility).

11. DELETE_RULE — `short` indicating what happens to the foreign key when the primary key is updated.

The possible values are:

| | |
|---|---|
| `importedKeyNoAction` | —If a primary key has been imported by another table, it cannot be deleted. |
| `importedKeyCascade` | —If a primary key has been deleted, delete rows that contain the foreign key. |
| `importedKeySetNull` | —If a primary key has been deleted, change the foreign key to `null`. |
| `importedKeySetDefault` | —If a primary key has been deleted, change the foreign key to its default value. |
| `importedKeyRestrict` | —This is the same as `importedKeyNoAction` (for ODBC 2.x compatibility). |
| 12. FK_NAME | `String` object containing the name of the foreign key, which may be `null`. |
| 13. PK_NAME | `String` object containing the name of the primary key, which may be `null`. |
| 14. DEFERRABILITY | `short` indicating whether the evaluation of foreign key constraints can be deferred until commit. |

Possible values are:

| | |
|---|---|
| `importedKeyInitiallyDeferred` | See SQL–92 for a definition. |
| `importedKeyInitiallyImmediate` | See SQL–92 for a definition. |
| `importedKeyNotDeferrable` | See SQL–92 for a definition. |

**EXAMPLE:**
```
ResultSet rs = dbmd.getImportedKeys(
                    "MYCATALOG", "MYSCHEMA", "TABLE1");
```

**SEE:**
`getExportedKeys`

"Sample Code 16" on page 114 for a complete example.

## getIndexInfo

```
ResultSet getIndexInfo(String catalog, String schema, String table,
        boolean unique, boolean approximate) throws SQLException
```

Gets a description of a table's indices and statistics. The descriptions are ordered by the columns NON_UNIQUE, TYPE, INDEX_NAME, and ORDINAL_POSITION.

**PARAMETERS:**

| | |
|---|---|
| *catalog* | String object representing a catalog name; "" retrieves those without a catalog; null indicates that the catalog name should be dropped from the selection criteria. |
| *schema* | String object representing a schema name; "" retrieves those without a schema; null indicates that the schema name should be dropped from the selection criteria. |
| *table* | String object representing a table name. |
| *unique* | true means that only indices for unique values will be returned; false means that all indices will be returned regardless of whether they are unique or not. |
| *approximate* | true means that results are allowed to reflect approximate or out-of-date values; false requests that results be accurate. |

**RETURNS:**

a ResultSet object, with each row being a description of an index column.

Each row of the ResultSet object has the following columns:

| | |
|---|---|
| 1. TABLE_CAT | String object giving the table catalog name; may be null. |
| 2. TABLE_SCHEM | String object giving the table schema name; may be null. |
| 3. TABLE_NAME | String object giving the table name. |
| 4. NON_UNIQUE | true means that index values can be non-unique; false means that index values must be unique or that TYPE is tableIndexStatistic. |
| 5. INDEX_QUALIFIER | String object giving the index catalog, which may be null; null when TYPE is tableIndex-Statistic. |
| 6. INDEX_NAME | String object giving the index name; null when TYPE is tableIndexStatistic. |
| 7. TYPE | short indicating the index type. The possible values are: |
|    tableIndexStatistic | —identifies table statistics that are returned in conjunction with a table's index descriptions. |
|    tableIndexClustered | —identifies this index as a clustered index. |
|    tableIndexHashed | —identifies this index as a hashed index. |
|    tableIndexOther | —identifies this index as some other style of index. |

| | |
|---|---|
| 8. ORDINAL_POSITION | short indicating the column sequence number within the index; 0 is returned when TYPE is tableIndexStatistic. |
| 9. COLUMN_NAME | String object giving the column name; null when TYPE is tableIndexStatistic. |
| 10. ASC_OR_DESC | String object indicating the column sort sequence. "A" indicates ascending; "D" indicates descending; "null" indicates that a sort sequence is not supported or that TYPE is tableIndexStatistic. |
| 11. CARDINALITY | int indicating the number of unique values in the index. When TYPE is tableIndexStatistic, however, it indicates the number of rows in the table. |
| 12. PAGES | int indicating the number of pages used for the current index. When TYPE is tableIndexStatistic, however, it indicates the number of pages used for the table. |
| 13. FILTER_CONDITION | String object giving the filter condition, if any; may be null. |

**EXAMPLE:**

```
ResultSet rs = dbmd.getIndexInfo(
                "MYCATALOG", "MYSCHEMA", "TABLE1", false, false);
```

## getMaxBinaryLiteralLength

```
int getMaxBinaryLiteralLength() throws SQLException
```

Gets the maximum number of hexadecimal characters allowed in an inline binary literal.

**RETURNS:**
an int representing the maximum number of hex characters.

**EXAMPLE:**
```
int max = dbmd.getMaxBinaryLiteralLength();
```

## getMaxCatalogNameLength

```
int getMaxCatalogNameLength() throws SQLException
```

Gets the maximum number of characters allowed in a catalog name.

**RETURNS:**
an int representing the maximum number of characters.

**EXAMPLE:**
```
int max = dbmd.getMaxCatalogNameLength();
```

## getMaxCharLiteralLength

```
int getMaxCharLiteralLength() throws SQLException
```

Gets the maximum number of characters allowed in a character literal.

**RETURNS:**
an int representing the maximum number of characters.

**EXAMPLE:**
```
int max = dbmd.getMaxCharLiteralLength();
```

## getMaxColumnNameLength

```
int getMaxColumnNameLength() throws SQLException
```

Gets the maximum number of characters allowed in a column name.

**RETURNS:**
an int representing the maximum number of characters.

**EXAMPLE:**
```
int max = dbmd.getMaxColumnNameLength();
```

## getMaxColumnsInGroupBy

```
int getMaxColumnsInGroupBy() throws SQLException
```

Gets the maximum number of columns allowed in a GROUP BY clause.

**RETURNS:**
an `int` representing the maximum number of columns.

**EXAMPLE:**
`int max = dbmd.getMaxColumnsInGroupBy();`

## getMaxColumnsInIndex

`int getMaxColumnsInIndex() throws SQLException`

Gets the maximum number of columns allowed in an index.

**RETURNS:**
an `int` representing the maximum number of columns.

**EXAMPLE:**
`int max = dbmd.getMaxColumnsInIndex();`

## getMaxColumnsInOrderBy

`int getMaxColumnsInOrderBy() throws SQLException`

Gets the maximum number of columns allowed in an ORDER BY clause.

**RETURNS:**
an `int` representing the maximum number of columns.

**EXAMPLE:**
`int max = dbmd.getMaxColumnsInOrderBy();`

## getMaxColumnsInSelect

`int getMaxColumnsInSelect() throws SQLException`

Gets the maximum number of columns allowed in a SELECT clause.

**RETURNS:**
an `int` representing the maximum number of columns.

**EXAMPLE:**
`int max = dbmd.getMaxColumnsInSelect();`

## getMaxColumnsInTable

```
int getMaxColumnsInTable() throws SQLException
```

Gets the maximum number of columns allowed in a table.

**RETURNS:**
an int representing the maximum number of columns.

**EXAMPLE:**
```
int max = dbmd.getMaxColumnsInTable();
```

## getMaxConnections

```
int getMaxConnections() throws SQLException
```

Gets the maximum number of active connections to this database that can be made through this driver instance.

**RETURNS:**
an int representing the maximum number of connections.

**EXAMPLE:**
```
int max = dbmd.getMaxConnections();
```

## getMaxCursorNameLength

```
int getMaxCursorNameLength() throws SQLException
```

Gets the maximum number of characters allowed in a cursor name.

**RETURNS:**
an int representing the maximum number of characters.

**EXAMPLE:**
```
int max = dbmd.getMaxCursorNameLength();
```

## getMaxIndexLength

```
int getMaxIndexLength() throws SQLException
```

Gets the maximum number of bytes allowed in an index.

**RETURNS:**
an int representing the maximum number of bytes.

**EXAMPLE:**
```
int max = dbmd.getMaxIndexLength();
```

## getMaxProcedureNameLength

```
int getMaxProcedureNameLength() throws SQLException
```

Gets the maximum number of characters allowed in a procedure name.

**RETURNS:**
an int representing the maximum number of characters.

**EXAMPLE:**
```
int max = dbmd.getMaxProcedureNameLength();
```

## getMaxRowSize

```
int getMaxRowSize() throws SQLException
```

Gets the maximum number of bytes allowed in a single row.

**RETURNS:**
an int representing the maximum number of bytes.

**EXAMPLE:**
```
int max = dbmd.getMaxRowSize();
```

## getMaxSchemaNameLength

```
int getMaxSchemaNameLength() throws SQLException
```

Gets the maximum number of characters allowed in a schema name.

**RETURNS:**
an int representing the maximum number of characters.

## getMaxStatementLength

```
int getMaxStatementLength() throws SQLException
```

Gets the maximum number of characters allowed in an SQL statement.

RETURNS:
an int representing the maximum number of characters.

EXAMPLE:
int max = dbmd.getMaxStatementLength();

## getMaxStatements

```
int getMaxStatements() throws SQLException
```

Gets the maximum number of active statements to this database that may be open at the same time.

RETURNS:
an int representing the maximum number of statements.

EXAMPLE:
int max = dbmd.getMaxStatements();

## getMaxTableNameLength

```
int getMaxTableNameLength() throws SQLException
```

Gets the maximum number of characters allowed in a table name.

RETURNS:
an int representing the maximum number of characters.

EXAMPLE:
int max = dbmd.getMaxTableNameLength();

## getMaxTablesInSelect

```
int getMaxTablesInSelect() throws SQLException
```

Gets the maximum number of tables allowed in a SELECT clause.

**RETURNS:**
an int representing the maximum number of tables.

**EXAMPLE:**
```
int max = dbmd.getMaxTablesInSelect();
```

## getMaxUserNameLength

```
int getMaxUserNameLength() throws SQLException
```

Gets the maximum number of characters allowed in a user name.

**RETURNS:**
an int representing the maximum number of characters.

**EXAMPLE:**
```
int max = dbmd.getMaxUserNameLength();
```

## getNumericFunctions

```
String getNumericFunctions() throws SQLException
```

Gets a list of a database's math functions.

**RETURNS:**
a String object that is a comma-separated list of math functions.

**EXAMPLE:**
```
String s = dbmd.getNumericFunctions();
```

## getPrimaryKeys

```
ResultSet getPrimaryKeys(String catalog, String schema,
            String table) throws SQLException
```

Gets a description of a table's primary key columns. Descriptions are returned only if all of the following are true: the table's catalog name matches *catalog*, the table's schema name matches *schema,* and the column's table name matches *table.* The descriptions are ordered by the column COLUMN_NAME.

**PARAMETERS:**

| | |
|---|---|
| *catalog* | a String object representing a catalog name; "" retrieves primary key columns in tables without a catalog; null indicates that the catalog name should be dropped from the selection criteria. |
| *schema* | a String object representing a schema name; "" retrieves primary key columns in tables without a schema; null indicates that the schema name should be dropped from the selection criteria. |
| *table* | a String object representing a table name. |

**RETURNS:**

a ResultSet object, with each row being a description of a table's primary key column(s).

Each primary key column description has the following columns:

| | |
|---|---|
| 1. TABLE_CAT | String object giving the table catalog, which may be null. |
| 2. TABLE_SCHEM | String object giving the table schema, which may be null. |
| 3. TABLE_NAME | String object giving the table name. |
| 4. COLUMN_NAME | String object giving the column name. |
| 5. KEY_SEQ | short giving the sequence number within a primary key (useful if the primary key consists of more than one column). |
| 6. PK_NAME | String object giving the primary key name, which may be null. |

**EXAMPLE:**

```
ResultSet rs = dbmd.getPrimaryKeys("MYCATALOG", "MYSCHEMA",
                                   "TABLE1");
```

**SEE:**

"Sample Code 15" on page 111 for a complete example.

## getProcedureColumns

```
ResultSet getProcedureColumns(String catalog, String schemaPattern,
          String procedureNamePattern, String columnNamePattern)
                                        throws SQLException
```

Gets a description of the input, output, and results associated with certain stored procedures available in catalog *catalog*. The input, output, and results include the IN, OUT, and INOUT parameters; the return value, if there is one; and the columns in a ResultSet object generated by the execution of a stored procedure.

Descriptions are returned for input, output, and results associated with all stored procedures that satisfy the following critera: the procedure schema name matches *schemaPattern*, the procedure name matches *procedureName-Pattern*, and the column name matches *columnNamePattern*. The descriptions are ordered by the columns PROCEDURE_SCHEM and PROCE-DURE_NAME. Within this, the stored procedure's return value, if any, is first. Next are the parameter descriptions in call order. Last are the descriptions of result set columns, given in column number order.

**PARAMETERS:**

*catalog*            a String object representing a catalog name; "" retrieves procedures without a catalog; null indicates that the catalog name should be dropped from the selection criteria.

*schemaPattern*      a String object representing a schema name pattern; "" retrieves procedures without a schema; null indicates that the schema name should be dropped from the selection criteria.

*procedureNamePattern* a String object representing a procedure name pattern.

*columnNamePattern*  a String object representing the name pattern of a column in a ResultSet object that was generated by the stored procedure.

**RETURNS:**

a ResultSet object, with each row being a description of one of the following: a parameter for this stored procedure, the return value for this stored procedure, or a column in a ResultSet object derived from this stored procedure.

Each row in the ResultSet object is a parameter description or a ResultSet column description with the following fields:

1. PROCEDURE_CAT      `String` object giving the procedure catalog name, which may be `null`.

2. PROCEDURE_SCHEM    `String` object giving the procedure schema name, which may be `null`.

3. PROCEDURE_NAME     `String` object giving the procedure name.

4. COLUMN_NAME      `String` object giving the result set column name or the parameter name.

5. COLUMN_TYPE       `short` indicating what this row describes. The possible values are:

      `procedureColumnUnknown` —kind of column unknown.

      `procedureColumnIn` —column contains an IN parameter.

      `procedureColumnInOut` —column contains an INOUT parameter.

      `procedureColumnOut` —column contains an OUT parameter.

      `procedureColumnReturn` —column contains the return value for the procedure.

      `procedureColumnResult` —column is a result column in a `ResultSet` object.

6. DATA_TYPE        `short` indicating the JDBC type from `java.sql.Types`.

7. TYPE_NAME       `String` object giving the local type name used by the data source.

8. PRECISION        `int` indicating the total number of digits.

9. LENGTH         `int` indicating the length of data in bytes.

10. SCALE         `short` indicating the number of digits to the right of the decimal point.

11. RADIX         `int` indicating the radix.

12. NULLABLE       `short` indicating whether this column can contain a null value. The possible values are:

      `procedureNoNulls` —null values are not allowed.

      `procedureNullable` —null values are allowed.

      `procedureNullableUnknown` —not known whether null values are allowed.

13. REMARKS        `String` object containing an explanatory comment on the parameter or column. This column may be `null`.

Note that some databases may not return the parameter or `ResultSet` column descriptions for a procedure. Additional columns beyond REMARKS can be defined by the database.

**EXAMPLE:**
```
ResultSet rs = getProcedureColumns("MYCATALOG", "MYSCHEMA%",
                                    "MYPROCEDURE%", "MYCOLUMN%");
```

**SEE:**
`java.sql.Types`
"String Patterns as Arguments" on page 164.

## getProcedures

```
ResultSet getProcedures(String catalog, String schemaPattern,
        String procedureNamePattern) throws SQLException
```

Gets a description of the stored procedures available in catalog *catalog*. Only descriptions of those procedures whose schema name matches *schemaPattern* and whose procedure name matches *procedureNamePattern* are returned. The descriptions are ordered by the columns PROCEDURE_SCHEM and PROCEDURE_NAME.

**PARAMETERS:**

| | |
|---|---|
| *catalog* | a `String` object representing a catalog name; "" retrieves procedures without a catalog; `null` indicates that the catalog name should be dropped from the selection criteria. |
| *schemaPattern* | a `String` object representing a schema name pattern; "" retrieves procedures without a schema; `null` indicates that the schema name should be dropped from the selection criteria. |

*procedureNamePattern* a `String` object representing a procedure name pattern.

**RETURNS:**
a `ResultSet` object, with each row being a description of a stored procedure.

Each procedure description has the following columns:
1. PROCEDURE_CAT    `String` object giving the procedure catalog, which may be `null`.
2. PROCEDURE_SCHEM   `String` object giving the procedure schema, which may be `null`.
3. PROCEDURE_NAME    `String` object giving the procedure name.
4. Reserved for future use.
5. Reserved for future use.

6. Reserved for future use.

7. REMARKS — `String` object containing an explanatory comment on the procedure. This column may be `null`.

8. PROCEDURE_TYPE — `short` indicating the kind of procedure. The possible values are:

`procedureResultUnknown`—procedure may return a result.

`procedureNoResult` —procedure does not return a result.

`procedureReturnsResult`—procedure returns a result.

**EXAMPLE:**
```
ResultSet rs = getProcedures("MYCATALOG", "MYSCHEMA%",
                                       "MYPROCEDURE%");
```

**SEE:**
"String Patterns as Arguments" on page 164.

## getProcedureTerm

```
String getProcedureTerm() throws SQLException
```

Gets the database vendor's preferred term for "procedure."

**RETURNS:**
a `String` object containing the vendor term for "procedure."

**EXAMPLE:**
```
String s = dbmd.getProcedureTerm();
```

## getSchemas

```
ResultSet getSchemas() throws SQLException
```

Gets the schema names available in this database. The results are ordered by schema name.

**RETURNS:**
a `ResultSet` object, with each row representing a schema name available in this database.

Each row of the `ResultSet` object has a single `String` column that is a schema name. The `ResultSet` object has the following column:

1. TABLE_SCHEM          `String` object containing a schema name.

**EXAMPLE:**
```
ResultSet rs = dbmd.getSchemas();
```

## getSchemaTerm

```
String getSchemaTerm() throws SQLException
```

Gets the database vendor's preferred term for "schema."

**RETURNS:**
a `String` object containing the vendor term for "schema."

**EXAMPLE:**
```
String s = dbmd.getSchemaTerm();
```

## getSearchStringEscape

```
String getSearchStringEscape() throws SQLException
```

Gets the string that can be used to escape "_"or "%" wildcards in the string search pattern used for catalog search parameters.

The character "_" represents any single character. The character "%" represents any sequence of zero or more characters.

**RETURNS:**
a `String` object that is used to escape wildcard characters.

**EXAMPLE:**
```
String s = dbmd.getSearchStringEscape();
```

**SEE:**
"Methods that Return a String" on page 101 for a more complete example.

## getSQLKeywords

```
String getSQLKeywords() throws SQLException
```

Gets a list of all a database's keywords that are NOT also SQL–92 keywords.

**RETURNS:**

a `String` object that is a comma-separated list of keywords used by the database that are not also SQL–92 keywords.

**EXAMPLE:**

```
String s = dbmd.getSQLKeywords();
```

## getStringFunctions

```
String getStringFunctions() throws SQLException
```

Gets a list of all a database's string functions.

**RETURNS:**

a `String` object that is a comma-separated list of string functions.

**EXAMPLE:**

```
String s = dbmd.getStringFunctions();
```

## getSystemFunctions

```
String getSystemFunctions() throws SQLException
```

Gets a list of all a database's system functions.

**RETURNS:**

a `String` object that is a comma-separated list of system functions.

**EXAMPLE:**

```
String s = dbmd.getSystemFunctions();
```

## getTablePrivileges

```
ResultSet getTablePrivileges(String catalog, String schemaPattern,
            String tableNamePattern) throws SQLException
```

Gets a description of the access rights for each table available in catalog *catalog*. Descriptions of privileges are returned only if all of the following are true: the table's catalog name matches *catalog*, the table's schema name matches *schemaPattern,* and the column's table name matches *tableName-Pattern.* The descriptions are ordered by the columns TABLE_SCHEM, TABLE_NAME, and PRIVILEGE.

Note that the method getTablePrivileges returns privileges that were set at the table level and also those that were set at the column level. A table privilege applies to one or more columns in a table; it cannot be assumed that a table privilege applies to all columns. In some RDBMSs a table privilege applies to all columns, but this is not necessarily true for all RDBMSs.

**PARAMETERS:**

| | |
|---|---|
| *catalog* | a String object representing a catalog name; "" retrieves columns in tables without a catalog; null indicates that the catalog name should be dropped from the selection criteria. |
| *schemaPattern* | a String object representing a schema name pattern; "" retrieves privileges in tables without a schema; null indicates that the schema name should be dropped from the selection criteria. |
| *tableNamePattern* | a String object representing a table name pattern. |

**RETURNS:**
a ResultSet object, with each row being a description of the access rights for a table.

Each privilege description has the following columns:

| | |
|---|---|
| 1. TABLE_CAT | String object giving the table catalog, which may be null. |
| 2. TABLE_SCHEM | String object giving the table schema, which may be null. |
| 3. TABLE_NAME | String object giving the table name. |
| 4. GRANTOR | String object giving the grantor of access, which may be null. |
| 5. GRANTEE | String object giving the grantee of access. |
| 6. PRIVILEGE | String object naming the type of access (SELECT, INSERT, UPDATE, REFERENCES, and so on). |
| 7. IS_GRANTABLE | String object; "YES" indicates that the grantee is permitted to grant access to others, "NO" indicates that the grantee cannot grant access to others, and null indicates that it is unknown. |

**EXAMPLE:**
```
ResultSet rs = dbmd.getTablePrivileges(
                        "MYCATALOG", "MYSCHEMA%", "EMPLOY%");
```

**SEE:**
"String Patterns as Arguments" on page 164.

## getTables

```
ResultSet getTables(String catalog, String schemaPattern,
    String tableNamePattern, String types[]) throws SQLException
```

Gets a description of the tables available in catalog *catalog*. Only descriptions of those tables whose catalog name matches *catalogPattern*, whose schema name matches *schemaPattern*, and whose table name matches *tableNamePattern* are returned. The descriptions are ordered by the columns TABLE_TYPE, TABLE_SCHEM, and TABLE_NAME.

**PARAMETERS:**

| | |
|---|---|
| *catalog* | a String object representing a catalog name; "" retrieves tables without a catalog; null indicates that the catalog name should be dropped from the selection criteria. |
| *schemaPattern* | a String object representing a schema name pattern; "" retrieves tables without a schema; null indicates that the schema name should be dropped from the selection criteria. |
| *tableNamePattern* | a String object representing a table name pattern. |
| *types[]* | a list of String objects representing the table types to include; null indicates that all table types should be returned. |

**RETURNS:**
a ResultSet object, with each row being a description of a table.

Each table description has the following columns:

| | |
|---|---|
| 1. TABLE_CAT | String object giving the table catalog, which may be null. |
| 2. TABLE_SCHEM | String object giving the table schema, which may be null. |
| 3. TABLE_NAME | String object giving the table name. |

| | |
|---|---|
| 4. TABLE_TYPE | String object giving the table type. Typical types are "TABLE", "VIEW", "SYSTEM TABLE", "GLOBAL TEMPORARY", "LOCAL TEMPORARY", "ALIAS", "SYNONYM". |
| 5. REMARKS | String object containing an explanatory comment on the table. This column may be null. |

Note that some databases may not return information for all tables.

**EXAMPLE:**
```
String [] s = { "TABLE", "VIEW" };
ResultSet rs = dbmd.getTables(
                    "MYCATALOG", "MYSCHEMA%", "MYTABLE%", s);
```

**SEE:**
"String Patterns as Arguments" on page 164.

## getTableTypes

```
ResultSet getTableTypes() throws SQLException
```

Gets the table types available in this database system. The results are ordered by table type.

**RETURNS:**
a ResultSet object, with each row representing a table type available in this DBMS.

Each row of the ResultSet object has a single String column that is a table type. The ResultSet object has the following column:

| | |
|---|---|
| 1. TABLE_TYPE | String object containing a table type. Typical types are "TABLE", "VIEW", "SYSTEM TABLE", "GLOBAL TEMPORARY", "LOCAL TEMPORARY", "ALIAS", "SYNONYM". |

**EXAMPLE:**
```
ResultSet rs = dbmd.getTableTypes();
```

**SEE:**
"Sample Code 13" on page 104 for a complete example.

## getTimeDateFunctions

```
String getTimeDateFunctions() throws SQLException
```

Gets a list of all a database's time and date functions.

**RETURNS:**
a String object that is a comma-separated list of time and date functions.

**EXAMPLE:**
```
String s = dbmd.getTimeDateFunctions();
```

## getTypeInfo

```
ResultSet getTypeInfo() throws SQLException
```

Gets a description of all the datatypes supported by this database. Each row describes a DBMS datatype with the name of TYPE_NAME. The type in the column DATA_TYPE is the JDBC SQL type that is the best mapping for this local DBMS type.

The results are ordered first by DATA_TYPE and then by how closely the local type matches the definition of DATA_TYPE. Therefore, if two or more rows have the same value for the column DATA_TYPE, the first row gives the best local type to use for the JDBC type in DATA_TYPE.

**RETURNS:**
a ResultSet object, with each row being a description of a local DBMS type.

Each row in the ResultSet object has the following columns:

1. TYPE_NAME — String object giving the local DBMS name for a type supported by this DBMS.
2. DATA_TYPE — short indicating the JDBC datatype from java.sql.Types that corresponds to the local datatype in column TYPE_NAME. If there is more than one row for a datatype, the first entry is the preferred one.
3. PRECISION — int indicating the maximum precision.
4. LITERAL_PREFIX — String object giving the prefix used to quote a literal; may be null.
5. LITERAL_SUFFIX — String object giving the suffix used to quote a literal; may be null.

6. CREATE_PARAMS      `String` object giving the parameters used in creating the type; may be `null`.

7. NULLABLE           `int` indicating whether a column can be `NULL`. The possible values are:

   `typeNoNulls`          —does not allow `NULL` values.

   `typeNullable`         —allows `NULL` values.

   `typeNullableUnknown`  —nullability unknown.

8. CASE_SENSITIVE     `true` to indicate that the type is case sensitive; `false` indicates that it is not case sensitive.

9. SEARCHABLE         `short` indicating whether it is possible to use a `WHERE` clause based on this type. The possible values are:

   `typePredNone`         —No `WHERE` clauses can be based on this type.

   `typePredChar`         —Only a `WHERE` . . . `LIKE` clause can be based on this type.

   `typePredBasic`        —All `WHERE` clauses except `WHERE` . . . `LIKE` can be based on this type.

   `typeSearchable`       —All `WHERE` clauses can be based on this type.

10. UNSIGNED_ATTRIBUTE    `true` indicates that the type is unsigned; `false` indicates that it is signed.

11. FIXED_PREC_SCALE      `true` indicates that the type can be a money value; `false` indicates that it cannot.

12. AUTO_INCREMENT        `true` indicates that the type can be used for an auto-increment value; `false` indicates that it cannot.

13. LOCAL_TYPE_NAME       `String` object containing the localized version of the type name. It may be `null`.

14. MINIMUM_SCALE         `short` indicating the minimum scale supported.

15. MAXIMUM_SCALE         `short` indicating the maximum scale supported.

16. SQL_DATA_TYPE         `int` ; unused.

17. SQL_DATETIME_SUB      `int` ; unused.

18. NUM_PREC_RADIX        `int` indicating the radix, which is usually 2 or 10.

**EXAMPLE:**
```
ResultSet rs = dbmd.getTypeInfo();
```

**SEE:**
"Sample Code 14" on page 106 for a complete example.

## getURL

```
String getURL() throws SQLException
```

Gets the URL for this database.

**RETURNS:**
a `String` object representing the URL for this database or `null` if the URL cannot be generated.

**EXAMPLE:**
```
String s = dbmd.getURL();
```

## getUserName

```
String getUserName() throws SQLException
```

Gets the user name as known to the database.

**RETURNS:**
a `String` object representing one's database user name.

**EXAMPLE:**
```
String s = dbmd.getUserName();
```

## getVersionColumns

```
ResultSet getVersionColumns(String catalog, String schema,
                            String table) throws SQLException
```

Gets a description of the columns in a table that are automatically updated when any value in a row is updated. The column descriptions are not ordered.

**PARAMETERS:**

*catalog*   a `String` object representing a catalog name; "" retrieves those without a catalog; `null` indicates that the catalog name should be dropped from the selection criteria.

*schema*                      a `String` object representing a schema name; `""` re-
                              trieves those without a schema; `null` indicates that the
                              schema name should be dropped from the selection cri-
                              teria.

*table*                       a `String` object representing a table name.

**RETURNS:**

a `ResultSet` object, with each row being a description of a table column that is
automatically updated whenever a value in a row is updated.

Each column description has the following columns:

  1. SCOPE                     `short`; not used.
  2. COLUMN_NAME               `String` object giving the column name.
  3. DATA_TYPE                 `short` indicating a JDBC datatype from
                                                `java.sql.Types`.
  4. TYPE_NAME                 `String` object giving the local type name used
                                                by the data source.
  5. COLUMN_SIZE               `int` giving the precision.
  6. BUFFER_LENGTH             `int` indicating the length of the column value in
                                                bytes.
  7. DECIMAL_DIGITS            `short` indicating the scale.
  8. PSEUDO_COLUMN             `short` indicating whether this is a pseudo col-
                                                umn, such as an Oracle ROWID.
                                                The possible values are:

     `versionColumnUnknown`      —may or may not be a pseudo column.
     `versionColumnNotPseudo`—is NOT a pseudo column.
     `versionColumnPseudo`       —is a pseudo column.

**EXAMPLE:**

```
ResultSet rs = dbmd.getVersionColumns("MYCATALOG", "MYSCHEMA",
                                               "MYTABLE");
```

## isCatalogAtStart

```
boolean isCatalogAtStart() throws SQLException
```

Checks whether a catalog name appears at the start of a fully qualified table
name. If it is not at the beginning, it appears at the end.

**RETURNS:**
true if the catalog name appears at the start of a fully qualified table name; false if it appears at the end.

**EXAMPLE:**
```
boolean b = dbmd.isCatalogAtStart();
```

## isReadOnly

```
boolean isReadOnly() throws SQLException
```

Checks whether the database is in read-only mode.

**RETURNS:**
true if so; false otherwise.

**EXAMPLE:**
```
boolean b = dbmd.isReadOnly();
```

## nullPlusNonNullIsNull

```
boolean nullPlusNonNullIsNull() throws SQLException
```

Checks whether the concatenation of a NULL value and a non-NULL value results in a NULL value. A JDBC Compliant driver always returns true.

**RETURNS:**
true if so; false otherwise.

**EXAMPLE:**
```
boolean b = dbmd.nullPlusNonNullIsNull();
```

## nullsAreSortedAtEnd

```
boolean nullsAreSortedAtEnd() throws SQLException
```

Checks whether NULL values are sorted at the end regardless of sort order.

**RETURNS:**
true if so; false otherwise.

EXAMPLE:
```
boolean b = dbmd.nullsAreSortedAtEnd();
```

## nullsAreSortedAtStart

```
boolean nullsAreSortedAtStart() throws SQLException
```

Checks whether NULL values are sorted at the start regardless of sort order.

RETURNS:
true if so; false otherwise.

EXAMPLE:
```
boolean b = dbmd.nullsAreSortedAtStart();
```

## nullsAreSortedHigh

```
boolean nullsAreSortedHigh() throws SQLException
```

Checks whether NULL values are sorted high.

RETURNS:
true if so; false otherwise.

EXAMPLE:
```
boolean b = dbmd.nullsAreSortedHigh();
```

## nullsAreSortedLow

```
boolean nullsAreSortedLow() throws SQLException
```

Checks whether NULL values are sorted low.

RETURNS:
true if so; false otherwise.

EXAMPLE:
```
boolean b = dbmd.nullsAreSortedLow();
```

## storesLowerCaseIdentifiers

```
boolean storesLowerCaseIdentifiers() throws SQLException
```

Checks whether the DBMS (1) treats mixed-case unquoted SQL identifiers used in SQL statements as case-insensitive and (2) stores them as all lowercase in its metadata tables.

**RETURNS:**
true if so; false otherwise.

**EXAMPLE:**
```
boolean b = dbmd.storesLowerCaseIdentifiers();
```

## storesLowerCaseQuotedIdentifiers

```
boolean storesLowerCaseQuotedIdentifiers() throws SQLException
```

Checks whether the DBMS (1) treats mixed-case quoted SQL identifiers used in SQL statements as case-insensitive and (2) stores them as all lowercase in its metadata tables.

**RETURNS:**
true if so; false otherwise.

**EXAMPLE:**
```
boolean b = dbmd.storesLowerCaseQuotedIdentifiers();
```

## storesMixedCaseIdentifiers

```
boolean storesMixedCaseIdentifiers() throws SQLException
```

Checks whether the DBMS (1) treats mixed-case unquoted SQL identifiers used in SQL statements as case-insensitive and (2) stores them in mixed case in its metadata tables.

**RETURNS:**
true if so; false otherwise.

**EXAMPLE:**
```
boolean b = dbmd.storesMixedCaseIdentifiers();
```

## storesMixedCaseQuotedIdentifiers

```
boolean storesMixedCaseQuotedIdentifiers() throws SQLException
```

Checks whether the DBMS (1) treats mixed-case quoted SQL identifiers used in SQL statements as case-insensitive and (2) stores them in mixed case in its metadata tables.

**RETURNS:**
true if so; false otherwise.

**EXAMPLE:**
```
boolean b = dbmd.storesMixedCaseQuotedIdentifiers();
```

## storesUpperCaseIdentifiers

```
boolean storesUpperCaseIdentifiers() throws SQLException
```

Checks whether the DBMS (1) treats mixed-case unquoted SQL identifiers used in SQL statements as case-insensitive and (2) stores them in all uppercase in its metadata tables.

**RETURNS:**
true if so; false otherwise.

**EXAMPLE:**
```
boolean b = dbmd.storesUpperCaseIdentifiers();
```

## storesUpperCaseQuotedIdentifiers

```
boolean storesUpperCaseQuotedIdentifiers() throws SQLException
```

Checks whether the DBMS (1) treats mixed-case quoted SQL identifiers used in SQL statements as case-insensitive and (2) stores them as all uppercase in its metadata tables.

**RETURNS:**
true if so; false otherwise.

**EXAMPLE:**
```
boolean b = dbmd.storesUpperCaseQuotedIdentifiers();
```

## supportsAlterTableWithAddColumn

boolean **supportsAlterTableWithAddColumn**() throws SQLException

Checks whether the database supports ALTER TABLE with add column.

**RETURNS:**
true if so; false otherwise.

**EXAMPLE:**
boolean b = dbmd.supportsAlterTableWithAddColumn();


## supportsAlterTableWithDropColumn

boolean **supportsAlterTableWithDropColumn**() throws SQLException

Checks whether the database supports ALTER TABLE with drop column.

**RETURNS:**
true if so; false otherwise.

**EXAMPLE:**
boolean b = dbmd.supportsAlterTableWithDropColumn();


## supportsANSI92EntryLevelSQL

boolean **supportsANSI92EntryLevelSQL**() throws SQLException

Checks whether the database supports ANSI–92 entry level SQL grammar. All JDBC Compliant drivers must return true.

**RETURNS:**
true if so; false otherwise.

**EXAMPLE:**
boolean b = dbmd.supportsANSI92EntryLevelSQL();


## supportsANSI92FullSQL

boolean **supportsANSI92FullSQL**() throws SQLException

Checks whether the database supports ANSI–92 full SQL grammar.

**RETURNS:**
true if so; false otherwise.

**EXAMPLE:**
```
boolean b = dbmd.supportsANSI92FullSQL();
```

## supportsANSI92IntermediateSQL

```
boolean supportsANSI92IntermediateSQL() throws SQLException
```

Checks whether the database supports ANSI–92 intermediate SQL grammar.

**RETURNS:**
true if so; false otherwise.

**EXAMPLE:**
```
boolean b = dbmd.supportsANSI92IntermediateSQL();
```

## supportsCatalogsInDataManipulation

```
boolean supportsCatalogsInDataManipulation() throws SQLException
```

Checks whether this database supports using a catalog name in a data manipulation statement.

**RETURNS:**
true if so; false otherwise.

**EXAMPLE:**
```
boolean b = dbmd.supportsCatalogsInDataManipulation();
```

## supportsCatalogsInIndexDefinitions

```
boolean supportsCatalogsInIndexDefinitions() throws SQLException
```

Checks whether this database supports using a catalog name in an index definition statement.

**RETURNS:**
true if so; false otherwise.

EXAMPLE:
```
boolean b = dbmd.supportsCatalogsInIndexDefinitions();
```

## supportsCatalogsInPrivilegeDefinitions

```
boolean supportsCatalogsInPrivilegeDefinitions()
                                            throws SQLException
```

Checks whether this database supports using a catalog name in a privilege definition statement.

RETURNS:
true if so; false otherwise.

EXAMPLE:
```
boolean b = dbmd.supportsCatalogsInPrivilegeDefinitions();
```

## supportsCatalogsInProcedureCalls

```
boolean supportsCatalogsInProcedureCalls() throws SQLException
```

Checks whether this database supports using a catalog name in a procedure call statement.

RETURNS:
true if so; false otherwise.

EXAMPLE:
```
boolean b = dbmd.supportsCatalogsInProcedureCalls();
```

## supportsCatalogsInTableDefinitions

```
boolean supportsCatalogsInTableDefinitions() throws SQLException
```

Checks whether this database supports using a catalog name in a table definition statement.

RETURNS:
true if so; false otherwise.

**EXAMPLE:**
```
boolean b = dbmd.supportsCatalogsInTableDefinitions();
```

## supportsColumnAliasing

```
boolean supportsColumnAliasing() throws SQLException
```

Checks whether the database supports column aliasing. If true, the SQL AS clause can be used to provide names for computed columns or to provide alias names for columns as required. A JDBC Compliant driver always returns true.

**RETURNS:**
true if so; false otherwise.

**EXAMPLE:**
```
boolean b = dbmd.supportsColumnAliasing();
```

## supportsConvert

```
boolean supportsConvert() throws SQLException
```

Checks whether the database supports CONVERT between JDBC types.

**RETURNS:**
true if so; false otherwise.

**EXAMPLE:**
```
boolean b = dbmd.supportsConvert();
```

## supportsConvert

```
boolean supportsConvert(int fromType, int toType)
                                              throws SQLException
```

Checks whether the database supports CONVERT between the JDBC types *fromType* and *toType*.

**PARAMETERS:**

*fromType*          the SQL type to convert from

*toType*             the SQL type to convert to

**RETURNS:**
true if so; false otherwise.

**EXAMPLE:**
```
boolean b = dbmd.supportsConvert(TIMESTAMP, CHAR);
```

## supportsCoreSQLGrammar

```
boolean supportsCoreSQLGrammar() throws SQLException
```

Checks whether the database supports the ODBC Core SQL grammar.

**RETURNS:**
true if so; false otherwise.

**EXAMPLE:**
```
boolean b = dbmd.supportsCoreSQLGrammar();
```

## supportsCorrelatedSubqueries

```
boolean supportsCorrelatedSubqueries() throws SQLException
```

Checks whether this database supports correlated subqueries. A JDBC Compliant driver always returns true.

**RETURNS:**
true if so; false otherwise.

**EXAMPLE:**
```
boolean b = dbmd.supportsCorrelatedSubqueries();
```

## supportsDataDefinitionAndDataManipulationTransactions

```
boolean supportsDataDefinitionAndDataManipulationTransactions()
                                        throws SQLException
```

Checks whether this database supports both data definition and data manipulation statements within a transaction.

**RETURNS:**
true if so; `false` otherwise.

**EXAMPLE:**
```
boolean b =
    dbmd.supportsDataDefinitionAndDataManipulationTransactions();
```

## supportsDataManipulationTransactionsOnly

```
boolean supportsDataManipulationTransactionsOnly() throws SQLException
```

Checks whether this database supports only data manipulation statements within a transaction.

**RETURNS:**
true if so; `false` otherwise.

**EXAMPLE:**
```
boolean b = dbmd.supportsDataManipulationTransactionsOnly();
```

## supportsDifferentTableCorrelationNames

```
boolean supportsDifferentTableCorrelationNames() throws SQLException
```

Checks whether it is true that if table correlation names are supported, they are restricted to be different from the names of the tables.

**RETURNS:**
true if so; `false` otherwise.

**EXAMPLE:**
```
boolean b = dbmd.supportsDifferentTableCorrelationNames();
```

## supportsExpressionsInOrderBy

```
boolean supportsExpressionsInOrderBy() throws SQLException
```

Checks whether the database supports expressions in `ORDER BY` lists.

**RETURNS:**
true if so; `false` otherwise.

**EXAMPLE:**
`boolean b = dbmd.supportsExpressionsInOrderBy();`

## supportsExtendedSQLGrammar

`boolean supportsExtendedSQLGrammar() throws SQLException`

Checks whether the database supports the ODBC Extended SQL grammar.

**RETURNS:**
true if so; `false` otherwise.

**EXAMPLE:**
`boolean b = dbmd.supportsExtendedSQLGrammar();`

## supportsFullOuterJoins

`boolean supportsFullOuterJoins() throws SQLException`

Checks whether the database supports full nested outer joins.

**RETURNS:**
true if so; `false` otherwise.

**EXAMPLE:**
`boolean b = dbmd.supportsFullOuterJoins();`

## supportsGroupBy

`boolean supportsGroupBy() throws SQLException`

Checks whether the database supports some form of the GROUP BY clause.

**RETURNS:**
true if so; `false` otherwise.

**EXAMPLE:**
`boolean b = dbmd.supportsGroupBy();`

## supportsGroupByBeyondSelect

```
boolean supportsGroupByBeyondSelect() throws SQLException
```

Checks whether a GROUP BY clause can use columns that are not in the SELECT clause, provided that it specifies all the columns in the SELECT clause.

**RETURNS:**
true if so; false otherwise.

**EXAMPLE:**
```
boolean b = dbmd.supportsGroupByBeyondSelect();
```

## supportsGroupByUnrelated

```
boolean supportsGroupByUnrelated() throws SQLException
```

Checks whether a GROUP BY clause can use columns that are not in the SELECT clause.

**RETURNS:**
true if so; false otherwise.

**EXAMPLE:**
```
boolean b = dbmd.supportsGroupByUnrelated();
```

## supportsIntegrityEnhancementFacility

```
boolean supportsIntegrityEnhancementFacility() throws SQLException
```

Checks whether the database supports the SQL Integrity Enhancement Facility.

**RETURNS:**
true if so; false otherwise.

**EXAMPLE:**
```
boolean b = dbmd.supportsIntegrityEnhancementFacility();
```

## supportsLikeEscapeClause

```
boolean supportsLikeEscapeClause() throws SQLException
```

Checks whether the database supports escape characters in LIKE clauses. A JDBC Compliant driver always returns true.

**RETURNS:**
true if so; false otherwise.

**EXAMPLE:**
```
boolean b = dbmd.supportsLikeEscapeClause();
```

## supportsLimitedOuterJoins

```
boolean supportsLimitedOuterJoins() throws SQLException
```

Checks whether the database provides limited support for outer joins. Note that this method returns true if the method supportsFullOuterJoins returns true.

**RETURNS:**
true if so; false otherwise.

**EXAMPLE:**
```
boolean b = dbmd.supportsLimitedOuterJoins();
```

## supportsMinimumSQLGrammar

```
boolean supportsMinimumSQLGrammar() throws SQLException
```

Checks whether the database supports the ODBC Minimum SQL grammar. All JDBC Compliant drivers must return true.

**RETURNS:**
true if so; false otherwise.

**EXAMPLE:**
```
boolean b = dbmd.supportsMinimumSQLGrammar();
```

## supportsMixedCaseIdentifiers

boolean **supportsMixedCaseIdentifiers**() throws SQLException

Checks whether the DBMS treats mixed-case unquoted SQL identifiers used in SQL statements as case sensitive and as a result stores them in mixed case in its metadata tables. A JDBC Compliant driver will always return false.

**RETURNS:**
true if so; false otherwise.

**EXAMPLE:**
boolean b = dbmd.supportsMixedCaseIdentifiers();

## supportsMixedCaseQuotedIdentifiers

boolean **supportsMixedCaseQuotedIdentifiers**() throws SQLException

Checks whether the database treats mixed-case quoted SQL identifiers used in SQL statements as case sensitive and as a result stores them in mixed case in its metadata tables. A JDBC Compliant driver will always return true.

**RETURNS:**
true if so; false otherwise.

**EXAMPLE:**
boolean b = dbmd.supportsMixedCaseQuotedIdentifiers();

## supportsMultipleResultSets

boolean **supportsMultipleResultSets**() throws SQLException

Checks whether the database supports multiple result sets from a single execute statement.

**RETURNS:**
true if so; false otherwise.

**EXAMPLE:**
boolean b = dbmd.supportsMultipleResultSets();

## supportsMultipleTransactions

```
boolean supportsMultipleTransactions() throws SQLException
```

Checks whether there can be multiple transactions open at once (on different connections).

**RETURNS:**
true if so; false otherwise.

**EXAMPLE:**
```
boolean b = dbmd.supportsMultipleTransactions();
```

## supportsNonNullableColumns

```
boolean supportsNonNullableColumns() throws SQLException
```

Checks whether the database supports defining columns as nonnullable. A JDBC Compliant driver will always return true.

**RETURNS:**
true if so; false otherwise.

**EXAMPLE:**
```
boolean b = dbmd.supportsNonNullableColumns();
```

## supportsOpenCursorsAcrossCommit

```
boolean supportsOpenCursorsAcrossCommit() throws SQLException
```

Checks whether this database supports having cursors remain open across commits. Note that a return value of false does not mean that cursors are always closed on commit; rather, false means that cursors are not always left open across commits.

**RETURNS:**
true if cursors always remain open after commits; false if cursors are sometimes or always closed on commit.

**EXAMPLE:**
```
boolean b = dbmd.supportsOpenCursorsAcrossCommit();
```

## supportsOpenCursorsAcrossRollback

boolean **supportsOpenCursorsAcrossRollback**() throws SQLException

Checks whether this database supports having cursors remain open across rollbacks. Note that a return value of false does not mean that cursors are always closed on rollback; rather, false means that cursors are not always left open across rollbacks.

**RETURNS:**
true if cursors always remain open after rollbacks; false if cursors are sometimes or always closed on rollback.

**EXAMPLE:**
boolean b = dbmd.supportsOpenCursorsAcrossRollback();

## supportsOpenStatementsAcrossCommit

boolean **supportsOpenStatementsAcrossCommit**() throws SQLException

Checks whether this database supports having statements remain open across commits. Note that a return value of false does not mean that statements are always closed on commit; rather, false means that statements are not always left open across commits.

**RETURNS:**
true if statements always remain open across commits; false if statements are sometimes or always closed on commit.

**EXAMPLE:**
boolean b = dbmd.supportsOpenStatementsAcrossCommit();

## supportsOpenStatementsAcrossRollback

boolean **supportsOpenStatementsAcrossRollback**() throws SQLException

Checks whether this database supports having statements remain open across rollbacks. Note that a return value of false does not mean that statements are always closed on rollback; rather, false means that statements are not always left open across rollbacks.

**RETURNS:**
true if statements always remain open across rollbacks; `false` if statements are sometimes or always closed on rollback.

**EXAMPLE:**
```
boolean b = dbmd.supportsOpenStatementsAcrossRollback();
```

## supportsOrderByUnrelated

```
boolean supportsOrderByUnrelated() throws SQLException
```

Checks whether an `ORDER BY` clause can use columns that are not in the `SELECT` clause.

**RETURNS:**
true if so; `false` otherwise.

**EXAMPLE:**
```
boolean b = dbmd.supportsOrderByUnrelated();
```

## supportsOuterJoins

```
boolean supportsOuterJoins() throws SQLException
```

Checks whether the database supports some form of outer join.

**RETURNS:**
true if so; `false` otherwise.

**EXAMPLE:**
```
boolean b = dbmd.supportsOuterJoins();
```

## supportsPositionedDelete

```
boolean supportsPositionedDelete() throws SQLException
```

Checks whether this database supports positioned `DELETE` statements.

**RETURNS:**
true if so; `false` otherwise.

**EXAMPLE:**
```
boolean b = dbmd.supportsPositioned Delete();
```

## supportsPositionedUpdate

```
boolean supportsPositionedUpdate() throws SQLException
```

Checks whether this database supports positioned UPDATE statements.

**RETURNS:**
true if so; false otherwise.

**EXAMPLE:**
```
boolean b = dbmd.supportsPositionedUpdate();
```

## supportsSchemasInDataManipulation

```
boolean supportsSchemasInDataManipulation() throws SQLException
```

Checks whether this database supports using a schema name in a data manipulation statement.

**RETURNS:**
true if so; false otherwise.

**EXAMPLE:**
```
boolean b = dbmd.supportsSchemasInDataManipulation();
```

## supportsSchemasInIndexDefinitions

```
boolean supportsSchemasInIndexDefinitions() throws SQLException
```

Checks whether this database supports using a schema name in an index definition statement.

**RETURNS:**
true if so; false otherwise.

**EXAMPLE:**
```
boolean b = dbmd.supportsSchemasInIndexDefinitions();
```

## supportsSchemasInPrivilegeDefinitions

```
boolean supportsSchemasInPrivilegeDefinitions() throws SQLException
```

Checks whether this database supports using a schema name in a privilege definition statement.

**RETURNS:**
true if so; false otherwise.

**EXAMPLE:**
```
boolean b = dbmd.supportsSchemasInPrivilegeDefinitions();
```

## supportsSchemasInProcedureCalls

```
boolean supportsSchemasInProcedureCalls() throws SQLException
```

Checks whether this database supports using a schema name in a procedure call statement.

**RETURNS:**
true if so; false otherwise.

**EXAMPLE:**
```
boolean b = dbmd.supportsSchemasInProcedureCalls();
```

## supportsSchemasInTableDefinitions

```
boolean supportsSchemasInTableDefinitions() throws SQLException
```

Checks whether this database supports using a schema name in a table definition statement.

**RETURNS:**
true if so; false otherwise.

**EXAMPLE:**
```
boolean b = dbmd.supportsSchemasInTableDefinition();
```

## supportsSelectForUpdate

```
boolean supportsSelectForUpdate() throws SQLException
```

Checks whether this database supports SELECT FOR UPDATE statements.

**RETURNS:**
true if so; false otherwise.

**EXAMPLE:**
```
boolean b = dbmd.supportsSelectForUpdate();
```

## supportsStoredProcedures

```
boolean supportsStoredProcedures() throws SQLException
```

Checks whether this database supports stored procedure calls using the stored procedure escape syntax.

**RETURNS:**
true if so; false otherwise.

**EXAMPLE:**
```
boolean b = dbmd.supportsStoredProcedures();
```

## supportsSubqueriesInComparisons

```
boolean supportsSubqueriesInComparisons() throws SQLException
```

Checks whether this database supports subqueries in comparison expressions. A JDBC Compliant driver always returns true.

**RETURNS:**
true if so; false otherwise.

**EXAMPLE:**
```
boolean b = dbmd.supportsSubqueriesInComparisons();
```

## supportsSubqueriesInExists

```
boolean supportsSubqueriesInExists() throws SQLException
```

Checks whether this database supports subqueries in EXISTS expressions.

**RETURNS:**
true if so; false otherwise.

**EXAMPLE:**
```
boolean b = dbmd.supportsSubqueriesInExists();
```

## supportsSubqueriesInIns

```
boolean supportsSubqueriesInIns() throws SQLException
```

Checks whether this database supports subqueries in IN statements. A JDBC Compliant driver always returns true.

**RETURNS:**
true if so; false otherwise.

**EXAMPLE:**
```
boolean b = dbmd.supportsSubqueriesInIns();
```

## supportsSubqueriesInQuantifieds

```
boolean supportsSubqueriesInQuantifieds() throws SQLException
```

Checks whether this database supports subqueries in quantified expressions. A JDBC Compliant driver always returns true.

**RETURNS:**
true if so; false otherwise.

**EXAMPLE:**
```
boolean b = dbmd.supportsSubqueriesInQuantifieds();
```

## supportsTableCorrelationNames

```
boolean supportsTableCorrelationNames() throws SQLException
```

Checks whether this database supports table correlation names. A JDBC Compliant driver always returns true.

**RETURNS:**
true if so; false otherwise.

**EXAMPLE:**
```
boolean b = dbmd.supportsTableCorrelationNames();
```


## supportsTransactionIsolationLevel

```
boolean supportsTransactionIsolationLevel(int level)
                                          throws SQLException
```

Checks whether this database supports the transaction isolation level *level*.

**PARAMETERS:**

*level*              int representing one of the constants defined in java.sql.Connection; possible values are TRANSACTION_NONE, TRANSACTION_READ_UNCOMMITTED, TRANSACTION_READ_COMMITTED, TRANSACTION_REPEAT-ABLE_READ, or TRANSACTION_SERIALIZABLE.

**RETURNS:**
true if this database supports the given transaction isolation level; false otherwise.

**EXAMPLE:**
```
boolean b = dbmd.supportsTransactionIsolationLevel(
                               TRANSACTION_SERIALIZABLE);
```

**SEE:**
"Connection Fields" on page 161.

## supportsTransactions

```
boolean supportsTransactions() throws SQLException
```

Checks whether this database supports transactions. If this method returns false, the method commit does nothing, and the transaction isolation level is TRANSACTION_NONE. Drivers that are JDBC Compliant are required to support transactions.

**RETURNS:**
true if this database supports transactions; false otherwise.

**EXAMPLE:**
```
boolean b = dbmd.supportsTransactions();
```

## supportsUnion

```
boolean supportsUnion() throws SQLException
```

Checks whether this database supports SQL UNION.

**RETURNS:**
true if so; false otherwise.

**EXAMPLE:**
```
boolean b = dbmd.supportsUnion();
```

## supportsUnionAll

```
boolean supportsUnionAll() throws SQLException
```

Checks whether this database supports SQL UNION ALL.

**RETURNS:**
true if so; false otherwise.

**EXAMPLE:**
```
boolean b = dbmd.supportsUnionAll();
```

## usesLocalFilePerTable

```
boolean usesLocalFilePerTable() throws SQLException
```

Checks whether this database uses a separate local file to store each table.

**RETURNS:**
true if the database uses a local file for each table; false otherwise.

**EXAMPLE:**
```
boolean b = dbmd.usesLocalFilePerTable();
```

## usesLocalFiles

```
boolean usesLocalFiles() throws SQLException
```

Checks whether the database stores tables in a local file.

**RETURNS:**
true if so; false otherwise.

**EXAMPLE:**
```
boolean b = dbmd.usesLocalFiles();
```

# 6.4   DatabaseMetaData Fields

## bestRowNotPseudo

```
public final static int bestRowNotPseudo = 1
```
A possible value for column PSEUDO_COLUMN in the ResultSet object returned by the method getBestRowIdentifier.
Indicates that the best row identifier is not a pseudo column.

## bestRowPseudo

```
public final static int bestRowPseudo = 2
```
A possible value for column PSEUDO_COLUMN in the ResultSet object returned by the method getBestRowIdentifier.
Indicates that the best row identifier is a pseudo column.

## bestRowSession

```
public final static int bestRowSession = 2
```
A possible value for column SCOPE in the ResultSet object returned by the method getBestRowIdentifier.

Indicates that the best row identifier is valid for the remainder of the current session.

## bestRowTemporary

```
public final static int bestRowTemporary = 0
```
A possible value for column SCOPE in the ResultSet object returned by the method getBestRowIdentifier.

Indicates that the best row identifier is very temporary, being valid only while using this row.

## bestRowTransaction

```
public final static int bestRowTransaction = 1
```
A possible value for column SCOPE in the ResultSet object returned by the method getBestRowIdentifier.

Indicates that the best row identifier is valid for the remainder of the current transaction.

## bestRowUnknown

```
public final static int bestRowUnknown = 0
```
A possible value for column PSEUDO_COLUMN in the ResultSet object returned by the method getBestRowIdentifier.

Indicates that the best row identifier may or may not be a pseudo column.

## columnNoNulls

```
public final static int columnNoNulls = 0
```
> A possible value for column NULLABLE in the ResultSet object returned by the method getColumns.
>
> Indicates that a column might not allow NULL values.

## columnNullable

```
public final static int columnNullable = 1
```
> A possible value for column NULLABLE in the ResultSet object returned by the method getColumns.
>
> Indicates that a column definitely allows NULL values.

## columnNullableUnknown

```
public final static int columnNullableUnknown = 2
```
> A possible value for column NULLABLE in the ResultSet object returned by the method getColumns.
>
> Indicates that it is not known whether a column allows NULL values.

## importedKeyCascade

```
public final static int importedKeyCascade = 0
```
> A possible value for the columns UPDATE_RULE and DELETE_RULE in the ResultSet objects returned by getImportedKeys, getExportedKeys, and get-CrossReference.
>
> For the column UPDATE_RULE, it indicates that when the primary key is updated, the foreign key (imported key) is changed to agree with it.
>
> For the column DELETE_RULE, it indicates that when the primary key is deleted, rows that imported that key are deleted.

## importedKeyInitiallyDeferred

```
public final static int importedKeyInitiallyDeferred = 5
```

A possible value for the column DEFERRABILITY in the ResultSet objects returned by getImportedKeys, getExportedKeys, and getCrossReference. Indicates deferrability. See SQL–92 for a definition.

## importedKeyInitiallyImmediate

`public final static int importedKeyInitiallyImmediate = 6`

A possible value for the column DEFERRABILITY in the ResultSet objects returned by getImportedKeys, getExportedKeys, and getCrossReference. Indicates deferrability. See SQL–92 for a definition.

## importedKeyNoAction

`public final static int importedKeyNoAction = 3`

A possible value for the columns UPDATE_RULE and DELETE_RULE in the ResultSet objects returned by getImportedKeys, getExportedKeys, and getCrossReference.

For the columns UPDATE_RULE and DELETE_RULE, it indicates that if the primary key has been imported, then it cannot be updated or deleted.

## importedKeyNotDeferrable

`public final static int importedKeyNotDeferrable = 7`

A possible value for the column DEFERRABILITY in the ResultSet objects returned by getImportedKeys, getExportedKeys, and getCrossReference. Indicates deferrability. See SQL–92 for a definition.

## importedKeyRestrict

`public final static int importedKeyRestrict = 1`

A possible value for the columns UPDATE_RULE and DELETE_RULE in the ResultSet objects returned by getImportedKeys, getExportedKeys, and getCrossReference.

For the column UPDATE_RULE, it indicates that a primary key may not be updated if it has been imported by another table as a foreign key.

For the column DELETE_RULE, it indicates that a primary key may not be deleted if it has been imported by another table as a foreign key.

## importedKeySetDefault

`public final static int` **`importedKeySetDefault`** `= 4`

A possible value for the columns UPDATE_RULE and DELETE_RULE in the ResultSet objects returned by getImportedKeys, getExportedKeys, and get-CrossReference.

For the columns UPDATE_RULE and DELETE_RULE, it indicates that if the primary key has been updated or deleted, then the foreign key (imported key) should be set to the default value.

## importedKeySetNull

`public final static int` **`importedKeySetNull`** `= 2`

A possible value for the columns UPDATE_RULE and DELETE_RULE in the ResultSet objects returned by getImportedKeys, getExportedKeys, and get-CrossReference.

For the columns UPDATE_RULE and DELETE_RULE, it indicates that if the primary key has been updated or deleted, then the foreign key (imported key) is changed to NULL.

## procedureColumnIn

`public final static int` **`procedureColumnIn`** `= 1`

A possible value for column COLUMN_TYPE in the ResultSet object returned by the method getProcedureColumns.

Indicates that this row of the ResultSet object describes an IN parameter.

## procedureColumnInOut

`public final static int` **`procedureColumnInOut`** `= 2`

A possible value for column COLUMN_TYPE in the ResultSet object returned by the method getProcedureColumns.

Indicates that this row of the ResultSet object describes an INOUT parameter.

## procedureColumnOut

public final static int **procedureColumnOut** = 4

A possible value for column COLUMN_TYPE in the ResultSet object returned by the method getProcedureColumns.

Indicates that this row of the ResultSet object describes an OUT parameter.

## procedureColumnResult

public final static int **procedureColumnResult** = 3

A possible value for column COLUMN_TYPE in the ResultSet object returned by the method getProcedureColumns.

Indicates that this row describes a result column in a ResultSet object produced by a stored procedure.

## procedureColumnReturn

public final static int **procedureColumnReturn** = 5

A possible value for column COLUMN_TYPE in the ResultSet object returned by the method getProcedureColumns.

Indicates that this row describes a procedure's return value.

## procedureColumnUnknown

public final static int **procedureColumnUnknown** = 0

A possible value for column COLUMN_TYPE in the ResultSet object returned by the method getProcedureColumns.

Indicates that the type of the column described in this row is unknown.

## procedureNoNulls

public final static int **procedureNoNulls** = 0

A possible value for column NULLABLE in the ResultSet object returned by the method getProcedureColumns.

Indicates that the procedure does not allow NULL values.

## procedureNoResult

```
public final static int procedureNoResult = 1
```
> A possible value for column PROCEDURE_TYPE in the ResultSet object returned by the method getProcedures.
> Indicates that the procedure does not return a result.

## procedureNullable

```
public final static int procedureNullable = 1
```
> A possible value for column NULLABLE in the ResultSet object returned by the method getProcedureColumns.
> Indicates that the procedure allows NULL values.

## procedureNullableUnknown

```
public final static int procedureNullableUnknown = 2
```
> A possible value for column NULLABLE in the ResultSet object returned by the method getProcedureColumns.
> Indicates that whether or not the procedure allows NULL values is unknown.

## procedureResultUnknown

```
public final static int procedureResultUnknown = 0
```
> A possible value for column PROCEDURE_TYPE in the ResultSet object returned by the method getProcedures.
> Indicates that it is not known whether the procedure returns a result.

## procedureReturnsResult

```
public final static int procedureReturnsResult = 2
```
> A possible value for column PROCEDURE_TYPE in the ResultSet object returned by the method getProcedures.
> Indicates that the procedure returns a result.

## tableIndexClustered

```
public final static short tableIndexClustered = 1
```
>    A possible value for column TYPE in the ResultSet object returned by the method getIndexInfo.
>    Indicates that this table index is a clustered index.

## tableIndexHashed

```
public final static short tableIndexHashed = 2
```
>    A possible value for column TYPE in the ResultSet object returned by the method getIndexInfo.
>    Indicates that this table index is a hashed index.

## tableIndexOther

```
public final static short tableIndexOther = 3
```
>    A possible value for column TYPE in the ResultSet object returned by the method getIndexInfo.
>    Indicates that this is not a clustered index, a hashed index, or table statistics that are returned in conjunction with a table's index descriptions; it is something other than these.

## tableIndexStatistic

```
public final static short tableIndexStatistic = 0
```
>    A possible value for column TYPE in the ResultSet object returned by the method getIndexInfo.
>    Indicates that this column contains table statistics that are returned in conjunction with a table's index descriptions.

## typeNoNulls

```
public final static int columnNoNulls = 0
```
> A possible value for column NULLABLE in the ResultSet object returned by the method getTypeInfo.
>
> Indicates that NULL values are not allowed for this datatype.

## typeNullable

```
public final static int columnNullable = 1
```
> A possible value for column NULLABLE in the ResultSet object returned by the method getTypeInfo.
>
> Indicates that a NULL value is allowed for this datatype.

## typeNullableUnknown

```
public final static int columnNullableUnknown = 2
```
> A possible value for column NULLABLE in the ResultSet object returned by the method getTypeInfo.
>
> Indicates that it is not known whether NULL values are allowed for this datatype.

## typePredBasic

```
public final static int typePredBasic = 2
```
> A possible value for column SEARCHABLE in the ResultSet object returned by the method getTypeInfo.
>
> Indicates that one can base all WHERE search clauses except WHERE . . . LIKE on this type.

## typePredChar

```
public final static int typePredChar = 1
```
> A possible value for column SEARCHABLE in the ResultSet object returned by the method getTypeInfo.

Indicates that the only WHERE search clause that can be based on this type is WHERE . . . LIKE.

## typePredNone

`public final static int typePredNone = 0`

A possible value for column SEARCHABLE in the ResultSet object returned by the method getTypeInfo.

Indicates that WHERE search clauses are not supported for this type.

## typeSearchable

`public final static int typeSearchable = 3`

A possible value for column SEARCHABLE in the ResultSet object returned by the method getTypeInfo.

Indicates that all WHERE search clauses can be based on this type.

## versionColumnNotPseudo

`public final static int versionColumnNotPseudo = 1`

A possible value for column PSEUDO_COLUMN in the ResultSet object returned by the method getVersionColumns.

Indicates that this column, which is automatically updated when any value in a row is updated, is *not* a pseudo column.

## versionColumnPseudo

`public final static int versionColumnPseudo = 2`

A possible value for column PSEUDO_COLUMN in the ResultSet object returned by the method getVersionColumns.

Indicates that this column, which is automatically updated when any value in a row is updated, is a pseudo column.

## versionColumnUnknown

`public final static int versionColumnUnknown = 0`

A possible value for column PSEUDO_COLUMN in the ResultSet object returned by the method getVersionColumns.

Indicates that this column, which is automatically updated when any value in a row is updated, may or may not be a pseudo column.

# CHAPTER 7

# DataTruncation

## 7.1  DataTruncation Overview

THE class DataTruncation, a subclass of SQLWarning, provides information when JDBC unexpectedly truncates a data value. Under some circumstances, only part of a data field will be read from or written to a database. How this is handled will depend on the circumstances. In general, when data is unexpectedly truncated while being read from a database, an SQLWarning is reported, whereas unexpected data truncation during a write operation to a database will generally cause an SQLException to be thrown.

### 7.1.1  Data Truncation with No Warning or Exception

If an application imposes a limit on the size of a field (using the Connection method setMaxFieldSize) and attempts to read or write a field larger than the limit, the data will be silently truncated to that size limit. In this case, even though the data is truncated, no SQLException will be thrown, and no SQLWarning will be reported.

For maximum portability, an application should set the maximum field size to at least 256 bytes.

### 7.1.2  Data Truncation on Reads

The application programmer does not need to be concerned about data truncation exceptions when reading data from a database. The JDBC API does not require the programmer to pass in fixed-size buffers; instead, Java allocates appropriate data space as needed. This means that JDBC puts no limits on the size of data that can be read and accommodates varying field sizes.

### 7.1.3   Data Truncation on Writes

It is possible that an application may attempt to send more data to a database than the driver or the database is prepared to accept. In this case, the failing method should throw a DataTruncation object as an SQLException. It should be noted that even when a data truncation exception has been thrown, the data has still been sent to the database, and depending on the driver, the truncated data may have been written.

### 7.1.4   What a DataTruncation Object Contains

Each DataTruncation object contains the following kinds of information:

- the string "Data truncation" to describe the warning or exception.

- an "SQLState" string set to "01004".

- a boolean to indicate whether a column or parameter was truncated.

- an int giving the index of the column or parameter that was truncated.

- a boolean to indicate whether the truncation occurred on a read or a write operation.

- an int indicating the number of bytes that should have been transferred.

- an int indicating the number of bytes that were actually transferred.

- a chain to the next SQLWarning or SQLException object, which can be used if there is more than one warning or exception.

### 7.1.5   Retrieving DataTruncation Information

The method getWarnings will retrieve the first SQLWarning. The interfaces Connection, Statement (including PreparedStatement and CallableStatement), and ResultSet all have their own versions of the method getWarnings to retrieve the first SQLWarning or DataTruncation object reported. Any subsequent warnings are retrieved by calling the SQLWarning method getNextWarning.

The first DataTruncation object thrown as an SQLException object can be caught in a catch block. Second and subsequent exceptions are retrieved by calling the SQLException method getNextException.

Once a DataTruncation object has been accessed, the information stored in it is retrieved by calling the following methods: getMessage, getSQLState, getIndex, getParameter, getRead, getDataSize, and getTransferSize.

The `DataTruncation` class defines one constructor for creating instances of `DataTruncation`. The inherited methods `getMessage` and `getSQLState` return the default values with which every `DataTruncation` object is initialized: `getMessage` returns "Data truncation", and `getSQLState` returns "01004". The five methods for getting components specific to this class return the values supplied to the constructor.

## 7.2    **DataTruncation** Class Definition

```
package java.sql;
public class DataTruncation extends SQLWarning {
    public DataTruncation(int index, boolean parameter,
            boolean read, int dataSize, int transferSize);
    public int getIndex();
    public boolean getParameter();
    public boolean getRead();
    public int getDataSize();
    public int getTransferSize();
}
```

## 7.3    **DataTruncation** Constructor

The following constructor is defined in `java.sql.DataTruncation`:

### DataTruncation

```
public DataTruncation(int index, boolean parameter,
                boolean read, int dataSize, int transferSize);
```

Constructs a fully specified `DataTruncation` object.

**PARAMETERS:**

| | |
|---|---|
| *index* | an int indicating the index of the parameter or column in which data was truncated. |
| *parameter* | true to indicate that the value truncated is a parameter value; false to indicate that the value truncated is a column value. |

| | |
|---|---|
| *read* | true to indicate that data was truncated while being read from the database; false to indicate that data was truncated while being written to the database. |
| *dataSize* | an int indicating the number of bytes that should have been read or written. |
| *transferSize* | an int indicating the number of bytes that were actually read or written. |

**RETURNS:**

a DataTruncation object initialized with "Data truncation", "01004", *index*, *parameter*, *read*, *dataSize,* and *transferSize.*

**EXAMPLE:**

```
DataTruncation dt = new DataTruncation(3, false, false, 1000, 255);
// dt contains a DataTruncation object with the message "Data trunca-
// tion", the SQLState of "01004", and the information that only 255
// bytes out of 1000 were written to column 3
```

## 7.4    DataTruncation Methods

The following methods are inherited from the class java.lang.Exception, which inherited them from the class java.lang.Throwable:

```
fillInStackTrace
getMessage
printStackTrace
toString
```

The following methods are inherited from the class java.sql.SQLException:

```
getSQLState
getErrorCode
getNextException
setNextException
```

The following methods are inherited from the class java.sql.SQLWarning:

```
getNextWarning
setNextWarning
```

The following methods are defined in the class java.sql.DataTruncation:

## getDataSize

public int **getDataSize**();

Gets the number of bytes of data that should have been transferred. This number may be approximate if data conversions were performed. The value will be -1 if the size is unknown.

**RETURNS:**
an int indicating the number of bytes of data that should have been transferred or -1 if the size is unknown.

**EXAMPLE:**
```
int numberOfBytes = myDataTruncation.getDataSize();
```

## getIndex

public int **getIndex**()

Gets the index of the column or parameter that was truncated. This may be -1 if the column or parameter index is unknown, in which case the parameter and read fields should be ignored.

**RETURNS:**
an int representing the DataTruncation object's index value or -1 if the index of the column or parameter is unknown.

**EXAMPLE:**
```
int ix = myDataTruncation.getIndex();
```

## getParameter

public boolean **getParameter**()

Indicates whether data truncation occurred in a parameter or a result set column. The parameter field should be ignored if the method getIndex returns -1.

**RETURNS:**
true if data truncation occurred in a parameter or false if it occurred in a result set column.

**EXAMPLE:**
```
boolean b = myDataTruncation.getParameter();
```

**SEE:**
```
DataTruncation.getIndex
```

## getRead

```
public boolean getRead()
```

Indicates whether the data truncation occurred during a read or a write operation. The read field should be ignored if the method getIndex returns -1.

**RETURNS:**
true if data truncation occurred during a read from the database or false if it occurred during a write to the database.

**EXAMPLE:**
```
boolean b = myDataTruncation.getRead();
```

**SEE:**
```
DataTruncation.getIndex
```

## getTransferSize

```
public int getTransferSize()
```

Gets the number of bytes of data actually transferred. This number may be -1 if the size is unknown.

**RETURNS:**
an int indicating the number of bytes that were actually transferred or -1 if the size is unknown.

**EXAMPLE:**
```
int numberOfBytes = myDataTruncation.getTransferSize();
```

# CHAPTER 8

# Date

## 8.1 Date Overview

THE class `java.sql.Date` provides a convenient way to represent an SQL DATE value. The class `java.util.Date` is not used because it contains both date and time information, and the type SQL DATE contains only date information (year, month, and day). The class `java.sql.Date` is implemented as a thin wrapper around `java.util.Date` and uses only the date part. The class `java.sql.Time` works in a similar fashion, using only the time part of `java.util.Date`.

It should be noted that early versions of the JDK worked for dates from January 1, 1970 on. JDK version 1.1 works with dates preceding 1970 as well.

The JDBC Date class adds methods for formatting and parsing so that the JDBC escape syntax for date values can be used. See "SQL Escape Syntax in `Statement` Objects" starting on page 345 for information about escape syntax for dates.

### 8.1.1  Creating a Date Object

There are two ways to create a `Date` object. The first way is to use one of the constructors, and the second is to create one from a string using the method `valueOf`.

1. using a constructor to create a `Date` object :

```
Date d = new Date(99, 4, 31);
```

The variable d now contains a `Date` object that represents the date May 31, 1999.

Note that the first argument supplied to the constructor, which specifies the year, is the result of subtracting 1900 from it. Also, the month is specified using 0 for January, 1 for February, and so on through 11 for December.

2. using the method `valueOf` to convert a string to a `Date` object:

```
Date d = Date.valueOf("1999-05-31");
```

The variable d contains a `Date` object representing May 31, 1999.

Technically, a `java.sql.Date` object includes the time component inherited from `java.util.Date`, but the time is set to 00:00:00 and is not accessible. Trying to set or get a time component will generate an exception.

## 8.2    Date Class Definition

```
package java.sql;
public class Date extends java.util.Date {
    public Date(int year, int month, int day);
    public Date(long date);
    public static Date valueOf(String s);
    public String toString();
}
```

## 8.3    Date Constructors

### Date

---

```
public Date(int year, int month, int day)
```

Constructs a `java.sql.Date` object initialized with *year*, *month*, and *day* to represent a date value that can be used as an SQL DATE value.

**PARAMETERS:**

| | |
|---|---|
| *year* | a Java `int` representing the year minus 1900. |
| *month* | a Java `int` from 0 to 11 (0 is January; 11 is December). |
| *day* | a Java `int` from 1 to 31. |

**RETURNS:**
a `java.sql.Date` object representing a date.

**EXAMPLE:**
```
Date d = new Date(100, 0, 1); // d represents January 1, 2000
```

## Date

`public Date(long date)`

Constructs a `java.sql.Date` object from *date,* a milliseconds time value*,* to represent a date value that can be used as an SQL DATE value.

Since `java.sql.Date` is a subclass of `java.util.Date`, it inherits a time component, but any time component of *date* is ignored and replaced with 00:00:00. Only the date components (day, month, and year) are accessible. If any of the following methods is called on a `java.sql.Date` object, it will throw a `java.lang.IllegalArgumentException`: getHours, getMinutes, get-Seconds, setHours, setMinutes, setSeconds.

**PARAMETERS:**

| | |
|---|---|
| *date* | a Java `long` representing the number of milliseconds since January 1, 1970, 00:00:00 GMT. A negative value represents the number of milliseconds before January 1, 1970, 00:00:00 GMT. |

**RETURNS:**
a `java.sql.Date` object representing a date.

**EXAMPLE:**
```
Date d = new Date(864000000); // d represents January 10, 1970
```

## 8.4   Date Methods

## toString

`public String toString()`

Formats the calling `Date` object as a `String` object in the JDBC date escape format yyyy-mm-dd.

**RETURNS:**

A `String` object with the format "yyyy-mm-dd".

**EXAMPLE:**
```
Date d = new Date(100, 0, 1);
String s = d.toString(); // s contains "2000-01-01"
```

## valueOf

```
public static Date valueOf(String s)
```

Converts *s*, a string in JDBC date escape format, to a `Date` value.

**PARAMETERS:**

*s*                         a `String` object in the format "yyyy-mm-dd", which is
                            referred to as the *date escape format.*

**RETURNS:**

a `Date` object representing the year, month, and day specified in the `String` object *s.*

**EXAMPLE:**
```
String s = new String("2000-01-01");
java.sql.Date d = java.sql.Date.valueOf(s);
// d contains a Date object representing January 1, 2000
```

CHAPTER 9

# Driver

## 9.1 Driver Overview

IN most cases, only developers writing drivers will need to understand the `java.sql.Driver` interface. It provides six methods. One method sets up a connection between a driver and a database, and the others give information about the driver or get information necessary for making a connection to a database.

Driver methods most often work behind the scenes, being called by the generic `java.sql.DriverManager` class. For example, the usual way for a user to establish a connection with a database is to call the `DriverManager.getConnection` method. The driver manager calls the `Driver` method `connect` on each registered driver in turn, and the first driver that can make the connection is the one to do it. See "DriverManager" on page 263 for a more detailed explanation. It is possible, however, for users to bypass the driver manager and call the `connect` method directly if they want to specify that a particular driver be used. Similarly, although it is possible for anyone to call `getPropertyInfo`, most users will probably never call it. Its intended purpose is to allow a GUI tool to find out for what information it should prompt the human user in order to be able to make a connection.

### 9.1.1 Loading and Registering a Driver

A driver should be implemented with a static section that automatically does two things when it is loaded: (1) creates an instance of itself and (2) registers that instance by calling the method `DriverManager.registerDriver`. See the section "Implement a Special Static Section" on page 402 for an example. When a driver includes this static section, the user can simply invoke the method `Class.forName`, supplying the classname of the driver as a string, to load and register that driver. For example, the following code loads and registers the `Driver` class `foo.bah.Driver`:

```
Class.forName("foo.bah.Driver");
```

### 9.1.2   JDBC Implementation Alternatives

The Java SQL framework allows for multiple database drivers, and there are various choices for JDBC driver implementations. One alternative is an implementation of JDBC on top of ODBC, called a JDBC–ODBC bridge. JavaSoft provides such a bridge as part of the JDK. Since JDBC is patterned after ODBC, this implementation is small and efficient.

Another useful driver, called a net driver, is one that goes directly to a DBMS-independent network protocol supported by a database middleware server. A JDBC net driver is a very small and fast all Java client-side implementation, and it speaks to many databases via the middleware server. Several vendors have already implemented JDBC net drivers.

A third alternative is a driver that is even smaller and more efficient because it works directly with a particular DBMS. This implementation, known as a two-tier

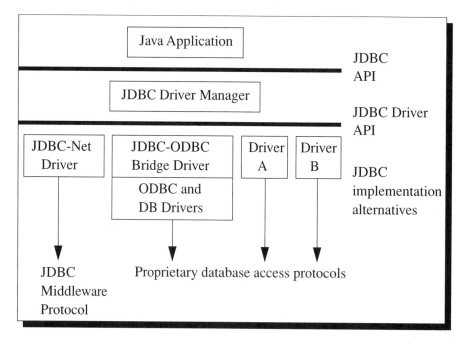

**Figure 9.1:** JDBC Driver Implementations

driver, has nothing intervening between the driver and the underlying data source. In contrast, the JDBC–ODBC bridge and JDBC net drivers require various intermediate components.

There are two variations of two-tier drivers: those that are all-Java and those that are not. A two-tier driver that is all-Java is the ideal JDBC driver, since it is platform-independent and can be automatically installed.

Figure 9.1 (opposite page) illustrates driver implementation alternatives. The `java.sql.Driver` interface works between the `DriverManager` class and the various drivers implemented in JDBC.

## 9.2   Driver Interface Definition

```
package java.sql;
public interface Driver {
    Connection connect(String url, java.util.Properties info)
                                            throws SQLException;
    boolean acceptsURL(String url) throws SQLException;
    DriverPropertyInfo[] getPropertyInfo(String url,
                    java.util.Properties info) throws SQLException;
    int getMajorVersion();
    int getMinorVersion();
    boolean jdbcCompliant();
}
```

## 9.3   Driver Methods

### acceptsURL

```
boolean acceptsURL(String url) throws SQLException
```

Tests to see if this driver understands the subprotocol specified in *url*.

Typically, drivers will return `true` if they understand the URL and `false` if they do not.

**PARAMETERS:**

*url*                         The URL of the database to which to connect.

**RETURNS:**
true if this driver can connect to *url* and `false` if it cannot.

**EXAMPLE:**
`boolean b = myDriver.acceptsURL(url);`

## connect

---

`Connection connect(String url, java.util.Properties info)`
                                    `throws SQLException`

Tries to make a database connection to *url*. The driver will return `null` if it is the wrong kind of driver to connect to *url*. This might not be uncommon because when the JDBC driver manager is asked to connect to a given URL, it passes the URL to each loaded driver in turn. The first driver may be the correct one to make the connection, but often it will not be. In that case, the driver returns `null` and the driver manager passes the URL to the next driver, and so on.

**PARAMETERS:**

| | |
|---|---|
| *url* | The URL of the database to which to connect. |
| *info* | A list of arbitrary string tag/value pairs as connection arguments; normally at least a "user" and "password" property should be included in `Properties`. |

**RETURNS:**
a `Connection` object that represents a connection to the database located at *url* or `null` if the driver realizes it is the wrong kind of driver to connect to *url*. The driver will raise an `SQLException` if it is the right driver to connect to the given URL but has trouble connecting to the database.

**EXAMPLE:**
`Connection con = myDriver.connect(url, info);`

## getMajorVersion

---

`int getMajorVersion()`

Returns the driver's major version number, which should initially be 1.

**RETURNS:**
the driver's major version number.

**EXAMPLE:**
```
int x = d.getMajorVersion(); // x = 1 to begin with
```

**SEE ALSO:**
```
getMinorVersion
```

## getMinorVersion

```
int getMinorVersion()
```

Returns the driver's minor version number, which should initially be 0.

**RETURNS:**
the driver's minor version number.

**EXAMPLE:**
```
int x = d.getMajorVersion();
int y = d.getMinorVersion();
System.out.println("This driver version is " + x + "." + y);
➡ This driver version is 1.0   // initial version
```

## getPropertyInfo

```
DriverPropertyInfo[] getPropertyInfo(String url,
                    java.util.Properties info) throws SQLException
```

The getPropertyInfo method is intended to allow a generic GUI tool to discover for what properties it should prompt a human user in order to get enough information to connect to a database.

The second argument should be null the first (and generally only) time this method is called. The second argument is included so that it is possible for an application to process input and present the human user with a list of properties from which to choose. Depending on the values the human has supplied so far, it is conceivable that additional values may be needed. In such cases, and assuming that the application has been written to handle the results of multiple calls to getPropertyInfo, it may be necessary to iterate through several calls to getPropertyInfo. If the application uses the information it gets to fill in values for a `java.util.Properties` object, then that object can be supplied to `getPropertyInfo` in subsequent calls to the method.

**PARAMETERS:**

*url*              The URL of the database to which to connect.

*info*             `null`; on second and later invocations, a `java.sql.DriverPropertyInfo` object that contains a proposed list of tag/value pairs that will be sent when the method `Driver.connect` is called.

**RETURNS:**

an array of `java.sql.DriverPropertyInfo` objects describing possible properties. This may be an empty array if no properties are required.

**EXAMPLE:**
```
String url = "jdbc:miracle:winners";
DriverPropertyInfo [] propArray = myDriver.getPropertyInfo(
                                                  url, null);
```

**SEE :**
`DriverPropertyInfo`

## jdbcCompliant

```
boolean jdbcCompliant()
```

Tests whether a driver can be designated JDBC Compliant. A driver may report `true` only if it passes the JDBC compliance tests; otherwise, it is required to return `false`. JDBC compliance requires full support for the JDBC API and full support for SQL–92 Entry Level. It is expected that JDBC Compliant drivers will be available for all the major commercial databases.

This method is not intended to encourage the development of JDBC drivers that are not compliant; rather, it is a recognition of the fact that some vendors are interested in using the JDBC API and framework for lightweight databases that do not support full database functionality or for special databases, such as document information retrieval, where a SQL implementation may not be feasible.

**RETURNS:**

true if the driver is a genuine JDBC Compliant driver or `false` if it is not.

**EXAMPLE:**
```
boolean b = myDriver.jdbcCompliant();
```

# CHAPTER 10

# DriverManager

## 10.1 DriverManager Overview

THE DriverManager class is the management layer of JDBC, working between the user and the drivers. It keeps track of the drivers that are available and handles establishing a connection between a database and the appropriate driver. In addition, the DriverManager class attends to things like driver login time limits and the printing of log and tracing messages.

For simple applications, the only method in this class that a general programmer needs to use directly is DriverManager.getConnection. As its name implies, this method establishes a connection to a database. JDBC allows the user to call the DriverManager methods getDriver, getDrivers, and registerDriver as well as the Driver method connect, but in most cases it is better to let the DriverManager class manage the details of establishing a connection.

### 10.1.1 Keeping Track of Available Drivers

The DriverManager class maintains a list of Driver classes that have registered themselves by calling the method DriverManager.registerDriver. All Driver classes should be written with a static section that creates an instance of the class and then registers it with the DriverManager class when it is loaded. Thus, a user would not normally call DriverManager.registerDriver directly; it should be called automatically by a driver when it is loaded. A Driver class is loaded, and therefore automatically registered with the DriverManager, in one of two ways:

1. by calling the method Class.forName. This explicitly loads the driver class. Since it does not depend on any external setup, this way of loading a driver is

the recommended one. The following code loads the class `acme.db.Driver`:

```
Class.forName("acme.db.Driver");
```

If `acme.db.Driver` has been written so that loading it causes an instance to be created and also calls `DriverManager.registerDriver` with that instance as the parameter (as it should do), then it is in the `DriverManager`'s list of drivers and available for creating a connection.

2. by adding the driver to the `java.lang.System` property `jdbc.drivers`. This is a list of driver classnames, separated by colons, that the `DriverManager` class loads. When the `DriverManager` class is initialized, it looks for the system property "`jdbc.drivers`," and if the user has entered one or more drivers, the `DriverManager` class attempts to load them. The following code illustrates how a programmer might enter three driver classes in ~/.hotjava/properties (HotJava loads these into the system properties list on startup):

```
jdbc.drivers=foo.bah.Driver:wombat.sql.Driver:bad.test.ourDriver
```

The first call to a `DriverManager` method will automatically cause these driver classes to be loaded.

Note that this second way of loading drivers requires a preset environment that is persistent. If there is any doubt about that being the case, it is safer to call the method `Class.forName` to explicitly load each driver. This is also the right method to use to bring in a particular driver since once the `DriverManager` class has been initialized, it will never recheck the `jdbc.drivers` property list.

In both of these cases, it is the responsibility of the newly loaded `Driver` class to register itself by calling `DriverManager.registerDriver`. As mentioned, this should be done automatically when the class is loaded.

For security reasons, the JDBC management layer will keep track of which class loader provided which driver. Then when the `DriverManager` class is opening a connection, it will use only drivers that come from the local file system or from the same class loader as the code issuing the request for a connection.

### 10.1.2  Establishing a Connection

Once the `Driver` classes have been loaded and registered with the `DriverManager` class, they are available for establishing a connection with a database. When a request for a connection is made with a call to the `DriverManager.getConnection` method, the `DriverManager` tests each driver in turn to see if it can establish a connection.

It may sometimes be the case that more than one JDBC driver is capable of connecting to a given URL. For example, when connecting to a given remote database, it might be possible to use a JDBC–ODBC bridge driver, a JDBC-to-generic-network-protocol driver, or a driver supplied by the database vendor. In such cases, the order in which the drivers are tested is significant because the DriverManager will use the first driver it finds that can successfully connect to the given URL.

First the `DriverManager` tries to use each of the drivers in the order it was registered. (The drivers listed in `jdbc.drivers` are always registered first.) It will skip any drivers that are untrusted code, unless they have been loaded from the same source as the code that is trying to open the connection.

It tests the drivers by calling the method `Driver.connect` on each one in turn, passing them the URL that the user originally passed to the method `DriverManager.getConnection`. The first driver that recognizes the URL makes the connection.

At first glance this may seem inefficient, but it requires only a few procedure calls and string comparisons per connection since it is unlikely that dozens of drivers will be loaded concurrently.

The following code is an example of all that is normally needed to set up a connection with a driver such as a JDBC–ODBC bridge driver:

```
Class.forName("jdbc.odbc.JdbcOdbcDriver"); //loads the driver
String url = "jdbc:odbc:fred";
Connection con = DriverManager.getConnection(
                                        url, "userID", "passwd");
```

The variable *con* represents a connection to the data source "fred" and can be used to create and execute SQL statements.

### 10.1.3 **DriverManager** Methods Are Static

All `DriverManager` methods are declared `static`, which means that they operate on the class as a whole and not on particular instances. In fact, the constructor for `DriverManager` is declared `private` to prevent users from instantiating it. Logically, there is one instance of the `DriverManager` class. This means that methods are called by qualifying them with DriverManager, as in the following code fragment:

```
DriverManager.setLogStream(System.out);
```

## 10.2  DriverManager Class Definition

```
package java.sql;
public class DriverManager {
    private static DriverManager();
    public static Connection getConnection(String url,
                java.util.Properties info) throws SQLException;
    public static Connection getConnection(String url,
                String user, String password) throws SQLException;
    public static Connection getConnection(String url)
                                              throws SQLException;
    public static Driver getDriver(String url) throws SQLException;
    public static void registerDriver(java.sql.Driver
                                    driver) throws SQLException;
    public static void deregisterDriver(Driver driver) throws
                                                SQLException;
    public static java.util.Enumeration getDrivers();
    public static void setLoginTimeout(int seconds);
    public static int getLoginTimeout();
    public static void setLogStream(java.io.PrintStream out);
    public static java.io.PrintStream getLogStream();
    public static void println(String message);
}
```

## 10.3  DriverManager Methods

### deregisterDriver

public static void **deregisterDriver**(Driver *driver*) throws SQLException

Removes the first entry for *driver* (if one exists) from the DriverManager's list of registered drivers. If there are duplicate entries, only the first one is removed. If there is no entry for *driver*, deregisterDriver does nothing. (Its definition specifies that it throws an SQLException, but this is only included for future use if needed.) For security reasons, applets can deregister drivers only from their own classloaders.

Normally users do not call either registerDriver or deregisterDriver; the easiest way to keep track of which drivers have been registered is by simply leaving registration up to the drivers and never deregistering them.

**PARAMETERS:**

*driver*                     the JDBC driver to drop.

**EXAMPLE:**

```
DriverManager.deregisterDriver(d);
```

## getConnection

There are three forms of the method getConnection. All three take a URL as a parameter; one takes a java.util.Properties object in addition, and one takes a password and user in addition. A URL may contain a user, password, and attributes, in which case all the information is contained in the URL, making the other parameters unnecessary. In order to allow applets to access databases in a generic way, we recommend that as much connection information as possible be encoded as part of the JDBC URL and that driver writers minimize their use of java.util.Properties. As a general rule, the more information contained in the URL the better, especially for Internet connections.

Since the only difference in the three forms is the parameter list, they are grouped together to avoid unnecessary repetition.

```
public static Connection getConnection(String url)
                                                    throws SQLException;
public static Connection getConnection(String url,
                    java.util.Properties info) throws SQLException;
public static Connection getConnection(String url,
                String user, String password) throws SQLException;
```

The method getConnection attempts to establish a connection to the database identified in *url*. The DriverManager attempts to select an appropriate driver from the set of registered JDBC drivers by calling the Driver method connect on each driver in turn, passing it *url* as the parameter to the method connect. The connection is made with the first driver to recognize *url*.

**PARAMETERS:**

| | |
|---|---|
| *url* | a JDBC URL of the form `jdbc:subprotocol:subname`. |
| *info* | an instance of the class `java.util.Properties` that contains a list of strings that are key/value pairs. If this parameter is used, it will normally include at least a user and password. |
| *user* | the database user on whose behalf the connection is being made. |
| *password* | the user's password. |

**RETURNS:**

a `Connection` object that represents a connection to the database specified in *url*.

**EXAMPLE 1:**
```
String url = "jdbc:myDriverProtocol:http://xyzcorp.com." +
            "myLogin.myPassword:123/personnel/employees";
DriverManager.getConnection(url);
```

**EXAMPLE 2:**
```
// normally only an application that prompts the user for input
// in order to get enough information to make a connection would use
// this version of getConnection, and it would set up the properties
// in info
String url = "jdbc:odbc:myDataSourceName";
DriverManager.getConnection(url, info);
```

**SEE:**

`DriverPropertyInfo` and `Driver.getPropertyInfo`

**EXAMPLE 3:**
```
String url = "jdbc:myDriverProtocol://acme.com/personnel/" +
            "employees";
DriverManager.getConnection(url, "myLogin", "myPassword");
```

# getDriver

```
public static Driver getDriver(String url) throws SQLException
```

Attempts to locate a driver that understands *url*. A user might want to call getDriver directly in the rare case where the `Driver` object rather than a connection is desired.

**PARAMETERS:**

*url*

a JDBC URL of the form `jdbc:subprotocol:subname`. If the method `DriverManager.getConnection` was called, this should be the same URL that was passed to it.

**RETURNS:**

a driver that understands *url* and can connect to the subprotocol it specifies.

**EXAMPLE:**

```
String url = "jdbc:odbc:superdb";
Driver d = DriverManager.getDriver(url);
```

## getDrivers

```
public static java.util.Enumeration getDrivers()
```

A user may call the method `getDrivers` to get a list of registered drivers. However, most users would never call this method.

**RETURNS:**

an `Enumeration` object containing a list of the JDBC drivers that have been loaded by the caller's class loader. These are the drivers that are available to the caller for making a connection to a database.

**EXAMPLE:**

```
Enumeration e = DriverManager.getDrivers();
```

## getLoginTimeout

```
public static int getLoginTimeout()
```

Indicates how many seconds a driver will wait to log in to a database before it times out.

**RETURNS:**

the maximum time in seconds that a driver can wait when attempting to log in to a database.

**EXAMPLE:**

```
int x = DriverManager.getLoginTimeout();
```

## getLogStream

```
public static java.io.PrintStream getLogStream()
```

Indicates where log and tracing messages will be printed.

**RETURNS:**
the PrintStream object that will be used by the DriverManager and all drivers for printing their logging and tracing messages.

**EXAMPLE:**
```
java.io.PrintStream outStream = DriverManager.getLogStream();
```

## println

```
public static void println(String message)
```

Prints message to the current JDBC log stream.

**PARAMETERS:**
message                  a log or tracing message.

**EXAMPLE:**
```
DriverManager.println("Loading driver d");
```

## registerDriver

```
public static void registerDriver(java.sql.Driver driver)
                                    throws SQLException
```

Adds driver to the list of drivers that DriverManager maintains. Driver-Manager will test each driver in the list to find the first one that recognizes the JDBC URL passed to the method DriverManager.getConnection.

Normally, a user will not call this method directly; it will be called by a driver when it is being loaded. The definition of a JDBC Driver class should include a static section such that when the Driver class is loaded, it creates an instance of itself and then calls the method registerDriver with that instance as the parameter driver.

Registering a driver adds an entry to the end of the list maintained by the `DriverManager` class, and this list is scanned from beginning to end. Note that duplicate registrations result in duplicate entries. A programmer who explicitly creates a new driver instance and registers it will create an unnecessary duplicate that will appear in the `DriverManager`'s list of drivers twice.

**PARAMETERS:**

*driver*                a JDBC `Driver` class that has been loaded.

**EXAMPLE:**
```
// The user calls Class.forName() to load the Driver class MyDriver.
Class.forName("MyDriver");
// Driver creates instance and registers it behind the scenes
Driver d = new Driver("myDriver");
DriverManager.registerDriver(d);
```

## setLoginTimeout

```
public static void setLoginTimeout(int seconds)
```

Sets to *seconds* the maximum time that a driver can wait to log in to a database before timing out.

**PARAMETERS:**

*seconds*               the maximum time in seconds that a driver can wait
                        when it is attempting to log in to a database.

**EXAMPLE:**
```
DriverManager.setLoginTimeout(10);
// a driver will timeout after waiting 10 seconds to log in
```

## setLogStream

```
public static void setLogStream(java.io.PrintStream out)
```

Sets the print stream for logging and tracing messages to *out*.

**PARAMETERS:**

*out*                   the print stream to which logging and tracing messages
                        will be printed.

**EXAMPLE:**

```
DriverManager.setLogStream(System.out);
// sets the logging and tracing print stream to the standard output
// stream.
DriverManager.setLogStream(null); // shuts off the log stream
```

# CHAPTER 11

# DriverPropertyInfo

## 11.1 `DriverPropertyInfo` Overview

**T**HE class `DriverPropertyInfo` is used only by advanced programmers who need to interact with a driver to discover and supply properties for connections. Its function is to be the return value for the method `Driver.getPropertyInfo`, which returns an array of `DriverPropertyInfo` objects. This method allows a generic GUI tool to discover for what properties it should prompt a human user in order to get enough information to connect to a database.

The class consists of a constructor and five fields; there are no methods. It can therefore be thought of as being similar to a `struct`.

### 11.1.1 Creating a `DriverPropertyInfo` Object

An instance of `DriverPropertyInfo` is created using the constructor, which takes two arguments:

```
DriverPropertyInfo info = new DriverPropertyInfo("fred", "foo");
```

The variable *info* contains a `DriverPropertyInfo` object initialized with "fred" as its `name` field and "foo" as its `value` field. The other three fields are initialized with their default values, which are the following:

```
description    null
required       false
choices        null
```

Since there are no set methods, a new value for a field is simply assigned to it, as in the following example:

```
info.required = true;
```

Similarly, since there are no get methods, the value of a field is accessed by simply using the field in an expression, as in the following example:

```
if(info.required) { // if required == true, do something
    . . . .
}
```

## 11.2  DriverPropertyInfo Class Definition

```
package java.sql;
public class DriverPropertyInfo {
    public DriverPropertyInfo(String name, String value);
    public String name;
    public String description = null;
    public boolean required = false;
    public String value;
    public String[] choices = null;
}
```

## 11.3  DriverPropertyInfo Constructor

### DriverPropertyInfo

```
public DriverPropertyInfo(String name, String value);
```

Constructs a DriverPropertyInfo object with the field name initialized to *name* and the field value initialized to *value*. Other fields are initialized with their default values: description and choices are null; required is false.

**PARAMETERS:**

name                          a String object indicating the name of the property.

| | |
|---|---|
| *value* | a String object indicating the current value; null if the current value is not known. |

**EXAMPLE:**
```
DriverPropertyInfo info2 = new DriverPropertyInfo("xyz", "abc");
```

## 11.4  DriverPropertyInfo Variables

### choices

```
public String[] choices = null;
```
An array of String objects, with each String object representing a possible value for the field DriverPropertyInfo.value. This field is used only if the value for the field value may be selected from a particular set of values. If there are no choices, this field should be null.

### description

```
public String description = null;
```
A String object giving a brief description of the property. It may be null, which is the default.

### name

```
public String name;
```
A String object that is the name of the property.

### required

```
public boolean required = false;
```
Indicates whether a value must be supplied for this property. It is required if it must be used by the method Driver.connect in order to make a connection. The property is required if required is true; false indicates that it is optional.

## value

`public String value = null;`

A String object specifying the current value of the property. This is based on a combination of three things: (1) the information supplied to getPropertyInfo, (2) the Java environment, and (3) any driver-supplied default values. It may be null if no value is known.

# CHAPTER 12

# PreparedStatement

## 12.1 `PreparedStatement` Overview

**T**HE `PreparedStatement` interface inherits from `Statement` and differs from it in two ways:

1. Instances of `PreparedStatement` contain an SQL statement that has already been compiled. This is what makes a statement "prepared."

2. The SQL statement contained in a `PreparedStatement` object may have one or more IN parameters. An IN parameter is a parameter whose value is not specified when the SQL statement is created. Instead the statement has a question mark (?) as a placeholder for each IN parameter. A value for each question mark must be supplied by the appropriate `setXXX` method before the statement is executed.

Because `PreparedStatement` objects are precompiled, their execution can be faster than that of `Statement` objects. Consequently, an SQL statement that is executed many times is often created as a `PreparedStatement` object to increase efficiency.

Being a subclass of `Statement`, `PreparedStatement` inherits all the functionality of `Statement`. In addition, it adds a set of methods that are needed for setting the values to be sent to the database in place of the placeholders for IN parameters. Also, the three methods `execute`, `executeQuery`, and `executeUpdate` are modified so that they take no argument. The `Statement` forms of these methods (the forms that take an SQL statement parameter) should never be used with a `PreparedStatement` object.

### 12.1.1    Creating `PreparedStatement` Objects

The following code fragment, where `con` is a `Connection` object, creates a `PreparedStatement` object containing an SQL statement with two placeholders for IN parameters:

```
PreparedStatement pstmt = con.prepareStatement(
                    "UPDATE table4 SET m = ? WHERE x = ?");
```

The object `pstmt` now contains the statement `"UPDATE table4 SET m = ? WHERE x = ?"`, which has already been sent to the DBMS and been prepared for execution.

### 12.1.2    Passing IN Parameters

Before a `PreparedStatement` object is executed, the value of each ? parameter must be set. This is done by calling a `setXXX` method, where `XXX` is the appropriate type for the parameter. For example, if the parameter has a Java type of `long`, the method to use is `setLong`. The first argument to the `setXXX` methods is the *ordinal position* of the parameter to be set, with numbering starting at 1. The second argument is the *value* to which the parameter is to be set. For example, the following code sets the first parameter to `123456789` and the second parameter to `100000000`:

```
pstmt.setLong(1, 123456789);
pstmt.setLong(2, 100000000);
```

Once a parameter value has been set for a given statement, it can be used for multiple executions of that statement until it is cleared by a call to the method `clearParameters` or until a new value is set.

In the default mode for a connection (auto-commit enabled), each statement is committed automatically when it is completed. Some database systems do not retain prepared statements across commits, so for them, the driver will have to recompile the prepared statement after each commit. This means that for these DBMSs, it may actually be less efficient to use a `PreparedStatement` object in place of a `Statement` object that is executed many times.

Using `pstmt`, the `PreparedStatement` object created above, the following code illustrates setting values for the two parameter placeholders and executing `pstmt` 10 times. In this example, the first parameter is set to "Hi" and remains constant.

The second parameter is set to a different value each time around the `for` loop, starting with 0 and ending with 9.

```
pstmt.setString(1, "Hi");
for (int i = 0; i < 10; i++) {
    pstmt.setInt(2, i);
    int rowCount = pstmt.executeUpdate();
}
```

### 12.1.3  Data Type Conformance on IN Parameters

The XXX in a `setXXX` method is a Java type. It also implicitly specifies a JDBC type because the driver will map the Java type to its corresponding JDBC type (following the mapping specified in Table 21.2 on page 394) and send that JDBC type to the database. For example, the following code fragment sets the second parameter of the `PreparedStatement` object *pstmt* to 44, with a Java type of `short`:

```
pstmt.setShort(2, 44);
```

The driver will send 44 to the database as a JDBC `SMALLINT`, which is the standard mapping from a Java `short`.

It is the programmer's responsibility to make sure that the Java type of each IN parameter maps to a JDBC type that is compatible with the JDBC data type expected by the database. Consider the case where the database expects a JDBC `SMALLINT`. If the method `setByte` is used, the driver will send a JDBC `TINYINT` to the database. This will probably work because many database systems convert from one related type to another, and generally a `TINYINT` can be used anywhere a `SMALLINT` is used. However, for an application to work with the most database systems possible, it is best to use Java types that correspond to the exact JDBC types expected by the database. If the expected JDBC type is `SMALLINT`, using `setShort` instead of `setByte` will make an application more portable. The table "Java Types Mapped to JDBC Types" on page 394 can be used to determine which `setXXX` method to use.

### 12.1.4  Using `setObject`

A programmer can explicitly convert an input parameter to a particular JDBC type by using the method `setObject`. This method can take a third argument, which specifies the target JDBC type. The driver will convert the Java `Object` to the specified JDBC type before sending it to the database.

If no JDBC type is given, the driver will simply map the Java `Object` to its default JDBC type (using Table 21.4 on page 396) and then send it to the database. This is similar to what happens with the regular `setXXX` methods; in both cases, the driver maps the Java type of the value to the appropriate JDBC type before sending it to the database. The difference is that the `setXXX` methods use the standard mapping from Java types to JDBC types (Table 21.2 on page 394), whereas the `setObject` method uses the mapping from Java `Object` types to JDBC types (Table 21.4 on page 396).

The capability of the method `setObject` to accept any Java object allows an application to be generic and accept input for a parameter at run time. In this situation the type of the input is not known when the application is compiled. By using `setObject`, the application can accept any Java object type as input and convert it to the JDBC type expected by the database. Table 21.5 on page 397 shows all the possible conversions that `setObject` can perform.

### 12.1.5   Sending JDBC `NULL` as an IN parameter

The `setNull` method allows a programmer to send a JDBC `NULL` (a generic SQL `NULL`) value to the database as an IN parameter. Note, however, that one must still specify the JDBC type of the parameter.

A JDBC `NULL` will also be sent to the database when a Java `null` value is passed to a `setXXX` method (if it takes Java objects as arguments). The method `setObject`, however, can take a `null` value only if the JDBC type is specified.

### 12.1.6   Sending Very Large IN Parameters

The methods `setBytes` and `setString` are capable of sending unlimited amounts of data. Sometimes, however, programmers prefer to pass in large blobs of data in smaller chunks. This can be accomplished by setting an IN parameter to a Java input stream. When the statement is executed, the JDBC driver will make repeated calls to this input stream, reading its contents and transmitting those contents as the actual parameter data.

JDBC provides three methods for setting IN parameters to input streams: `setBinaryStream` for streams containing uninterpreted bytes, `setAsciiStream` for streams containing ASCII characters, and `setUnicodeStream` for streams containing Unicode characters. These methods take one more argument than the other setXXX methods because the total length of the stream must be specified. This is necessary because some database systems need to know the total transfer size before any data is sent.

The following code illustrates using a stream to send the contents of a file as an IN parameter:

```
java.io.File file = new java.io.File("/tmp/data");
int fileLength = file.length();
java.io.InputStream fin = new java.io.FileInputStream(file);
java.sql.PreparedStatement pstmt = con.prepareStatement(
                "UPDATE Table5 SET stuff = ? WHERE index = 4");
pstmt.setBinaryStream (1, fin, fileLength);
pstmt.executeUpdate();
```

When the statement executes, the input stream fin will get called repeatedly to deliver up its data.

## 12.2  PreparedStatement Interface Definition

```
package java.sql;
public interface PreparedStatement extends Statement {
    ResultSet executeQuery() throws SQLException;
    int executeUpdate() throws SQLException;
    void setNull(int parameterIndex, int jdbcType) throws SQLException;
    void setBoolean(int parameterIndex, boolean x) throws SQLException;
    void setByte(int parameterIndex, byte x) throws SQLException;
    void setShort(int parameterIndex, short x) throws SQLException;
    void setInt(int parameterIndex, int x) throws SQLException;
    void setLong(int parameterIndex, long x) throws SQLException;
    void setFloat(int parameterIndex, float x) throws SQLException;
    void setDouble(int parameterIndex, double x) throws SQLException;
    void setBigDecimal(int parameterIndex, java.math.BigDecimal x)
                                            throws SQLException;
    void setString(int parameterIndex, String x) throws SQLException;
    void setBytes(int parameterIndex, byte x[]) throws SQLException;
    void setDate(int parameterIndex, java.sql.Date x) throws
                                    SQLException;
```

```
    void setTime(int parameterIndex, java.sql.Time x)
                                                throws SQLException;
    void setTimestamp(int parameterIndex, java.sql.Timestamp x)
                                                throws SQLException;
    void setAsciiStream(int parameterIndex, java.io.InputStream x, int
                            length) throws SQLException;
    void setUnicodeStream(int parameterIndex, java.io.InputStream x, int
                            length) throws SQLException;
    void setBinaryStream(int parameterIndex, java.io.InputStream x, int
                            length) throws SQLException;
    void clearParameters() throws SQLException;


//--------------------------------------------------------------------
        // Advanced features:
//--------------------------------------------------------------------
    void setObject(int parameterIndex, Object x, int targetJdbcType,
                                    int scale) throws SQLException;
    void setObject(int parameterIndex, Object x, int targetJdbcType)
                                                throws SQLException;
    void setObject(int parameterIndex, Object x) throws SQLException;
    boolean execute() throws SQLException;
}
```

## 12.3  PreparedStatement Methods

The following methods are inherited from `Statement`:

| | | |
|---|---|---|
| cancel | getMoreResults | setCursorName |
| clearWarnings | getQueryTimeout | setEscapeProcessing |
| close | getResultSet | setMaxFieldSize |
| getMaxFieldSize | getUpdateCount | setMaxRows |
| getMaxRows | getWarnings | setQueryTimeout |

### clearParameters

```
void clearParameters() throws SQLException
```

Clears the values set for the `PreparedStatement` object's IN parameters and releases the resources used by those values.

In general, parameter values remain in force for repeated use of a statement. Setting a new parameter value will automatically clear its previous value. In some cases, however, it is useful to immediately release the resources used by the current parameter values by calling the method clear-Parameters.

**EXAMPLE:**
```
pstmt.clearParameters();
```

## execute

```
boolean execute() throws SQLException
```

Executes the SQL statement contained in the PreparedStatement object and indicates whether the first result is a result set, an update count, or there are no results.

This method will execute any PreparedStatement object, but it is designed to handle a complex SQL statement that returns multiple result sets or a statement whose contents are unknown because it is being executed dynamically.

Note that when the execute method is used, one must call the method getResultSet or getUpdateCount to retrieve the first result and then getMore-Results to move to any subsequent result(s).

This version of the execute method does not override the execute method in the Statement interface; the Java compiler treats it as a different method because it takes no parameters and thus has a different signature. Programmers should act as if it does override the Statement version, however. Using the method PreparedStatement.execute with a query parameter is not appropriate and will throw an SQLException.

**RETURNS:**
true if the first result is a result set; false if it is an update count or there is no result.

**EXAMPLE:**
```
boolean b = pstmt.execute();
```

**SEE:**
"Using the Method execute" on page 348 for a fuller description.

## executeQuery

```
ResultSet executeQuery() throws SQLException
```

Executes a prepared SQL query and returns the result set in a `ResultSet` object. This method should be used only for SQL statements that return a result set; any other result will cause an exception.

This version of the `executeQuery` method does not override the `executeQuery` method in the `Statement` interface; the Java compiler treats it as a different method because it takes no parameters and thus has a different signature. Programmers should act as if it does override the `Statement` version, however. Using the method `PreparedStatement.executeQuery` with a query parameter is not appropriate and will throw an `SQLException`.

**RETURNS:**
the result set generated by the SQL statement contained in the calling `PreparedStatement` object.

**EXAMPLE:**
```
ResultSet rs = pstmt.executeQuery();
```

## executeUpdate

```
int executeUpdate() throws SQLException
```

Executes an SQL `INSERT`, `UPDATE` or `DELETE` statement and returns the number of rows that were affected. This method can also be used to execute SQL statements that have no return value, such as DDL statements that create or drop tables.

This method should be used for updates and data definition language statements only; an `SQLException` will be thrown if a result set is returned.

This version of the `executeUpdate` method does not override the `executeUpdate` method in the `Statement` interface; the Java compiler treats it as a different method because it takes no parameters and thus has a different signature. Programmers should act as if it does override the `Statement` version, however. Using the method `PreparedStatement.executeUpdate` with a query parameter is not appropriate and will throw an `SQLException`.

**RETURNS:**
an `int` indicating the number of rows that were affected; 0 indicates that zero rows were affected or that a DDL statement was executed.

**EXAMPLE:**
```
int rowCount = pstmt.executeUpdate();
```

## setAsciiStream

```
void setAsciiStream(int parameterIndex, java.io.InputStream fin,
                                   int length) throws SQLException
```

Sets the parameter in position *parameterIndex* to the input stream object *fin*, from which *length* bytes will be read and sent to the database.

This is useful when a very large ASCII value is input to a LONGVARCHAR parameter. JDBC will read the data from the stream as needed until it reaches end-of-file. The JDBC driver will do any necessary conversion from ASCII to the database CHAR format.

NOTE: This stream object can be either a standard Java stream object or the programmer's own subclass that implements the standard interface.

**PARAMETERS:**

| | |
|---|---|
| *parameterIndex* | 1 indicates the first parameter, 2 the second, and so on. |
| *fin* | the java.io.InputStream object which contains the input data in ASCII format. |
| *length* | the number of bytes to be read from the stream and sent to the database. Note that if the stream contains more or fewer bytes than are specified in *length*, an exception is thrown. |

**EXAMPLE:**
```
pstmt.setAsciiStream(3, fin, 4096);
// sets the third parameter to the input stream fin;
// 4096 bytes will be read
pstmt.setAsciiStream(1, (new StringBufferInputStream(text)),
               text.length()); // to get accurate length
```

## setBigDecimal

```
void setBigDecimal(int parameterIndex, java.math.BigDecimal n)
                                            throws SQLException
```

Sets parameter number *parameterIndex* to *n*. The driver converts this to a JDBC NUMERIC value when it sends it to the database.

**PARAMETERS:**

| | |
|---|---|
| *parameterIndex* | 1 is the first parameter, 2 is the second, and so on. |
| *n* | an instance of the class java.math.BigDecimal. |

**EXAMPLE:**
```
java.math.BigDecimal n = new java.math.BigDecimal(1234, 3);
pstmt.setBigDecimal(2, n); // sets second parameter to 1234.000
```

## setBinaryStream

```
void setBinaryStream(int parameterIndex, java.io.InputStream fin,
                             int length) throws SQLException
```

Sets the parameter in position *parameterIndex* to the input stream object *fin*, from which *length* bytes will be read and sent to the database.

This is useful when a very large binary value is input to a LONGVARBINARY parameter. JDBC will read the data from the stream as needed until it reaches end-of-file.

NOTE: This stream object can be either a standard Java stream object or the programmer's own subclass that implements the standard interface.

**PARAMETERS:**

| | |
|---|---|
| *parameterIndex* | 1 indicates the first parameter, 2 the second, and so on. |
| *fin* | the java.io.InputStream object which contains the input data in binary form. |
| *length* | the number of bytes to be read from the stream and sent to the database. Note that if the stream contains more or less bytes than are specified in *length*, an exception is thrown. |

**EXAMPLE:**
```
pstmt.setBinaryStream(2, fin, 10000);
// sets the second parameter to the input stream fin;
// 10000 bytes will be read
```

## setBoolean

```
void setBoolean(int parameterIndex, boolean b) throws SQLException
```

Sets parameter number *parameterIndex* to *x*, a Java boolean value. The driver converts this to a JDBC `BIT` value when it sends it to the database.

**PARAMETERS:**

| | |
|---|---|
| *parameterIndex* | 1 indicates the first parameter, 2 the second, and so on. |
| *b* | the parameter value—either `true` or `false`. |

**EXAMPLE:**
```
pstmt.setBoolean(3, false); // sets the third parameter to false
```

## setByte

```
void setByte(int parameterIndex, byte x) throws SQLException
```

Sets parameter number *parameterIndex* to *x*, a Java byte value. The driver converts this to a JDBC `TINYINT` value when it sends it to the database.

**PARAMETERS:**

| | |
|---|---|
| *parameterIndex* | 1 indicates the first parameter, 2 the second, and so on. |
| *x* | the parameter value. |

**EXAMPLE:**
```
pstmt.setByte(2, 31); // sets the second parameter to 31
```

## setBytes

```
void setBytes(int parameterIndex, byte x[]) throws SQLException
```

Sets parameter number *parameterIndex* to *x[]*, a Java array of bytes. The driver converts this to a JDBC `VARBINARY` or `LONGVARBINARY` value (depending on the argument's size relative to the driver's limits on `VARBINARY` values) when it sends it to the database.

**PARAMETERS:**

| | |
|---|---|
| *parameterIndex* | 1 is the first parameter, 2 is the second, and so on. |
| *x* | a Java array of bytes. |

**EXAMPLE:**
```
byte x[] = {1, 2, 3, 4, 5};
pstmt.setBytes(1, x); // sets the first parameter to the array x
```

## setDate

```
void setDate(int parameterIndex, java.sql.Date x) throws SQLException
```

Sets parameter number *parameterIndex* to *x*. The driver converts this to a JDBC DATE value when it sends it to the database.

**PARAMETERS:**

| | |
|---|---|
| *parameterIndex* | 1 is the first parameter, 2 is the second, and so on. |
| *x* | a java.sql.Date object. |

**EXAMPLE:**
```
Date x = new Date(101, 11, 31);
pstmt.setDate(1, x);
// sets first parameter to December 31, 2001
// (months are numbered 0 to 11; days, 1 to 31)
```

## setDouble

```
void setDouble(int parameterIndex, double x) throws SQLException
```

Sets parameter number *parameterIndex* to *x*. The driver converts this to a JDBC DOUBLE value when it sends it to the database.

**PARAMETERS:**

| | |
|---|---|
| *parameterIndex* | 1 is the first parameter, 2 is the second, and so on. |
| *x* | a double value. |

**EXAMPLE:**
```
pstmt.setDouble(1, 3958325.89);
// sets first parameter to 3958325.89
```

## setFloat

```
void setFloat(int parameterIndex, float x) throws SQLException
```

Sets parameter number *parameterIndex* to *x*. The driver converts this to a JDBC REAL value when it sends it to the database.

**PARAMETERS:**

| | |
|---|---|
| *parameterIndex* | 1 is the first parameter, 2 is the second, and so on. |
| *x* | a float value. |

**EXAMPLE:**

```
pstmt.setFloat(2, 18.0f); // sets second parameter to 18.0f
```

## setInt

```
void setInt(int parameterIndex, int x) throws SQLException
```

Sets parameter number *parameterIndex* to *x*. The driver converts this to a JDBC INTEGER value when it sends it to the database.

**PARAMETERS:**

| | |
|---|---|
| *parameterIndex* | 1 is the first parameter, 2 is the second, and so on. |
| *x* | an integer value. |

**EXAMPLE:**

```
pstmt.setInt(2, 18); // sets second parameter to 18
```

## setLong

```
void setLong(int parameterIndex, long x) throws SQLException
```

Sets parameter number *parameterIndex* to *x*. The driver converts this to a JDBC BIGINT value when it sends it to the database.

**PARAMETERS:**

| | |
|---|---|
| *parameterIndex* | 1 is the first parameter, 2 is the second, and so on. |
| *x* | a long value. |

**EXAMPLE:**

```
pstmt.setLong(2, 18000000); // sets second parameter to 18000000
```

## setNull

```
void setNull(int parameterIndex, int jdbcType) throws SQLException
```

Sets parameter number *parameterIndex* to JDBC NULL (the generic SQL NULL defined in java.sql.Types). Note that the JDBC type of the parameter to be set to JDBC NULL must be specified.

**PARAMETERS:**

| | |
|---|---|
| *parameterIndex* | 1 is the first parameter, 2 is the second, and so on. |
| *jdbcType* | a JDBC type code defined by java.sql.Types. |

**EXAMPLE:**

```
pstmt.setNull(2, java.sql.Types.INTEGER);
// sets the second parameter, whose type is JDBC INTEGER, to JDBC
// NULL
```

Note that it is also possible to set the value of an input parameter to JDBC NULL using setXXX methods if the XXX is a Java object type.

The following example sets the second parameter, a String value, to JDBC NULL:

```
pstmt.setString(2, null);
```

**SEE:**
java.sql.Types

## setObject

```
void setObject(int parameterIndex, Object x, int targetJdbcType,
                                   int scale) throws SQLException
```

Sets parameter number *parameterIndex* to *x*. The driver converts *x* to *targetJdbcType* before sending it to the database. If *targetJdbcType* is NUMERIC or DECIMAL, *scale* indicates the number of digits to the right of the decimal point; for all other data types, *scale* is ignored.

This form of the method setObject should be used when the target JDBC type is DECIMAL or NUMERIC.

Note that the setXXX methods for specific types convert their arguments to the JDBC type that is the default mapping for that particular type. Methods other than setObject do not, however, perform any general data type conversions. A setObject method can take any type (in the form of a generic Object object) and convert it to the specified JDBC type before sending it to the database. In order to be objects, values for built-in types need to be expressed in their java.lang equivalents. For example, an int needs to be an instance of class Integer.

This method may be used to pass database-specific abstract data types by using a driver-specified Java type for *x* and using `java.sql.Types.OTHER` for *targetJdbcType*.

**PARAMETERS:**

| | |
|---|---|
| *parameterIndex* | 1 is the first parameter, 2 is the second, and so on. |
| *x* | an instance of a Java `Object` containing the input parameter value. |
| *targetJdbcType* | an integer constant representing the JDBC type (as defined in `java.sql.Types`) to be sent to the database. The *scale* argument may further qualify this type. |
| *scale* | the number of digits to the right of the decimal point. This applies only to `java.sql.Types.DECIMAL` and `java.sql.Types.NUMERIC` types. For all other types, this value will be ignored. |

**EXAMPLE:**
```
Object x = new Integer(1234);
pstmt.setObject(1, x, java.sql.Types.DECIMAL, 5);
// sets first parameter to 1234.00000 after converting it to a JDBC
// DECIMAL
```

**SEE:**
`java.sql.Types`
"Using setObject" on page 279.

## setObject

```
void setObject(int parameterIndex, Object x, int targetJdbcType)
                                           throws SQLException
```

Sets parameter number *parameterIndex* to *x* and assumes a scale of zero. The driver converts *x* to *targetJdbcType* before sending it to the database.

Note that the `setXXX` methods for specific types convert their arguments to the JDBC type that is the default mapping for that particular type. Methods other than `setObject` do not, however, perform any general data type conversions. A `setObject` method can take any type (in the form of a generic `Object` object) and convert it to the specified JDBC type before sending it to the database. In order to be objects, values for built-in types need to be expressed in their java.lang class equivalents. For example, an `int` needs to be an instance of class `Integer`.

This method may be used to pass database-specific abstract data types by using a driver-specified Java type for *x* and using `java.sql.Types.OTHER` for *targetJdbcType*.

**PARAMETERS:**

| | |
|---|---|
| *parameterIndex* | 1 is the first parameter, 2 is the second, and so on. |
| *x* | an instance of a Java `Object` containing the input parameter value. |
| *targetJdbcType* | an integer constant representing the JDBC type (as defined in `java.sql.Types`) to be sent to the database. |

**EXAMPLE:**
```
Object x = new Integer(1234);
pstmt.setObject(1, x, java.sql.Types.VARCHAR);
// sets first parameter to 1234 and converts it to JDBC type VARCHAR
```

**SEE:**
`java.sql.Types`
"Using setObject" on page 279.


## setObject

```
void setObject(int parameterIndex, Object x) throws SQLException
```

Sets parameter number *parameterIndex* to *x* and converts it using the standard mapping of Java `Object` types to JDBC types before sending it to the database. This standard mapping is shown in Table 21.4 on page 396.

**PARAMETERS:**

| | |
|---|---|
| *parameterIndex* | 1 is the first parameter, 2 is the second, and so on. |
| *x* | an instance of a Java `Object` containing the input parameter value. |

**EXAMPLE:**
```
Object x = new Integer(1234);
pstmt.setObject(1, x);
// sets the first parameter to 1234 and converts it to a JDBC INTEGER
```

**SEE:**
"Using setObject" on page 279.

## setShort

```
void setShort(int parameterIndex, short x) throws SQLException
```

Sets parameter number *parameterIndex* to *x*. The driver converts this to a JDBC SMALLINT value when it sends it to the database.

**PARAMETERS:**

*parameterIndex*    1 is the first parameter, 2 is the second, and so on.

*x*    a short value.

**EXAMPLE:**
```
pstmt.setShort(2, 8); // sets second parameter to 8.
```

## setString

```
void setString(int parameterIndex, String x) throws SQLException
```

Sets parameter number *parameterIndex* to *x*. The driver converts this to a JDBC VARCHAR or LONGVARCHAR value (depending on the argument's size relative to the driver's limits on VARCHARs) when it sends it to the database.

**PARAMETERS:**

*parameterIndex*    1 is the first parameter, 2 is the second, and so on.

*x*    a Java String object.

**EXAMPLE:**
```
String x = "Happy days are here again"
pstmt.setString(2, x); // sets second parameter to "Happy days ...
```

## setTime

```
void setTime(int parameterIndex, java.sql.Time x) throws SQLException
```

Sets parameter number *parameterIndex* to *x*. The driver converts this to a JDBC TIME value when it sends it to the database.

**PARAMETERS:**

*parameterIndex*    1 is the first parameter, 2 is the second, and so on.

*x*    a java.sql.Time object.

**EXAMPLE:**
```
Time x = new Time(23, 30, 15);
pstmt.setTime(2, x); // sets second parameter to 11:30:15 p.m.
```

**SEE:**
```
java.sql.Time
```

## setTimestamp

```
void setTimestamp(int parameterIndex, java.sql.Timestamp x)
                                              throws SQLException
```

Sets parameter number *parameterIndex* to *x*. The driver converts this to a JDBC TIMESTAMP value when it sends it to the database.

**PARAMETERS:**

| | |
|---|---|
| *parameterIndex* | 1 is the first parameter, 2 is the second, and so on. |
| *x* | a java.sql.Timestamp object. |

**EXAMPLE:**
```
Timestamp x = new Timestamp(98, 0, 1, 12, 30, 0, 0);
pstmt.setTime(1, ); // sets first parameter to 12:30 p.m. on January
                    //1, 1998.
```

**SEE:**
```
java.sql.Timestamp
```

## setUnicodeStream

```
void setUnicodeStream(int parameterIndex, java.io.InputStream fin,
                                  int length) throws SQLException
```

Sets the parameter in position *parameterIndex* to the input stream object *fin*, from which *length* bytes will be read and sent to the database.

This is useful when a very large Unicode value is input to a LONGVARCHAR parameter. JDBC will read the data from the stream as needed until it reaches end-of-file. The JDBC driver will do any necessary conversion from Unicode to the database CHAR format.

NOTE: This stream object can be either a standard Java stream object or the programmer's own subclass that implements the standard interface.

**PARAMETERS:**

| | |
|---|---|
| *parameterIndex* | 1 indicates the first parameter, 2 the second, and so on. |
| *fin* | the java.io.InputStream object that contains the input data in Unicode format. |
| *length* | the number of bytes to be read from the stream and sent to the database. Note that if the stream contains more or fewer bytes than are specified in *length*, an exception is thrown. |

**EXAMPLE:**

```
pstmt.setUnicodeStream(1, fin, 256);
// sets the first parameter to the input stream fin;
// 256 bytes will be read
```

# CHAPTER 13

# ResultSet

## 13.1 ResultSet Overview

A `ResultSet` object is a table that contains the results of executing an SQL query. In other words, it contains the rows that satisfy the conditions of the query.

The data stored in a `ResultSet` object is retrieved through a set of `get` methods that allows access to the various columns of the current row. The `ResultSet.next` method is used to move to the next row of the `ResultSet`, making it the current row.

The general form of a result set is a table with column headings and the corresponding values returned by a query. For example, if your query is `SELECT a, b, c FROM Table1`, your result set will have the following form:

```
a               b               c
----------      ------------    -----------
12345           Cupertino       2459723.495
83472           Redmond         1.0
83492           Boston          35069473.43
```

The following code fragment is an example of executing an SQL statement that will return a collection of rows, with column 1 as an `int`, column 2 as a `String`, and column 3 as a float:

```
java.sql.Statement stmt = con.createStatement();
ResultSet rs = stmt.executeQuery("SELECT a, b, c FROM Table2");
while (rs.next()) {
```

```
    // print the values for the current row.
    int i = rs.getInt("a");
    String s = rs.getString("b");
    float f = rs.getFloat("c");
    System.out.println("ROW = " + i + " " + s + " " + f);
}
```

### 13.1.1  Rows and Cursors

A ResultSet object maintains a cursor, which points to its current row of data. The cursor moves down one row each time the method next is called. Initially it is positioned before the first row, so that the first call to next puts the cursor on the first row, making it the current row. ResultSet rows are retrieved in sequence from the top row down as the cursor moves down one row with each successive call to next.

A cursor remains valid until the ResultSet object or its parent Statement object is closed.

### 13.1.2  Retrieving Column Values

The getXXX methods provide the means for retrieving column values from the current row. Within each row, column values may be retrieved in any order, but for maximum portability, one should retrieve values from left to right and read column values only once.

Either the column name or the column number can be used to designate the column from which to retrieve data. For example, if the second column of a ResultSet object *rs* is named "title", and it stores values as strings, either of the following will retrieve the value stored in that column:

```
String s = rs.getString(2);
String s = rs.getString("title");
```

Note that columns are numbered from left to right starting with column 1. Also, column names used as input to getXXX methods are case insensitive.

The option of using the column name was provided so that a user who specifies column names in a query can use those same names as the arguments to getXXX methods. If, on the other hand, the select statement does not specify column names (as in "select * from table1" or in cases where a column is derived), column numbers should be used. In such situations, there is no way for the user to know for sure what the column names are.

In some cases, it is possible for an SQL query to return a result set that has more than one column with the same name. If a column name is used as the parameter to a getXXX method, getXXX will return the value of the first matching column name. Thus, if there are multiple columns with the same name, one needs to use a column index to be sure that the correct column value is retrieved. It may also be slightly more efficient to use column numbers.

If the name of a column is known but not its index, the method findColumn can be used to find the column number.

Information about the columns in a ResultSet is available by calling the method ResultSet.getMetaData. The ResultSetMetaData object returned gives the number, types, and properties of its ResultSet object's columns. Refer to "ResultSetMetaData" on page 319 for more information.

### 13.1.3  Datatypes and Conversions

For the getXXX methods, the JDBC driver attempts to convert the underlying data to the specified Java type and then returns a suitable Java value. For example, if the getXXX method is getString, and the datatype of the data in the underlying database is VARCHAR, the JDBC driver will convert VARCHAR to Java String. The return value of getString will be a Java String object.

Table 13.1 shows which JDBC types a getXXX method is *allowed* to retrieve and which JDBC types are *recommended* for it to retrieve. A small x indicates a legal getXXX method for a particular datatype; a large X indicates the recommended getXXX method for a datatype. For example, any getXXX method except getBytes or getBinaryStream can be used to retrieve the value of a LONGVARCHAR, but getAsciiStream or getUnicodeStream are recommended, depending on whether ASCII or Unicode characters are being returned. The method getObject will return any datatype as a Java Object and is useful when the underlying datatype is a database-specific type or when a generic application needs to be able to accept any datatype.

| | TINYINT | SMALLINT | INTEGER | BIGINT | REAL | FLOAT | DOUBLE | DECIMAL | NUMERIC | BIT | CHAR | VARCHAR | LONGVARCHAR | BINARY | VARBINARY | LONGVARBINARY | DATE | TIME | TIMESTAMP |
|---|---|---|---|---|---|---|---|---|---|---|---|---|---|---|---|---|---|---|---|
| getByte | X | x | x | x | x | x | x | x | x | x | x | x | x | | | | | | |
| getShort | x | X | x | x | x | x | x | x | x | x | x | x | x | | | | | | |
| getInt | x | x | X | x | x | x | x | x | x | x | x | x | x | | | | | | |
| getLong | x | x | x | X | x | x | x | x | x | x | x | x | x | | | | | | |
| getFloat | x | x | x | x | X | x | x | x | x | x | x | x | x | | | | | | |
| getDouble | x | x | x | x | x | X | X | x | x | x | x | x | x | | | | | | |
| getBigDecimal | x | x | x | x | x | x | x | X | X | x | x | x | x | | | | | | |
| getBoolean | x | x | x | x | x | x | x | x | x | X | x | x | x | | | | | | |
| getString | x | x | x | x | x | x | x | x | x | x | X | X | x | x | x | x | x | x | x |
| getBytes | | | | | | | | | | | | | | X | X | x | | | |
| getDate | | | | | | | | | | | x | x | x | | | | X | | x |
| getTime | | | | | | | | | | | x | x | x | | | | | X | x |
| getTimestamp | | | | | | | | | | | x | x | x | | | | x | x | X |
| getAsciiStream | | | | | | | | | | | x | x | X | x | x | x | | | |
| getUnicodeStream | | | | | | | | | | | x | x | X | x | x | x | | | |
| getBinaryStream | | | | | | | | | | | | | | x | x | X | | | |
| getObject | x | x | x | x | x | x | x | x | x | x | x | x | x | x | x | x | x | x | x |

**Table 13.1: Use of `ResultSet.getXXX` Methods to Retrieve JDBC Types**

An "x" indicates that the `getXXX` method may legally be used to retrieve the given JDBC type.
An "X" indicates that the `getXXX` method is recommended for retrieving the given JDBC type.

### 13.1.4 Positioned Updates

Some DBMSs support a concept called *positioned update*. A positioned update is used to change a row that has been fetched with a result set.

In SQL, the cursor for a result table can be named. If a DBMS allows positioned updates or positioned deletes, the name of the cursor needs to be supplied as a parameter to the update or delete command. This cursor name can be obtained by calling the `ResultSet` method `getCursorName`.

If there is any doubt as to whether a DBMS supports positioned update and delete, one can call the `DatabaseMetaData` methods `supportsPositionedDelete` and `supportsPositionedUpdate` to discover whether a particular connection supports these operations. When they are supported, the DBMS/driver must ensure that rows selected are properly locked so that positioned updates do not result in update anomalies or other concurrency problems.

### 13.1.5 Using Streams for Very Large Row Values

A `ResultSet` makes it possible to retrieve arbitrarily large `LONGVARBINARY` or `LONG-VARCHAR` data. The methods `getBytes` and `getString` return data as one large chunk (up to the limits imposed by the return value of `Statement.getMaxFieldSize`). However, it may be more convenient to retrieve very large data in smaller, fixed-size chunks. This is done by having the `ResultSet` class return `java.io.Input` streams from which data can be read in chunks. Note that these streams must be accessed immediately because they will be closed automatically on the next `getXXX` call on `ResultSet`. (This behavior is not a limitation of JDBC but rather a constraint on large blob access imposed by the underlying implementations in some database systems.)

JDBC has three separate methods for getting streams, each with a different return value:

- **getBinaryStream**—returns a stream that simply provides the raw bytes from the database without any conversion.

- **getAsciiStream**—returns a stream that provides one-byte ASCII characters.

- **getUnicodeStream**—returns a stream that provides two-byte Unicode characters.

Note that this differs from Java streams, which return untyped bytes and can (for example) be used for both ASCII and Unicode characters. Note also that

JDBC Unicode streams expect big-endian data; that is, they expect data with the high byte first and the low byte second. This conforms to the standard endian defined by Java, which is important if a program is to be portable.

The following code demonstrates using the method `getAsciiStream`:

```
java.sql.Statement stmt = con.createStatement();
ResultSet rs = stmt.executeQuery("SELECT x FROM Table2");
// Now retrieve the column 1 results in 4 K chunks:
byte [] buff = new byte[4096];
while (rs.next()) {
    java.io.InputStream fin = rs.getAsciiStream(1);
    for (;;) {
        int size = fin.read(buff);
        if (size == -1) { // at end of stream
                break;
        }
        // Send the newly filled buffer to some ASCII output stream:
        output.write(buff, 0, size);
    }
}
```

### 13.1.6  NULL Result Values

To determine if a given result value is JDBC NULL, one must first read the column and then use the `ResultSet.wasNull` method to discover if the read returned a JDBC NULL.

When one has read a JDBC NULL using one of the `ResultSet.getXXX` methods, the `getXXX` method will return one of the following:

- A Java `null` value for those getXXX methods that return Java objects (`get-String`, `getBigDecimal`, `getBytes`, `getDate`, `getTime`, `getTimestamp`, `getAsciiStream`, `getUnicodeStream`, `getBinaryStream`, `getObject`).

- A zero value for `getByte`, `getShort`, `getInt`, `getLong`, `getFloat`, and `getDouble`.

- A `false` value for `getBoolean`.

### 13.1.7   Optional or Multiple Result Sets

Normally SQL statements are executed using either executeQuery (which returns a single ResultSet) or executeUpdate (which can be used for database modification statements, which return a count of the rows updated, or for data definition language statements). However, under some circumstances an application may not know whether a given statement will return a result set until the statement has executed. In addition, some stored procedures may return several different result sets and/or update counts.

To accommodate these situations, JDBC provides a mechanism so that an application can execute a statement and then process an arbitrary collection of result sets and update counts. This mechanism is based on first calling a fully general execute method, and then calling three other methods, getResultSet, getUpdateCount, and getMoreResults. These methods allow an application to explore the statement results one at a time and to determine if a given result was a ResultSet or an update count. Most programmers will never need to use these methods. For those who do, a full explanation with a code example can be found in the section "Using the Method execute" on page 348.

### 13.1.8   Closing a **ResultSet** Object

Normally, nothing needs to be done to close a ResultSet object; it is automatically closed by the Statement object that generated it when that Statement object is closed, is re-executed, or is used to retrieve the next result from a sequence of multiple results. The method close is provided so that a ResultSet object can be closed explicitly, thereby immediately releasing the resources held by the ResultSet object. This could be necessary when several statements are being used and the automatic close does not occur soon enough to prevent database resource conflicts.

## 13.2   ResultSet Interface Definition

```
package java.sql;
public interface ResultSet {
    boolean next() throws SQLException;
    void close() throws SQLException;
    boolean wasNull() throws SQLException;
    //==============================================================
    // Methods for accessing results by column number:
    //==============================================================
```

```
String getString(int columnIndex) throws SQLException;
boolean getBoolean(int columnIndex) throws SQLException;
byte getByte(int columnIndex) throws SQLException;
short getShort(int columnIndex) throws SQLException;
int getInt(int columnIndex) throws SQLException;
long getLong(int columnIndex) throws SQLException;
float getFloat(int columnIndex) throws SQLException;
double getDouble(int columnIndex) throws SQLException;
java.math.BigDecimal getBigDecimal(int columnIndex, int scale)
                                            throws SQLException;
byte[] getBytes(int columnIndex) throws SQLException;
java.sql.Date getDate(int columnIndex) throws SQLException;
java.sql.Time getTime(int columnIndex) throws SQLException;
java.sql.Timestamp getTimestamp(int columnIndex)
                                            throws SQLException;
java.io.InputStream getAsciiStream(int columnIndex)
                                            throws SQLException;
java.io.InputStream getUnicodeStream(int columnIndex)
                                            throws SQLException;
java.io.InputStream getBinaryStream(int columnIndex)
                                            throws SQLException;
//=============================================================
// Methods for accessing results by column name:
//=============================================================
String getString(String columnName) throws SQLException;
boolean getBoolean(String columnName) throws SQLException;
byte getByte(String columnName) throws SQLException;
short getShort(String columnName) throws SQLException;
int getInt(String columnName) throws SQLException;
long getLong(String columnName) throws SQLException;
float getFloat(String columnName) throws SQLException;
double getDouble(String columnName) throws SQLException;
java.math.BigDecimal getBigDecimal(String columnName, int scale)
                                            throws SQLException;
byte[] getBytes(String columnName) throws SQLException;
java.sql.Date getDate(String columnName) throws SQLException;
java.sql.Time getTime(String columnName) throws SQLException;
java.sql.Timestamp getTimestamp(String columnName)
                                            throws SQLException;
```

```
java.io.InputStream getAsciiStream(String columnName)
                                             throws SQLException;
java.io.InputStream getUnicodeStream(String columnName)
                                             throws SQLException;
java.io.InputStream getBinaryStream(String columnName)
                                             throws SQLException;
//===========================================================
// Advanced features:
//===========================================================
SQLWarning getWarnings() throws SQLException;
void clearWarnings() throws SQLException;
String getCursorName() throws SQLException;
ResultSetMetaData getMetaData() throws SQLException;
Object getObject(int columnIndex) throws SQLException;
Object getObject(String columnName) throws SQLException;
int findColumn(String columnName) throws SQLException;
}
```

## 13.3  ResultSet Methods

NOTE: All getXXX methods except getCursorName, getMetaData, and getWarnings have two versions, one that takes a column name and one that takes a column number. Since this is the only difference between them, the two versions have been combined into one entry to avoid unnecessary repetition. Also, the explanation of parameters for all getXXX methods is given here once and is not repeated in the individual method explanations.

The parameter for each getXXX method is one of the following:

| | |
|---|---|
| *columnIndex* | the number of the column in the current row from which data is to be retrieved. The first column is 1, the second column is 2, and so on. |
| or | |
| *columnName* | the name of the column in the current row from which data is to be retrieved. |

## clearWarnings

void **clearWarnings**() throws SQLException

Clears any warnings for the ResultSet. After calling clearWarnings, a call to getWarnings will return null until a new warning is reported for this ResultSet.

**EXAMPLE:**
rs.clearWarnings();

## close

void **close**() throws SQLException

Immediately releases a ResultSet's database and JDBC resources.

A ResultSet is automatically closed by the Statement that generated it when that Statement is closed, re-executed, or used to retrieve the next result from a sequence of multiple results. A ResultSet is also automatically closed when it is garbage collected. The method close is used to close a ResultSet object immediately instead of waiting for it to be closed automatically.

**EXAMPLE:**
rs.close();

## findColumn

int **findColumn**(String *columnName*) throws SQLException

Maps a ResultSet object's column name to its column index.

**PARAMETERS:**
*columnName*          The name of a column in the current row.

**RETURNS:**
the column index for *columnName*.

**EXAMPLE:**
String s = rs.getString(rs.findColumn("Name"));

## getAsciiStream

```
java.io.InputStream getAsciiStream(int columnIndex) throws SQLException
java.io.InputStream getAsciiStream(String columnName) throws
                                                         SQLException
```

A column value can be retrieved as a stream of ASCII characters and then read in chunks from the stream. This method is particularly suitable for retrieving large LONGVARCHAR values. The JDBC driver will do any necessary conversion from the database format into ASCII.

Note that all the data in the returned stream must be read prior to getting the value of any other column. The next call to a getXXX method implicitly closes the stream.

**RETURNS:**
a Java input stream that delivers the value of *columnIndex* (or *columnName*) as a stream of one-byte ASCII characters. If the value is SQL NULL, then the return value is null.

**EXAMPLE:**
```
java.io.InputStream in = rs.getAsciiStream(2);
```
or
```
java.io.InputStream in = rs.getAsciiStream("Comments");
```

## getBigDecimal

```
java.math.BigDecimal getBigDecimal(int columnIndex, int scale)
                                                   throws SQLException
java.math.BigDecimal getBigDecimal(String columnName, int scale)
                                                   throws SQLException
```

Gets the value of the designated column as a java.math.BigDecimal object with *scale* digits to the right of the decimal point.

**PARAMETER:**
*scale*               The number of digits to the right of the decimal point.

**RETURNS:**
the value of column *columnIndex* (or *columnName*) as a java.math.BigDecimal object or null if the value is SQL NULL.

**EXAMPLES:**
```
java.math.BigDecimal num = rs.getBigDecimal(1, 8);
```

```
// retrieves a BigDecimal with 8 digits after the decimal point
// from column 1 of the ResultSet rs
or
java.math.BigDecimal num = rs.getBigDecimal("Number", 2);
// retrieves a BigDecimal with 2 digits after the decimal point
// from column "Number" of the ResultSet rs
```

## getBinaryStream

```
java.io.InputStream getBinaryStream(int columnIndex) throws
                                                    SQLException
java.io.InputStream getBinaryStream(String columnName) throws
                                                    SQLException
```

A column value can be retrieved as a stream of uninterpreted bytes and then read in chunks from the stream. This method is particularly suitable for retrieving large LONGVARBINARY values.

Note that all the data in the returned stream must be read prior to getting the value of any other column. The next call to a getXXX method implicitly closes the stream.

**RETURNS:**
a Java input stream that delivers the value of column *columnIndex* (or *columnName*) as a stream of uninterpreted bytes. If the value is SQL NULL, then the result is null.

**EXAMPLES:**
```
java.io.InputStream in = rs.getBinaryStream(2);
```
or
```
java.io.InputStream in = rs.getBinaryStream("Data");
```

## getBoolean

```
boolean getBoolean(int columnIndex) throws SQLException
boolean getBoolean(String columnName) throws SQLException
```

Gets the value of the designated column as a boolean.

**RETURNS:**
the value of column *columnIndex* (or *columnName*) as a Java boolean. If the value is SQL NULL, getBoolean will return false.

**EXAMPLES:**
```
boolean bool = rs.getBoolean(5);
```
or
```
boolean bool = rs.getBoolean("Completed");
```

## getByte

```
byte getByte(int columnIndex) throws SQLException
byte getByte(String columnName) throws SQLException
```

Gets the value of the designated column as a byte.

**RETURNS:**
the value of column *columnIndex* (or *columnName*) as a Java byte or 0 if the value is SQL NULL.

**EXAMPLES:**
```
byte b = rs.getByte(5);
```
or
```
byte b = rs.getByte("Completed");
```

## getBytes

```
byte[] getBytes(int columnIndex) throws SQLException
byte[] getBytes(String columnName) throws SQLException
```

Gets the value of the designated column as an array of bytes.

**RETURNS:**
the value of column *columnIndex* (or *columnName*) as a Java byte array or null if the value is JDBC NULL. The bytes represent the raw values returned by the driver.

**EXAMPLES:**
```
byte[] b = rs.getBytes(1);
```
or
```
byte[] b = rs.getBytes("Code");
```

## getCursorName

```
String getCursorName() throws SQLException
```

In SQL, a result table is retrieved through a named cursor. The current row of a result can be updated or deleted using a positioned update or positioned delete statement that references the cursor name.

JDBC supports this SQL feature by providing the name of the SQL cursor used by a ResultSet. The current row of a ResultSet is also the current row of this SQL cursor.

The cursor remains valid until the ResultSet object or its parent Statement object is closed.

If positioned update is not supported, an SQLException is thrown.

**RETURNS:**
the ResultSet's SQL cursor name.

**EXAMPLE:**
```
String s = rs.getCursorName();
```

## getDate

```
java.sql.Date getDate(int columnIndex) throws SQLException
java.sql.Date getDate(String columnName) throws SQLException
```

Gets the value of the designated column as a Date object.

**RETURNS:**
the value of column *columnIndex* (or *columnName*) as a java.sql.Date object or null if the value is SQL NULL.

**EXAMPLES:**
```
Date d = rs.getDate(1);
```
or
```
Date d = rs.getDate("Deadline")
```

## getDouble

```
double getDouble(int columnIndex) throws SQLException
double getDouble(String columnName) throws SQLException
```

Gets the value of the designated column as a double.

**RETURNS:**
the value of column *columnIndex* (or *columnName*) as a Java double or 0 if the value is SQL NULL.

**EXAMPLES:**
```
double d = rs.getFloat(3);
```
or
```
double d = rs.getDouble("Square_Root");
```

## getFloat

```
float getFloat(int columnIndex) throws SQLException
float getFloat(String columnName) throws SQLException
```

Gets the value of the designated column as a float.

**RETURNS:**
the value of column *columnIndex* (or *columnName*) as a Java float or 0 if the value is SQL NULL.

**EXAMPLES:**
```
float f = rs.getFloat(2);
```
or
```
float f = rs.getFloat("Cost");
```

## getInt

```
int getInt(int columnIndex) throws SQLException
int getInt(String columnName) throws SQLException
```

Gets the value of the designated column as an int.

**RETURNS:**
the value of column *columnIndex* (or *columnName*) as a Java int or 0 if the value is SQL NULL.

**EXAMPLES:**
```
int x = rs.getShort(1);
```
or
```
int x = rs.getShort("EmployeeID");
```

## getLong

```
long getLong(int columnIndex) throws SQLException
long getLong(String columnName) throws SQLException
```

Gets the value of the designated column as a `long`.

**RETURNS:**
the value of column *columnIndex* (or *columnName*) as a Java `long` or 0 if the value is SQL NULL.

**EXAMPLES:**
```
long q = rs.getLong(4);
```
or
```
long q = rs.getLong("Time_in_Secs");
```

## getMetaData

```
ResultSetMetaData getMetaData() throws SQLException
```

Gets the number, types, and properties of a `ResultSet` object's columns.

**RETURNS:**
a `ResultSetMetaData` object containing information about a `ResultSet` object's columns.

**EXAMPLE:**
```
ResultSetMetaData rsmd = rs.getMetaData();
```

**SEE:**
ResultSetMetaData

## getObject

```
Object getObject(int columnIndex) throws SQLException
Object getObject(String columnName) throws SQLException
```

Gets the value of the column *columnIndex* (or *columnName*) as a Java `Object`.

This method may be used to read database-specific abstract datatypes. It is also useful when an application wants to be generic and be able to read any datatype.

**RETURNS:**
the value of column *columnIndex* (or *columnName*) as a java.lang.Object. The type of the object will be the default Java Object type corresponding to the column's JDBC type. The table "JDBC Types Mapped to Java Object Types" on page 395 shows the Java Object type that getObject will return for each JDBC type. The result will be null if the value is SQL NULL.

**EXAMPLES:**
```
Object db_specific = rs.getObject(2);
```
or
```
Object db_specific = rs.getObject("Info");
```

**SEE:**
Table 21.3, "JDBC Types Mapped to Java Object Types" on page 395.

## getShort

```
short getShort(int columnIndex) throws SQLException
short getShort(String columnName) throws SQLException
```

Gets the value of the designated column as a short.

**RETURNS:**
the value of column *columnIndex* (or *columnName*) as a Java short or 0 if the value is SQL NULL.

**EXAMPLES:**
```
short n = rs.getShort(3);
```
or
```
short n = rs.getShort("Age");
```

## getString

```
String getString(int columnIndex) throws SQLException
String getString(String columnName) throws SQLException
```

Gets the value of the designated column as a String object.

**RETURNS:**
the value of column *columnIndex* (or *columnName*) as a Java String or null if the value is SQL NULL.

**EXAMPLES:**
```
String lastName = rs.getString(2);
```
or
```
String lastName = rs.getString("Last_Name");
```

## getTime

```
java.sql.Time getTime(int columnIndex) throws SQLException
java.sql.Time getTime(String columnName) throws SQLException
```

Gets the value of the designated column as a `Time` object.

**RETURNS:**
the value of column *columnIndex* (or *columnName*) as a `java.sql.Time` object or `null` if the value is SQL NULL.

**EXAMPLES:**
```
Time t = rs.getTime(3);
```
or
```
Time t = rs.getTime("Start_Time");
```

## getTimestamp

```
java.sql.Timestamp getTimestamp(int columnIndex) throws SQLException
java.sql.Timestamp getTimestamp(String columnName) throws SQLException
```

Gets the value of the designated column as a `Timestamp` object.

**RETURNS:**
the value of column *columnIndex* (or *columnName*) as a `java.sql.Timestamp` object or `null` if the value is SQL NULL.

**EXAMPLES:**
```
Timestamp ts = rs.getTimestamp(3);
```
or
```
Timestamp ts = rs.getTimestamp("Received");
```

## getUnicodeStream

```
java.io.InputStream getUnicodeStream(int columnIndex) throws
                                                    SQLException
java.io.InputStream getUnicodeStream(String columnName) throws
                                                    SQLException
```

A column value can be retrieved as a stream of Unicode characters and then read in chunks from the stream. This method is particularly suitable for retrieving large LONGVARCHAR values. The JDBC driver will do any necessary conversion from the database format into Unicode. Note that Unicode is produced in BigEndian order, that is, with the high byte first.

All the data in the returned stream must be read prior to getting the value of any other column because the next call to a getXXX method implicitly closes the stream.

**RETURNS:**
a Java input stream that delivers the database column value as a stream of two-byte Unicode characters. If the value is SQL NULL, getUnicodeStream returns null.

**EXAMPLES:**
```
java.io.InputStream in = rs.getUnicodeStream(2);
```
or
```
java.io.InputStream in = rs.getUnicodeStream("Comments_German");
```

## getWarnings

```
SQLWarning getWarnings() throws SQLException
```

Gets the first SQLWarning that has been reported for this ResultSet object. Subsequent warnings, if there are any, are chained to the first warning. The warning chain is automatically cleared each time a new row is read.

NOTE: This warning chain covers only warnings caused by ResultSet methods. Any warning caused by Statement methods (such as CallableStatement.getXXX methods for reading OUT parameters) will be chained on the Statement object.

**RETURNS:**
the first SQLWarning or null if there are no warnings.

**EXAMPLE:**
```
SQLWarning w = rs.getWarnings();
```

## next

```
boolean next() throws SQLException
```

Since the cursor of a ResultSet object is initially positioned before the first row, the first call to next makes the first row the current row; the second call makes the second row the current row, and so on. If a getXXX method is called before the first call to next, an exception will be thrown. An exception will also be thrown if a getXXX method is called after the method next returns false.

If an input stream from the previous row is open, it is implicitly closed.

The ResultSet object's warning chain is cleared when a new row is read; that is, the warning chain is cleared each time the method next is called.

**RETURNS:**
true if the move to the next row was successful; false if there are no more rows. This allows the use of next in a while loop, which is how it is typically used.

**EXAMPLE:**
```
ResultSet rs = stmt.executeQuery("SELECT a, b, c FROM Table1");
while (rs.next()) {
    // retrieve data with getXXX methods as long as next()
    // returns true (there is a valid current row)
}
```

## wasNull

```
boolean wasNull() throws SQLException
```

Checks to see if the last value read was SQL NULL or not.

**RETURNS:**
true if the last value read was SQL NULL and false otherwise.

**EXAMPLE:**

```
ResultSet rs = stmt.executeQuery("SELECT a, b, c FROM Table1");
while (rs.next()) {
    int x = rs.getInt(1);
    if (rs.wasNull()) {  // check to see if x was SQL NULL
        // do something if x was SQL NULL
    }else {
        // do something else if x was not SQL NULL
    }
    String s = rs.getString(2); // if s = null, it was SQL NULL
    Date d = rs.getDate(3); // if d = null, it was SQL NULL
}
```

CHAPTER 14

# ResultSetMetaData

## 14.1 `ResultSetMetaData` Overview

**T**HE interface `ResultSetMetaData` provides information about the types and properties of the columns in a `ResultSet` object.

An instance of `ResultSetMetaData` actually contains the information, and `ResultSetMetaData` methods give access to that information. The variables defined in `ResultSetMetaData` are constants that are the possible return values for the method `isNullable`.

### 14.1.1 Creating a `ResultSetMetaData` Object

The following code fragment, where *stmt* is a `Statement` object, illustrates creating a `ResultSetMetaData` object:

```
ResultSet rs = stmt.executeQuery("SELECT a, b, c FROM Table1");
ResultSetMetaData rsmd = rs.getMetaData();
```

The variable *rsmd* contains a `ResultSetMetaData` object that can be used for invoking `ResultSetMetaData` methods in order to get information about the `ResultSet` object *rs*.

### 14.1.2 Using `ResultSetMetaData`

Using the `ResultSetMetaData` object *rsmd* just created, the following method prints out the JDBC type and database name of that type for each column in the `ResultSet` object *rs*.

```
public static void printColumnTypes() throws SQLException {
    int numberOfColumns = rsmd.getColumnCount();
    for (int i=1; i <= numberOfColumns; i++) {
        int jdbcType = rsmd.getColumnType(i);
        String name = rsmd.getColumnTypeName(i);
        System.out.print("Column " + i + " is JDBC type " + jdbcType);
        System.out.println(", which is JDBC type " + name);
    }
}
```

The output for this code fragment might look something like the following:

➡ Column 1 is JDBC type 12, which is JDBC type VARCHAR
➡ Column 2 is JDBC type 4, which is JDBC type INTEGER
➡ Column 3 is JDBC type 8, which is JDBC type DOUBLE

The number of columns should be three because the SELECT statement that created the result set *rs* specified three column names (*a*, *b*, and *c*). So in this case it is not really necessary to invoke the method getColumnCount. However, by doing so, the method printColumnTypes is more general purpose because it can be used when the number of columns is not known at compile time. If, for example, the user did not already know the number of columns in Table 1 and the query that produced the ResultSet *rs* was SELECT * FROM TABLE1, invoking the method get-ColumnCount would be necessary to determine the number of columns.

The ResultSetMetaData interface is especially useful in the case where the method execute has been used to execute an SQL statement where the number and kind of results are not known at compile time. In such a case, a programmer could, for example, use ResultSetMetaData methods to ascertain which Result-Set.getXXX methods to use for retrieving data. "Getting Column Type Information" on page 93, has sample code that illustrates getting the JDBC type of a result set column. When the JDBC type is known, the table "Types Retrieved by Result-Set.getXXX Methods" on page 398 can be used to determine which getXXX method to use.

## 14.2  ResultSetMetaData Interface Definition

```
package java.sql;
public interface ResultSetMetaData {
    int getColumnCount() throws SQLException;
    boolean isAutoIncrement(int column) throws SQLException;
    boolean isCaseSensitive(int column) throws SQLException;
    boolean isCurrency(int column) throws SQLException;
    int isNullable(int column) throws SQLException;
    boolean isSigned(int column) throws SQLException;
    int getColumnDisplaySize(int column) throws SQLException;
    String getColumnLabel(int column) throws SQLException;
    String getColumnName(int column) throws SQLException;
    String getSchemaName(int column) throws SQLException;
    int getPrecision(int column) throws SQLException;
    int getScale(int column) throws SQLException;
    String getTableName(int column) throws SQLException;
    String getCatalogName(int column) throws SQLException;
    int getColumnType(int column) throws SQLException;
    String getColumnTypeName(int column) throws SQLException;
    boolean isReadOnly(int column) throws SQLException;
    boolean isWritable(int column) throws SQLException;
    boolean isDefinitelyWritable(int column) throws SQLException;
//-----------------------------------------------------------------
//         Possible return values for the method isNullable:
//-----------------------------------------------------------------
    int columnNoNulls         = 0;
    int columnNullable        = 1;
    int columnNullableUnknown = 2;
}
```

## 14.3  ResultSetMetaData Methods

### getCatalogName

```
String getCatalogName(int column) throws SQLException
```

Gets the catalog name for the table from which column *column* of this `ResultSet` was derived.

**PARAMETERS:**

*column*                    1 is the first column, 2 the second, and so on.

**RETURNS:**

a `String` object representing the catalog name or "" if not applicable.

**EXAMPLE:**
```
String s = rsmd.getCatalogName(1);
```

## getColumnCount

```
int getColumnCount() throws SQLException
```

Gets the number of columns in the `ResultSet` object.

**RETURNS:**

an `int` indicating the number of columns in the `ResultSet` object.

**EXAMPLE:**
```
int n = rsmd.getColumnCount();
```

## getColumnDisplaySize

```
int getColumnDisplaySize(int column) throws SQLException
```

Gets the normal maximum width in characters for column *column*.

**PARAMETERS:**

*column*                    1 is the first column, 2 the second, and so on.

**RETURNS:**

an `int` indicating the maximum width in characters.

**EXAMPLE:**
```
int n = rsmd.getColumnDisplaySize(1);
```

## getColumnLabel

```
String getColumnLabel(int column) throws SQLException
```

Gets the suggested column title for column *column*, to be used in printouts and displays.

**PARAMETERS:**

*column*                1 is the first column, 2 the second, and so on.

**RETURNS:**

a `String` object representing the suggested column title for use in printouts and displays.

**EXAMPLE:**
```
String s = rsmd.getColumnLabel(2);
```

## getColumnName

```
String getColumnName(int column) throws SQLException
```

Gets the name of column *column*.

**PARAMETERS:**

*column*                1 is the first column, 2 the second, and so on.

**RETURNS:**

a `String` object representing the column name.

**EXAMPLE:**
```
String s = rsmd.getColumnName(4);
```

## getColumnType

```
int getColumnType(int column) throws SQLException
```

Gets the JDBC type (from the class `java.sql.Types`) for the value stored in column *column*.

**PARAMETERS:**

*column*                1 is the first column, 2 the second, and so on.

**RETURNS:**

an `int` indicating the JDBC type.

**EXAMPLE:**

```
int n = rsmd.getColumnType(1);
// if the first column is a JDBC VARCHAR, n will be 12, which is the
// int value assigned to VARCHAR in the class java.sql.Types
```

**SEE:**

```
java.sql.Types
```

## getColumnTypeName

String **getColumnTypeName**(int *column*) throws SQLException

Gets the type name used by this particular DBMS for the value stored in column *column*.

**PARAMETERS:**

*column*                1 is the first column, 2 the second, and so on.

**RETURNS:**

a `String` object representing the type name used by the database.

**EXAMPLE:**

```
String s = rsmd.getColumnTypeName(2);
```

## getPrecision

int **getPrecision**(int *column*) throws SQLException

For number types, `getPrecision` gets the number of decimal digits in column *column*. For character types, it gets the maximum length in characters for column *column*. For binary types, it gets the maximum length in bytes for column *column*.

**PARAMETERS:**

*column*                1 is the first column, 2 the second, and so on.

**RETURNS:**

an `int` indicating the number of decimal digits for number types, the maximum number of characters for character types, or the maximum number of bytes for binary types.

**EXAMPLE:**
```
int n = rsmd.getPrecision(1);
```

## getScale

```
int getScale(int column) throws SQLException
```

Gets the number of digits to the right of the decimal point for values in column *column*.

**PARAMETERS:**
*column*                1 is the first column, 2 the second, and so on.

**RETURNS:**
an `int` indicating the number of digits to the right of the decimal point.

**EXAMPLE:**
```
int n = rsmd.getScale(5);
```

## getSchemaName

```
String getSchemaName(int column) throws SQLException
```

Gets the schema name for the table from which column *column* of this `ResultSet` was derived.

**PARAMETERS:**
*column*                1 is the first column, 2 the second, and so on.

**RETURNS:**
a `String` object representing the schema name or "" if not applicable.

**EXAMPLE:**
```
String s = rsmd.getSchemaName(1);
```

## getTableName

```
String getTableName(int column) throws SQLException
```

Gets the name of the table from which column *column* of this `ResultSet` was derived, or "" if there is none (for example, for a join).

**PARAMETERS:**

*column*                    1 is the first column, 2 the second, and so on.

**RETURNS:**

a `String` object representing the table name or "" if not applicable.

**EXAMPLE:**

```
String s = rsmd.getTableName(3);
```

## isAutoIncrement

```
boolean isAutoIncrement(int column) throws SQLException
```

Checks whether column *column* is automatically numbered and thus read-only.

**PARAMETERS:**

*column*                    1 is the first column, 2 the second, and so on.

**RETURNS:**

`true` if so; `false` otherwise.

**EXAMPLE:**

```
boolean b = rsmd.isAutoIncrement(3);
```

## isCaseSensitive

```
boolean isCaseSensitive(int column) throws SQLException
```

Checks whether column *column* is case sensitive.

**PARAMETERS:**

*column*                    1 is the first column, 2 the second, and so on.

**RETURNS:**

`true` if so; `false` otherwise.

**EXAMPLE:**

```
boolean b = rsmd.isCaseSensitive(1);
```

## isCurrency

```
boolean isCurrency(int column) throws SQLException
```

Checks whether column *column* is a cash value.

**PARAMETERS:**
*column*                1 is the first column, 2 the second, and so on.

**RETURNS:**
true if so; false otherwise.

**EXAMPLE:**
```
boolean b = rsmd.isCurrency(3);
```

## isDefinitelyWritable

```
boolean isDefinitelyWritable(int column) throws SQLException
```

Checks whether a write on column *column* will definitely succeed.

**PARAMETERS:**
*column*                1 is the first column, 2 the second, and so on.

**RETURNS:**
true if so; false otherwise.

**EXAMPLE:**
```
boolean b = rsmd.isDefinitelyWritable(2);
```

## isNullable

```
int isNullable(int column) throws SQLException
```

Checks whether a NULL can be stored in column *column*.

**PARAMETERS:**
*column*                1 is the first column, 2 the second, and so on.

**RETURNS:**
one of the constants defined in ResultSetMetaData. Possible values are
| | |
|---|---|
| columnNoNulls | column does not allow Null values. |
| columnNullable | column allows NULL values. |
| columnNullableUnknown | nullability is unknown. |

**EXAMPLE:**
```
boolean b = rsmd.isNullable(2);
```

**SEE:**
```
    ResultSetMetaData.columnNoNulls
    ResultSetMetaData.columnNullable
    ResultSetMetaData.columnNullableUnknown
```

## isReadOnly

```
boolean isReadOnly(int column) throws SQLException
```

Checks whether column *column* is definitely not writable.

**PARAMETERS:**

*column*                1 is the first column, 2 the second, and so on.

**RETURNS:**
true if so; false otherwise.

**EXAMPLE:**
```
boolean b = rsmd.isReadOnly(3);
```

## isSearchable

```
boolean isSearchable(int column) throws SQLException
```

Checks whether the value stored in column *column* can be used in a WHERE clause.

**PARAMETERS:**

*column*                1 is the first column, 2 the second, and so on.

**RETURNS:**
true if so; false otherwise.

**EXAMPLE:**
```
boolean b = rsmd.isSearchable(1);
```

## isSigned

```
boolean isSigned(int column) throws SQLException
```

Checks whether the value stored in column *column* is a signed number.

**PARAMETERS:**
*column*                1 is the first column, 2 the second, and so on.

**RETURNS:**
true if so; false otherwise.

**EXAMPLE:**
```
boolean b = rsmd.isSigned(3);
```

## isWritable

```
boolean isWritable(int column) throws SQLException
```

Checks whether it is possible for a write on column *column* to succeed.

**PARAMETERS:**
*column*                1 is the first column, 2 the second, and so on.

**RETURNS:**
true if so; false otherwise.

**EXAMPLE:**
```
boolean b = rsmd.isWritable(2);
```

# 14.4  ResultSetMetaData Fields

## columnNoNulls

```
public final static int columnNoNulls = 0
```
A possible return value for the method isNullable.
Indicates that this column does not allow NULL values.

## columnNullable

```
public final static int columnNullable = 1
```
> A possible return value for the method isNullable.
> Indicates that this column allows NULL values.


## columnNullableUnknown

```
public final static int columnNullableUnknown = 2
```
> A possible return value for the method isNullable.
> Indicates that the nullability of this column is unknown.

# CHAPTER 15

# SQLException

## 15.1 SQLException Overview

THE class SQLException provides information about errors in accessing a database. It is derived from the more general class java.lang.Exception, which is in turn derived from Throwable. Methods that are defined with throws SQLException will use an instance of SQLException when they cause an error trying to access a database.

### 15.1.1 What an SQLException Object Contains

Each SQLException object contains the following kinds of information:

- a description of the error. This is a String object, which is used as the Java Exception message. It can be retrieved by calling the method getMessage, which is inherited from Throwable.

- an "SQLState" string. This is a String object identifying the exception, which follows the X/Open SQLState conventions. Values for the SQLState string are described in the X/Open SQL specification.

- an error code. This is an integer that is specific to each vendor. Normally this will be the actual error code returned by the underlying database.

- a chain to the next SQLException object. This can be used if there is more than one error.

The class SQLException defines four constructors for creating instances of SQLException, plus three methods for retrieving information and one method for setting the next exception.

The class SQLWarning, a subclass of SQLException, provides warnings about database access. The class DataTruncation, a subclass of SQLWarning, provides warnings about data being truncated.

### 15.1.2  Retrieving SQLException Information

Information is retrieved from an SQLException object by getting each of its components. The method getMessage (inherited from java.lang.Exception, which in turn inherited it from java.lang.Throwable) returns the description of the exception. Three methods defined in SQLException get the other components: getSQL-State gets the SQLState value, getErrorCode gets the exception code used by the database vendor, and getNextException retrieves the exception chained to this one.

The following code fragment, the catch block of a try . . . catch construction, illustrates getting the components of the first SQLException object and then getting any subsequent ones that are chained to it:

```
catch (SQLException ex) {
    // If an SQLException was generated, catch it and display the
    // error information. It is possible for there to be multiple
    // error objects chained together
    System.out.println ("\n--- SQLException caught---\n");
    while (ex != null) {
        System.out.println("SQLState: " + ex.getSQLState());
        System.out.println("Message:  " + ex.getMessage());
        System.out.println("Vendor code:   " + ex.getErrorCode());
        ex.printStackTrace(System.out);
        ex = ex.getNextException();
        System.out.println("");
    }
}
```

### 15.1.3  What an SQLException Means

When an SQLException is thrown, it does not always mean that the method that caused it to be thrown was not executed. This means that a programmer should not make any assumptions about the state of a transaction based on exceptions.

The safest course is to call the method `rollback` when there is any doubt and then to start again.

## 15.2  `SQLException` Class Definition

```
package java.sql;
public class SQLException extends java.lang.Exception {
    public SQLException(String reason, String SQLState, int vendorCode);
    public SQLException(String reason, String SQLState);
    public SQLException(String reason);
    public SQLException();
    public String getSQLState();
    public int getErrorCode();
    public SQLException getNextException();
    public synchronized void setNextException(SQLException ex);
}
```

## 15.3  `SQLException` Constructors

### SQLException

```
public SQLException(String reason, String SQLState, int vendorCode)
```

Constructs a fully specified `SQLException` object.

**PARAMETERS:**

| | |
|---|---|
| *reason* | a `String` object describing the exception. |
| *SQLState* | a `String` object containing an X/Open code identifying the exception. |
| *vendorCode* | an `int` indicating an exception code for a particular database vendor. |

**RETURNS:**
an `SQLException` object initialized with *reason*, *SQLState*, and *vendorCode*.

**EXAMPLE:**
```
throw new SQLException(
                "Operation invalid at this time", "S1011", 59);
```

## SQLException

public **SQLException**(String *reason*, String *SQLState*)

Constructs an SQLException object initialized with *reason* and *SQLState*. The vendor code is set to 0.

**PARAMETERS:**

*reason*          a String object describing the exception.

*SQLState*      a String object containing an X/Open code identifying the exception.

**RETURNS:**

an SQLException object initialized with *reason* , *SQLState*, and 0 for the vendor code.

**EXAMPLE:**

throw new SQLException("No suitable driver", "08001");

## SQLException

public **SQLException**(String *reason*)

Constructs an SQLException object initialized with *reason*. SQL state is set to null, and vendor code is set to 0.

**PARAMETERS:**

*reason*          a String object describing the exception.

**RETURNS:**

an SQLException object initialized with *reason*, null for the SQL state, and 0 for the vendor code.

**EXAMPLE:**

throw new SQLException("Unable to load JdbcOdbc.dll");

## SQLException

public **SQLException**()

Constructs a SQLException object with reason and SQL state set to null, and vendor code set to 0.

**RETURNS:**
an SQLException object initialized with null for the error message, null for the SQL state, and 0 for the vendor code.

**EXAMPLE:**
```
throw new SQLException();
```

## 15.4  SQLException Methods

The following methods are inherited from the class java.lang.Exception, which inherited them from the class java.lang.Throwable:

```
fillInStackTrace
getMessage
printStackTrace
toString
```

The following methods are defined in java.sql.SQLException:

### getSQLState

```
public String getSQLState();
```

Gets the SQL state for this SQLException object.

**RETURNS:**
a String object giving the SQL state.

**EXAMPLE:**
```
SQLException ex = new SQLException(
                  "Operation invalid at this time", "S1011", 59);
String s = ex.getSQLState(); // s = S1011
```

### getErrorCode

```
public int getErrorCode()
```

Gets the vendor-specific error code for this SQLException object.

**RETURNS:**
an int indicating the error code used by the vendor of this database.

**EXAMPLE:**
```
SQLException ex = new SQLException(
                      "Operation invalid at this time", "S1011", 59);
int n = ex.getErrorCode(); // n = 59
```

## getNextException

```
public SQLException getNextException()
```

Gets the next SQLException object chained to this one.

**RETURNS:**
the next SQLException object or null if there are no more.

**EXAMPLE:**
```
while(ex.getNextException() != null) {
    // print exceptions
}
```

## setNextException

```
public synchronized void setNextException(SQLException next)
```

Sets *next* as the next element in the exception chain. This method is normally used only by driver or tool writers.

**PARAMETERS:**

next                    an SQLException object that will become the new end
                        of the exception chain.

**EXAMPLE:**
```
SQLException next = new SQLException("No suitable driver", "08001");
ex.setNextException(next);
```

# CHAPTER 16

# SQLWarning

## 16.1 SQLWarning Overview

$\mathbf{T}$HE class SQLWarning provides information about database access warnings.

Warnings are silently chained to the object whose method caused the warning to be reported. Connection methods, Statement methods (including Prepared-Statement and CallableStatement methods), and ResultSet methods may all cause access warnings to be reported on the calling object. For example, a Connection object *con* would have a warning reported on it if a call to the method *con*.getConnection caused a database access warning. If a subsequent call to a method, for example, *con*.setTransactionIsolation, caused an access warning, it would be chained to the first warning reported on *con*.

Connection, Statement, and ResultSet have their own versions of the method getWarnings to retrieve the first SQLWarning object reported. Any subsequent warnings are retrieved by calling the SQLWarning method getNextWarning.

Note that executing a statement flushes warnings from the previous statement. This keeps warnings from building up and consequently forcing the user to manually clear warnings after each execution.

### 16.1.1 What an SQLWarning Object Contains

Each SQLWarning object contains the following kinds of information:

- a description of the warning. This is a String object that explains the warning.

- an "SQLState" string. This is a String object identifying the warning, which follows the X/Open SQLState conventions. Values for the SQLState string are described in the X/Open SQL specification.

- an error code. This is an integer that is specific to each vendor. Normally this will be the actual error code returned by the underlying database.

- a chain to the next SQLWarning object. This can be used if there is more than one warning.

The SQLWarning class defines four constructors for creating instances of SQL-Warning plus two methods for getting and setting the next warning.

### 16.1.2 Retrieving SQLWarning Information

Information is retrieved from an SQLWarning object by getting each of its components. The method getMessage (inherited from SQLException, which inherited it from java.lang.Exception, which in turn inherited it from java.lang.Throwable) returns the description of the warning. Methods defined in SQLException get two other components: getSQLState gets the SQLState value, and getErrorCode gets the warning code used by the database vendor. The method getNextWarning, defined in SQLWarning, retrieves the warning chained to this one.

The following code fragment defines a method that checks for and displays warnings. The while loop illustrates getting the components of the first SQLWarning object and then getting any subsequent ones that are chained to it:

```
private static boolean printWarnings (SQLWarning w) throws
                                         SQLException {
    // If an SQLWarning object was given, display the warning. It
    // is possible for there to be multiple warning objects chained
    // together.
    if (w != null {
        System.out.println("\n--- Warning---\n");
        while (w != null) {
            System.out.println("SQLState: " + w.getSQLState());
            System.out.println("Message:  " + w.getMessage());
            System.out.println("Vendor:   " + w.getErrorCode());
            w = w.getNextWarning();
            System.out.println("");
        }
    }
}
```

## 16.2  **SQLWarning** Class Definition

```
package java.sql;
public class SQLWarning extends java.sql.SQLException {
    public SQLWarning(String reason, String SQLState, int vendorCode);
    public SQLWarning(String reason, String SQLState);
    public SQLWarning(String reason);
    public SQLWarning();
    public SQLWarning getNextWarning();
    public void setNextWarning(SQLWarning nextw);
}
```

## 16.3  **SQLWarning**  Constructors

### SQLWarning

```
public SQLWarning(String reason, String SQLState, int vendorCode)
```

Constructs a fully specified SQLWarning object.

**PARAMETERS:**

| | |
|---|---|
| *reason* | a String object describing the warning. |
| *SQLState* | a String object containing an X/Open code identifying the warning. |
| *vendorCode* | an int indicating a warning code for a particular database vendor. |

**RETURNS:**
an SQLWarning object initialized with *reason*, *SQLState*, and *vendorCode*.

**EXAMPLE:**
```
SQLWarning w = new SQLWarning(
        "Attempt to revoke privilege not successful",  "01006", 5);
// w contains an SQLWarning object initialized with the message,
// "Attempt to revoke privilege not successful", the SQL state
// "01006", and the vendor code 5.
```

## SQLWarning

```
public SQLWarning(String reason, String SQLState)
```

Constructs an SQLWarning object initialized with *reason* and *SQLState,* and with the vendor code set to 0.

**PARAMETERS:**

*reason*              a String object describing the warning.

*SQLState*            a String object containing an X/Open code identifying the warning.

**RETURNS:**

an SQLWarning object initialized with *reason*, *SQLState.*, and 0 for the vendor code.

**EXAMPLE:**
```
SQLWarning w = new SQLWarning(
   "An error occurred during the requested disconnection", "01002");
```

## SQLWarning

```
public SQLWarning(String reason)
```

Constructs an SQLWarning object initialized with *reason*. The SQL state is set to null, and the vendor code is set to 0.

**PARAMETERS:**

*reason*              a String object describing the warning.

**RETURNS:**

an SQLWarning object initialized with *reason,* null for the SQL state, and 0 for the vendor code.

**EXAMPLE:**
```
SQLWarning w = new SQLWarning(
                  "Null value eliminated in set function");
```

## SQLWarning

```
public SQLWarning()
```

Constructs an `SQLWarning` object with the description and SQL state set to `null`. The vendor code is set to 0.

**RETURNS:**
an `SQLWarning` object initialized with `null` for the error message, `null` for the SQL state, and 0 for the vendor code.

**EXAMPLE:**
```
SQLWarning w = new SQLWarning();
```

## 16.4  SQLWarning Methods

The following methods are inherited from the class `java.lang.Exception`, which inherited them from the class `java.lang.Throwable`:

```
fillInStackTrace
getMessage
printStackTrace
toString
```

The following methods are inherited from the class `java.sql.SQLException`:

```
getSQLState
getErrorCode
```

The following methods are defined in the class `java.sql.SQLWarning`:

### getNextWarning

```
public SQLWarning getNextWarning()
```

Gets the next `SQLWarning` object chained to this one.

**RETURNS:**
the next `SQLWarning` object or `null` if there are no more warnings.

**EXAMPLE:**
```
while(w.getNextWarning() != null) {
    // print warnings
}
```

## setNextWarning

public void **setNextWarning**(SQLWarning *nextw*)

Adds an SQLWarning object to the end of the chain.

**PARAMETERS:**

*nextw*                         an SQLWarning object that will become the next warn-
                                ing in the warning chain.

**EXAMPLE:**

```
SQLWarning nextw = new SQLWarning(
                          "Null value eliminated in set function");
w.setNextWarning(nextw);
```

# CHAPTER 17

# Statement

## 17.1 Statement Overview

A Statement object is used to send SQL statements to a database. There are actually three kinds of Statement objects, all of which act as containers for executing SQL statements on a given connection: Statement, PreparedStatement, which inherits from Statement, and CallableStatement, which inherits from Prepared-Statement. They are specialized for sending particular types of SQL statements: A Statement object is used to execute a simple SQL statement with no parameters, a PreparedStatement object is used to execute a precompiled SQL statement with or without IN parameters, and a CallableStatement object is used to execute a call to a database stored procedure.

The Statement interface provides basic methods for executing statements and retrieving results. The PreparedStatement interface adds methods for dealing with IN parameters; CallableStatement adds methods for dealing with OUT parameters.

### 17.1.1 Creating Statement objects

Once a connection to a particular database is established, that connection can be used to send SQL statements. A Statement object is created with the Connection method createStatement, as in the following code fragment:

```
Connection con = DriverManager.getConnection(url, "sunny", "");
Statement stmt = con.createStatement();
```

The SQL statement that will be sent to the database is supplied as the argument to one of the execute methods on a Statement object. This is demonstrated in the following example, which uses the method executeQuery:

```
ResultSet rs = stmt.executeQuery("SELECT a, b, c FROM Table2");
```

### 17.1.2   Executing Statements Using Statement objects

The Statement interface provides three different methods for executing SQL statements, executeQuery, executeUpdate, and execute. The one to use is determined by what the SQL statement produces.

The method executeQuery is designed for statements that produce a single result set, such as SELECT statements.

The method executeUpdate is used to execute INSERT, UPDATE, or DELETE statements and also SQL DDL (Data Definition Language) statements like CREATE TABLE and DROP TABLE. The effect of an INSERT, UPDATE, or DELETE statement is a modification of one or more columns in zero or more rows in a table. The return value of executeUpdate is an integer (referred to as the update count) that indicates the number of rows that were affected. For statements such as CREATE TABLE or DROP TABLE, which do not operate on rows, the return value of executeUpdate is always zero.

The method execute is used to execute statements that return more than one result set, more than one update count, or a combination of the two. Because it is an advanced feature that the majority of programmers will never use, it is explained in its own section later in this overview.

All of the methods for executing statements close the calling Statement object's current result set if there is one open. This means that one needs to complete any processing of the current ResultSet object before re-executing a Statement object.

It should be noted that the PreparedStatement interface, which inherits all of the methods in the Statement interface, has its own versions of the methods executeQuery, executeUpdate and execute. Statement objects do not themselves contain an SQL statement; therefore, one must be provided as the argument to the Statement.execute methods. PreparedStatement objects do not supply an SQL statement as a parameter to these methods because they already contain a precompiled SQL statement. CallableStatement objects inherit the PreparedStatement forms of these methods. Supplying a parameter to the PreparedStatement or

CallableStatement versions of these methods will cause an SQLException to be thrown.

### 17.1.3  Statement Completion

When a connection is in auto-commit mode, the statements being executed within it are committed or rolled back when they are completed. A statement is considered complete when it has been executed and all its results have been returned. For the method executeQuery, which returns one result set, the statement is completed when all the rows of the ResultSet object have been retrieved. For the method executeUpdate, a statement is completed when it is executed. In the rare cases where the method execute is called, however, a statement is not complete until all of the result sets or update counts it generated have been retrieved.

Some DBMSs treat each statement in a stored procedure as a separate statement; others treat the entire procedure as one compound statement. This difference becomes important when auto-commit is enabled because it affects when the method commit is called. In the first case, each statement is individually committed; in the second, all are committed together.

### 17.1.4  Closing Statement Objects

Statement objects will be closed automatically by the Java garbage collector. Nevertheless, it is recommended as good programming practice that they be closed explicitly when they are no longer needed. This frees DBMS resources immediately and helps avoid potential memory problems. See "Using the Method close to Free DBMS Resources" on page 150 for more information.

### 17.1.5  SQL Escape Syntax in Statement Objects

Statement objects may contain SQL statements that use SQL escape syntax. Escape syntax signals the driver that the code within it should be handled differently. The driver will scan for any escape syntax and translate it into code that the particular database understands. This makes escape syntax DBMS-independent and allows a programmer to use features that might not otherwise be available.

An escape clause is demarcated by curly braces and a key word:

```
{keyword . . . parameters . . . }
```

The keyword indicates the kind of escape clause, as shown here.

**escape**   for LIKE escape characters

The percent sign (%) and underscore (_) characters work like wild cards in SQL LIKE clauses (% matches zero or more characters, and _ matches exactly one character). In order to interpret them literally, they can be preceded by a backslash (\), which is a special escape character in strings. One can specify which character to use as the escape character by including the following syntax at the end of a query:

```
{escape 'escape-character'}
```

For example, the following query, using the backslash character as an escape character, finds identifier names that begin with an underbar:

```
stmt.executeQuery("SELECT name FROM Identifiers
                WHERE Id LIKE '\_%' {escape '\'}");
```

**fn**   for scalar functions

Almost all DBMSs have numeric, string, time, date, system, and conversion functions on scalar values. One of these functions can be used by putting it in escape syntax with the keyword fn followed by the name of the desired function and its arguments. For example, the following code calls the function concat with two arguments to be concatenated:

```
{fn concat("Hot", "Java")};
```

The name of the current database user can be obtained with the following syntax:

```
{fn user()};
```

Scalar functions may be supported by different DBMSs with slightly different syntax, and they may not be supported by all drivers. Various DatabaseMetaData methods will list the functions that are supported. For example, the method get-NumericFunctions returns a comma-separated list of the names of numeric functions, the method getStringFunctions returns string functions, and so on.

The driver will either map the escaped function call into the appropriate syntax or implement the function directly itself. Refer to Appendix A, "Support Scalar Functions" on page 404 for a list of the scalar functions a driver is expected to support. A driver is required to implement these functions only if the DBMS supports them, however.

**d, t,** and **ts**   for date and time literals

DBMSs differ in the syntax they use for date, time, and timestamp literals. JDBC supports ISO standard format for the syntax of these literals, using an escape clause that the driver must translate to the DBMS representation.

For example, a date is specified in a JDBC SQL statement with the following syntax:

```
{d 'yyyy-mm-dd'}
```

In this syntax, yyyy is the year, mm is the month, and dd is the day. The driver will replace the escape clause with the equivalent DBMS-specific representation. For example, the driver might replace {d 1999-02-28} with '28-FEB-99' if that is the appropriate format for the underlying database.

There are analogous escape clauses for TIME and TIMESTAMP:

```
{t 'hh:mm:ss'}
{ts 'yyyy-mm-dd hh:mm:ss.f . . .'}
```

The fractional seconds (.f . . .) portion of the TIMESTAMP can be omitted.

**call** or **? = call**   for stored procedures

If a database supports stored procedures, they can be invoked from JDBC with the syntax shown below. Note that the square brackets ([ ]) indicate that what is between them is optional, and they are not part of the syntax.

```
{call procedure_name[(?, ?, . . .)]}
```

or, where a procedure returns a result parameter:

```
{? = call procedure_name[(?, ?, . . .)]}
```

Input arguments may be either literals or parameters. See "Numbering of Parameters" on page 132 for more information.

One can call the method `DatabaseMetaData.supportsStoredProcedures` to see if the database supports stored procedures.

**oj**    for outer joins

The syntax for an outer join is

```
{oj outer-join}
```

where `outer-join` is of the form

```
table LEFT OUTER JOIN [ table | outer-join ] ON search-condition
```

(Note that square brackets ([]) indicate that what is between them is optional; they are not part of the syntax.)

Outer joins are an advanced feature and are not supported by all DBMSs; consult the SQL grammar for an explanation of them. JDBC provides three `DatabaseMetaData` methods for determining the kinds of outer joins a driver supports: `supportsOuterJoins`, `supportsFullOuterJoins`, and `supportsLimitedOuterJoins`.

The method `Statement.setEscapeProcessing` turns escape processing on or off; the default is for it to be on. A programmer might turn it off to cut down on processing time when performance is paramount, but it would normally be turned on. It should be noted that the method `setEscapeProcessing` does not work for `PreparedStatement` objects because the statement may have already been sent to the database before it can be called. See `PreparedStatement` regarding precompilation.

### 17.1.6    Using the Method execute

The `execute` method should be used only when it is possible that a statement may return more than one `ResultSet` object, more than one update count, or a combination of `ResultSet` objects and update counts. These multiple possibilities for results, though rare, are possible when one is executing certain stored procedures or dynamically executing an unknown SQL string (that is, unknown to the application programmer at compile time). For example, a user might execute a stored procedure (using a `CallableStatement` object—see "CallableStatement" on page 129), and that stored procedure could perform an update, then a select, then an update, then a select, and so on. In more typical situations, someone using a stored procedure will already know what it returns.

Because the method `execute` handles the cases that are out of the ordinary, it is no surprise that retrieving its results requires some special handling. For instance, suppose it is known that a procedure returns two result sets. After using the method `execute` to execute the procedure, one must call the method `getResultSet` to get the first result set and then the appropriate `getXXX` methods to retrieve values from it. To get the second result set, one needs to call `getMoreResults` and then `getResultSet` a second time. If it is known that a procedure returns two update counts, the method `getUpdateCount` is called first, followed by `getMoreResults` and a second call to `getUpdateCount`.

Those cases where one does not know what will be returned present a more complicated situation. The method `execute` returns `true` if the result is a `ResultSet` object and `false` if it is a Java `int`. If it returns an `int`, that means that the result is either an update count or that the statement executed was a DDL command. The first thing to do after calling the method `execute` is to call either `getResultSet` or `getUpdateCount`. The method `getResultSet` is called to get what might be the first of two or more `ResultSet` objects; the method `getUpdateCount` is called to get what might be the first of two or more update counts.

When the result of an SQL statement is not a result set, the method `getResultSet` will return `null`. This can mean that the result is an update count or that there are no more results. The only way to find out what the `null` really means in this case is to call the method `getUpdateCount`, which will return an integer. This integer will be the number of rows affected by the calling statement or -1 to indicate either that the result is a result set or that there are no results. If the method `getResultSet` has already returned `null`, which means that the result is not a `ResultSet` object, then a return value of -1 has to mean that there are no more results. In other words, there are no results (or no more results) when the following is true:

```
((stmt.getResultSet() == null) && (stmt.getUpdateCount() == -1))
```

If one has called the method `getResultSet` and processed the `ResultSet` object it returned, it is necessary to call the method `getMoreResults` to see if there is another result set or update count. If `getMoreResults` returns `true`, then one needs to call `getResultSet` again to actually retrieve the next result set. As already stated, if getResultSet returns null, one has to call getUpdateCount to find out whether null means that the result is an update count or that there are no more results.

When getMoreResults returns false, it means that the SQL statement returned an update count or that there are no more results. So one needs to call the method getUpdateCount to find out which is the case. In this situation, there are no more results when the following is true:

```
((stmt.getMoreResults() == false) && (stmt.getUpdateCount() == -1))
```

The following code demonstrates an alternate way to be sure that one has accessed all the result sets and update counts generated by a call to the method execute. In this approach, the method getUpdateCount is called first to determine whether the result is (1) and update count, (2) a DDL command or an update with no rows affected, or (3) a result set or no more results.

```
stmt.execute(queryStringWithUnknownResults);
while (true) {
    int rowCount = stmt.getUpdateCount();
    if (rowCount > 0) {              // this is an update count
        System.out.println("Rows changed = " + count);
        stmt.getMoreResults();
        continue;
    }
    if (rowCount == 0) {             // DDL command or 0 updates
        System.out.println(" No rows changed or statement was DDL
                                                    command");
        stmt.getMoreResults();
        continue;
    }

    // if we have gotten this far, we have either a result set
    // or no more results

    ResultSet rs = stmt.getResultSet;
    if (rs != null) {
        // use metadata to get info about result set columns
        while (rs.next()) {
```

```
            // process results
            stmt.getMoreResults();
            continue;
        }
        break; // there are no more results
    }
```

## 17.2  Statement Interface Definition

```
public interface Statement {
    ResultSet executeQuery(String sql) throws SQLException;
    int executeUpdate(String sql) throws SQLException;
    void close() throws SQLException;
    SQLWarning getWarnings() throws SQLException;
    void clearWarnings() throws SQLException;
    int getMaxFieldSize() throws SQLException;
    void setMaxFieldSize(int max) throws SQLException;
    int getMaxRows() throws SQLException;
    void setMaxRows(int max) throws SQLException;
    void setEscapeProcessing(boolean enable) throws SQLException;
    int getQueryTimeout() throws SQLException;
    void setQueryTimeout(int seconds) throws SQLException;
    //----------------------------------------------------------------
    //                      Advanced features
    //----------------------------------------------------------------
    void cancel() throws SQLException;
    void setCursorName(String name) throws SQLException;
    boolean execute(String sql) throws SQLException;
    ResultSet getResultSet() throws SQLException;
    int getUpdateCount() throws SQLException;
    boolean getMoreResults() throws SQLException;
}
```

## 17.3  Statement Methods

### cancel

```
void cancel() throws SQLException
```

This method can be used by one thread to cancel a statement that is being executed by another thread if the driver and DBMS both support aborting an SQL statement.

**EXAMPLE:**
```
stmt.cancel(); // called from another thread to cancel stmt
```

### clearWarnings

```
void clearWarnings() throws SQLException
```

Clears the warnings reported for this Statement object. After a call to the method clearWarnings, a call to the method getWarnings will return null until a new warning is reported.

**EXAMPLE:**
```
stmt.clearWarnings();
```

### close

```
void close() throws SQLException
```

Releases a Statement object's database and JDBC resources immediately instead of waiting for this to happen when the Statement object is closed automatically during garbage collection.

It is recommended that Statement objects be closed explicitly when they are no longer needed, thereby freeing DBMS resources as soon as possible.

**EXAMPLE:**
```
stmt.close();
```

## execute

```
boolean execute(String sql) throws SQLException
```

Executes *sql*, an SQL statement that may return one or more result sets, one or more update counts, or any combination of result sets and update counts. It also closes the calling `Statement` object's current `ResultSet` if an open one exists.

In some rare situations, a single SQL statement may return multiple result sets and/or update counts. The method execute should be used instead of executeQuery or executeUpdate in such situations. This might be the case when one is executing a stored procedure that one knows may return multiple results. Execute might also be used when one is dynamically executing an unknown SQL string. Normally, however, one would use either the method executeQuery or executeUpdate.

A call to the method execute executes an SQL statement and returns `true` if the first result is a result set; it returns `false` if the first result is an update count. One needs to call either the method `getResultSet` or `getUpdateCount` to actually retrieve the result and then the method `getMoreResults` to move to any subsequent result(s).

**PARAMETERS:**

*sql*                         any SQL statement.

**RETURNS:**

`true` if the first result is a `ResultSet` or `false` if it is an integer.

**EXAMPLE:**

```
boolean b = stmt.execute(sqlStatementWithUnknownResults);
```

**SEE:**

the example code on page 350.

## executeQuery

```
ResultSet executeQuery(String sql) throws SQLException
```

Executes *sql*, an SQL statement that returns a single result set, and closes the calling `Statement` object's current `ResultSet` if an open one exists.

**PARAMETERS:**

*sql*                         typically an SQL SELECT statement.

**RETURNS:**

a ResultSet object representing the table of data (result set) produced by *sql*. It never returns null. An SQLException is thrown if an error occurs processing the SQL query.

**EXAMPLE:**
```
ResultSet rs = stmt.executeQuery("SELECT a, b, c FROM Table1");
```

## executeUpdate

```
int executeUpdate(String sql) throws SQLException
```

Executes an SQL INSERT, UPDATE, or DELETE statement that does not have parameter placeholders and closes the calling Statement object's current ResultSet if an open one exists.

This method may also be used to execute SQL statements that return nothing, such as SQL DDL statements (CREATE TABLE, DROP TABLE, CREATE INDEX, DROP INDEX, and so on).

This method may not be used to return a ResultSet object; if executeUpdate is given an SQL SELECT statement, it will throw an SQLException.

**PARAMETERS:**

*sql*                             an SQL INSERT, UPDATE, or DELETE statement or a DDL statement.

**RETURNS:**

an int indicating the number of rows affected by an INSERT, UPDATE or DELETE statement; 0 if no rows were affected or the statement executed was a DDL statement.

**EXAMPLE:**
```
Statement stmt = con.createStatement();
int x = stmt.executeUpdate("UPDATE Table2 SET m = 8 WHERE q = true");
    // x will be 0 or more, indicating the number of rows affected
int x = stmt.executeUpdate("DROP TABLE Table2");
    // x will be 0
```

## getMaxFieldSize

```
int getMaxFieldSize() throws SQLException
```

The maximum field size (in bytes) is set to limit the size of data that can be returned for any result set column value. This limit applies only to fields of type BINARY, VARBINARY, LONGVARBINARY, CHAR, VARCHAR, and LONGVARCHAR. If the limit is exceeded, the excess data is silently discarded.

For maximum portability, the maximum field size should be greater than 256. By default there is no limit.

**RETURNS:**
an int representing the current maximum number of bytes that a ResultSet column may contain; zero means that there is no limit.

**EXAMPLE:**
```
int x = stmt.getMaxFieldSize();
```

## getMaxRows

```
int getMaxRows() throws SQLException
```

The maxRows limit is the maximum number of rows that a ResultSet object may contain. If the limit is exceeded, the excess rows are silently dropped. By default there is no limit.

**RETURNS:**
an int representing the current maximum number of rows that a ResultSet object may contain; zero means that there is no limit.

**EXAMPLE:**
```
int x = stmt.getMaxRows();
```

## getMoreResults

```
boolean getMoreResults() throws SQLException
```

Moves to a Statement object's next result and implicitly closes any current ResultSet object (obtained by calling the method getResultSet). The method getMoreResults is used after a Statement has been executed with a

call to the method execute and the method getResultSet or getUpdateCount
has been called.

**RETURNS:**
true if the next result is a ResultSet object; false if it is an integer (indicating
that it is an update count or there are no more results). There are no more results when the following is true:

```
((getMoreResults() == false) && (getUpdateCount() == -1))
```

**EXAMPLE:**
boolean b = stmt.getMoreResults();

**SEE:**
execute() and getResultSet()
the example code on page 350.

## getQueryTimeout

```
int getQueryTimeout() throws SQLException
```

The query timeout limit is the number of seconds the driver will wait for a
Statement object to execute. If the limit is exceeded, an SQLException is
thrown. By default there is no limit.

**RETURNS:**
the current query timeout limit in seconds. Zero means that there is no time
limit.

**EXAMPLE:**
int x = stmt.getQueryTimeout();

## getResultSet

```
ResultSet getResultSet() throws SQLException
```

When the execute method has been used to execute a statement, the
method getResultSet must be called to actually retrieve the result. It should
be called only once per result.

**RETURNS:**

the current result as a ResultSet object; null if the result is an integer (indicating that the result is an update count or there are no more results).

**EXAMPLE:**
```
ResultSet rs = stmt.getResultSet();
```

**SEE:**
```
execute()
```
the example code on page 350.

## getUpdateCount

```
int getUpdateCount() throws SQLException
```

This method should be called only after a call to execute or getMoreResults, and it should be called only once per result.

If the method getUpdateCount returns an integer greater that zero, the integer represents the number of rows affected by a statement modifying a table. Zero indicates either that no rows were affected or that the SQL statement was a DDL command such as CREATE TABLE or DROP TABLE. A return value of -1 means that the result is a ResultSet object or that there are no more results.

The only way to tell for sure whether or not a return value of -1 indicates a result set is to call the method getResultSet. It will return a ResultSet object if there is one, and null otherwise. In other words, there are no more results under the following conditions:

```
((stmt.getUpdateCount() == -1) && (stmt.getResultSet() == null))
```

Another approach is to call the method getResultSet before calling getUpdateCount. If one has called getResultSet and determined that the result is not a result set (the return value is false), the method getUpdateCount can be called to determine whether the result is an update count or there are no more results. In this case, there are no more results when the following is true:

```
((stmt.getMoreResults() == false) && (stmt.getUpdateCount() == -1))
```

**RETURNS:**

(1) an int greater than 0 representing the number of rows affected by an update operation, (2) 0 meaning that no rows were affected or that the operation was a DDL command, or (3) –1 if the result is a ResultSet object or there are no more results.

**EXAMPLE:**

Note: for the purposes of this example, suppose that the argument *sqlStatementWithUnknownResult* is a string that has been returned from a procedure call and that the user does not know what it will return.

```
boolean b = stmt.execute(sqlStatementWithUnknownResult);
if (!b) {                       // result is not a ResultSet object
    int rowCount = stmt.getUpdateCount();
    if (rowCount > 0) {
        System.out.println("Number of rows updated = " + rowCount);
    } else if (rowCount == 0) {
        System.out.println("DDL command or no rows updated");
    } else {                             // rowCount == -1
        System.out.println("There are no results");
    }
}
```

**SEE:**
execute()
the example code on page 350.

## getWarnings

```
SQLWarning getWarnings() throws SQLException
```

Returns the first warning reported by calls on this Statement object. Subsequent warnings, if there are any, are chained to this first warning. A call to this method does not clear warnings.

The methods execute, executeQuery, and executeUpdate will clear a Statement object's warning chain. In other words, a Statement object's warning chain is automatically cleared each time it is (re)executed.

Warnings that are reported while a ResultSet object is being read will be chained on that ResultSet object rather than on the Statement object that generated the result set.

**RETURNS:**
the first SQLWarning or null if there are no warnings.

**EXAMPLE:**
SQLWarning w = stmt.getWarnings();

**SEE:**
SQLWarning.getNextWarning();

## setCursorName

void setCursorName(String *name*) throws SQLException

Sets to *name* the SQL cursor name that will be used by subsequent Statement execute methods. This name can then be used in SQL positioned update
and positioned delete statements to identify the current row in the ResultSet
object generated by this Statement object. If the database does not support
positioned updates or positioned deletes, this method does nothing.

Note that by definition, positioned updates and positioned deletes must be
executed by a different Statement object than the one which generated the
ResultSet object which is being used for positioning.

Also note that cursor names must be unique within a connection.

**PARAMETERS:**

*name*                        the new cursor name, which must be unique within a
                              connection.

**EXAMPLE:**
stmt.setCursorName("cursor1");

## setEscapeProcessing

void setEscapeProcessing(boolean *enable*) throws SQLException

Sets the Statement object's escape scanning mode to *enable*. When
*enable* is true (the default), the driver will scan for any escape syntax and do
escape substitution before sending the escaped SQL statement to the database.
When *enable* is false, the driver will ignore escaped SQL statements.

Note that this does not work for PreparedStatement objects because they
may have already been sent to the database for precompilation before being
called.

**PARAMETERS:**

*enable*                      either `true` to enable escape scanning or `false` to disable it.

**EXAMPLE:**

```
stmt.setEscapeProcessing(false); // disables escape scanning
```

## setMaxFieldSize

```
void setMaxFieldSize(int max) throws SQLException
```

Sets the maximum size for a column in a result set to *max* bytes.

This method sets the limit for the size of data (in bytes) that can be returned for any column value. The limit applies only to fields of type BINARY, VARBINARY, LONGVARBINARY, CHAR, VARCHAR, and LONGVARCHAR. If the limit is exceeded, the excess data is silently discarded. By default there is no limit.

For maximum portability, the maximum field size should be set to a value greater than 256.

**PARAMETER:**

*max*                      the new maximum column size limit in bytes. Zero means that there is no limit to the size of a column.

**EXAMPLE:**

```
stmt.setMaxFieldSize(1024);
```

## setMaxRows

```
void setMaxRows(int max) throws SQLException
```

Sets the limit for the maximum number of rows in a ResultSet object to *max*. If the limit is exceeded, the excess rows are silently dropped. By default there is no limit.

**PARAMETERS:**

*max*                      the new limit for the number of rows in a ResultSet. Zero means that there is no limit.

**EXAMPLE:**

```
stmt.setMaxRows(256);
```

## setQueryTimeout

```
void setQueryTimeout(int seconds) throws SQLException
```

Sets to *seconds* the time limit for the number of seconds a driver will wait for a `Statement` object to be executed. By default there is no limit.

**PARAMETERS:**

*seconds*  the new query timeout limit in seconds. Zero means that there is no time limit.

**EXAMPLE:**

```
stmt.setQueryTimeout(10);
```

# CHAPTER 18

# Time

## 18.1 Time Overview

THE class java.sql.Time provides a way to represent a JDBC TIME value. The class java.util.Date cannot be used because it contains both date and time information, and the type JDBC TIME contains only time information. To remedy this, java.sql.Time acts as a thin wrapper around java.util.Date, using only the time part. The class java.sql.Date works in a similar fashion, using only the date part of java.util.Date.

The JDBC Time class adds methods for formatting and parsing so that the JDBC escape syntax for time values can be used. See "SQL Escape Syntax in Statement Objects" starting on page 345.

### 18.1.1 Creating a Time Object

There are two ways to create a Time object. The first way is to use one of the constructors, and the second is to create one from a string using the method valueOf.

1. using a constructor to create a Time object :

```
Time t = new Time(18, 30, 0);
```

The variable t now contains a Time object that represents the time 6:30 p.m.

2. using the method valueOf to convert a string to a Time object:

```
Time t = Time.valueOf("18:30:00");
```

The variable t contains a `Time` object representing 6:30 p.m.

Technically, a `java.sql.Time` object includes the date component inherited from `java.util.Date`, and by default it is set to January 1, 1970. This date component is not accessible, however; a `java.lang.IllegalArgumentException` will be thrown if a `java.sql.Time` object invokes any of the following methods: `get-Year`, `getMonth`, `getDay`, `getDate`, `setYear`, `setMonth`, `setDate`.

## 18.2   Time Class Definition

```
package java.sql;
public class Time extends java.util.Date {
    public Time(int hour, int minute, int second);
    public Time(long milliseconds);
    public static Time valueOf(String s);
    public String toString();
}
```

## 18.3   Time Constructors

### Time

```
public Time(int hour, int minute, int second)
```

Constructs a `java.sql.Time` object initialized with *hour*, *minute*, and *second* to represent a time value that can be used as a JDBC TIME value.

Since `java.sql.Time` is a subclass of `java.util.Date`, it inherits the date component of `java.util.Date`. By default, the date is set to January 1, 1970, but it is not accessible from a `java.sql.Time` object. Trying to access a date component will cause an exception to be thrown.

**PARAMETERS:**

| | |
|---|---|
| *hour* | a Java int from 0 to 23. |
| *minute* | a Java int from 0 to 59. |
| *second* | a Java int from 0 to 59. |

**RETURNS:**

a `java.sql.Time` object representing a time.

**EXAMPLE:**
Time t = new Time(15, 45, 0); // t represents 3:45 p.m. exactly

## Time

public **Time**(long *milliseconds*)

Constructs a java.sql.Time object from *milliseconds*, a milliseconds time value, to represent a time value that can be used as a JDBC TIME value. Any date component of *time* will be ignored and replaced with January 1, 1970. Date components are not accessible from a java.sql.Time object.

**PARAMETERS:**

*milliseconds*          a long representing the number of milliseconds since January 1, 1970, 00:00:00 GMT.

**RETURNS:**
a java.sql.Time object representing a time.

**EXAMPLE:**
Time t = new Time(58930253); // t is 08:22:10

## 18.4  Time Methods

## toString

public String **toString**()

Formats the calling Time object as a String object with the format hh:mm:ss. The method Time.toString overrides the method Date.toString.

**RETURNS:**
A String object with the format "hh:mm:ss".

**EXAMPLE:**
Time t = new Time(15, 45, 0);
String s = t.toString(); // s contains "15:45:00"

**OVERRIDES:**
java.util.Date.toString

## valueOf

```
public static Time valueOf(String s)
```

Converts *s*, a formatted string, to a `Time` object. The method `Time.valueOf` overrides the method `Date.valueOf`.

**PARAMETERS:**

*s*                              a `String` object in the format "hh:mm:ss", where hh is hours, mm is minutes, and ss is seconds.

**RETURNS:**

a `Time` object representing the hours, minutes, and seconds specified in the `String` object *s*.

**EXAMPLE:**

```
String s = new String("15:45:00");
java.sql.Time t = java.sql.Time.valueOf(s);
```

**OVERRIDES:**

```
java.util.Date.valueOf
```

# CHAPTER 19

# Timestamp

## 19.1  **Timestamp** Overview

The class java.sql.Timestamp provides a way to represent a JDBC TIMESTAMP value. A JDBC TIMESTAMP value has date and time information and also a field for nanoseconds. (A nanosecond is a billionth of a second.) The class java.util.Date cannot be used as a JDBC TIMESTAMP value because although it contains both date and time information, it does not contain nanoseconds. To remedy this, java.sql.Timestamp extends java.util.Date, adding a field for nanoseconds. In other words, java.sql.Timestamp is a thin wrapper around java.util.Date and consists of two parts; one part is a java.util.Date, and the other part is a separate field for nanoseconds.

The JDBC Timestamp class adds methods for formatting and parsing so that the JDBC escape syntax for timestamp values can be used. See "SQL Escape Syntax in Statement Objects" starting on page 345. It also adds methods for getting and setting the nanoseconds field and for comparing two Timestamp objects.

### 19.1.1  Creating a **Timestamp** Object

There are two ways to create a Timestamp object. One is to use the constructor, and the second is to create one from a string using the method valueOf.

1. using the constructor to create a Timestamp object:

```
Timestamp ts = new Timestamp(99, 4, 31, 18, 30, 0, 345345345);
```

The variable ts now contains a Timestamp object that represents May 31, 1999 at 6:30 p.m. plus 345,345,345 billionths of a second (or 345 milliseconds).

2. using the method `valueOf` to convert a string to a `Timestamp` object:

```
Timestamp ts = Timestamp.valueOf("1999-05-31 18:30:00.9");
```

The variable `ts` contains a `Timestamp` object representing May 31, 1999 at 6:30 p.m. plus nine-tenths of a second (900 milliseconds).

## 19.2  `Timestamp` Class Definition

```
package java.sql;
public class Timestamp extends java.util.Date {
    public Timestamp(int year, int month, int day, int hour, int minute,
                                            int second, int nano);
    public Timestamp(long milliseconds);
    public static Timestamp valueOf(String s);
    public String toString();
    public int getNanos();
    public void setNanos(int n);
    public boolean equals(Timestamp ts);
    public boolean before(Timestamp ts);
    public boolean after(Timestamp ts);
}
```

## 19.3  `Timestamp` Constructors

### Timestamp

```
public Timestamp (int year, int month, int day, int hour, int minute,
                int second, int nano)
```

Constructs a `java.sql.Timestamp` object initialized with *year*, *month*, *day*, *hour*, *minute*, *second* and *nano* to represent a timestamp value that can be used as a JDBC `TIMESTAMP` value.

**PARAMETERS:**

| | |
|---|---|
| *year* | an `int` calculated by subtracting 1900 from the year. |
| *month* | an `int` from 0 to 11 (0 is January; 11 is December). |

| | |
|---|---|
| *day* | an int from 1 to 31, representing the day of the month. |
| *hour* | an int from 0 to 23, representing hours. |
| *minute* | an int from 0 to 59, representing minutes. |
| *second* | an int from 0 to 59, representing seconds. |
| *nano* | an int from 0 to 999,999,999, representing nanoseconds. |

**RETURNS:**

a java.sql.Timestamp object representing a timestamp.

**EXAMPLE:**

```
Timestamp ts = new Timestamp(100, 0, 1, 15, 45, 0, 999999999);
// ts represents one nanosecond before 3:45:01 p.m. on January 1,
// 2000
```

## Timestamp

```
public Timestamp (long milliseconds)
```

Constructs a java.sql.Timestamp object from *milliseconds*, a milliseconds time value. The integral seconds are stored in the underlying date value; the fractional seconds are stored in the nanos value.

Initialized with *year*, *month*, *day*, *hour*, *minute*, *second* and *nano* to represent a timestamp value that can be used as a JDBC TIMESTAMP value.

**PARAMETERS:**

| | |
|---|---|
| *milliseconds* | a long representing milliseconds since January 1, 1970, 00:00:00 GMT. |

**RETURNS:**

a java.sql.Timestamp object representing a timestamp.

**EXAMPLE:**

```
Timestamp ts = new Timestamp(58930253);
// ts represents 1970-01-01 08:22:10.253
```

## 19.4  `Timestamp` Methods

### after

```
public boolean after(Timestamp ts)
```

Tests the calling `Timestamp` object to see if it is later than `ts`.

**PARAMETERS:**

`ts`                 a `Timestamp` object with which to compare the calling `Timestamp` object.

**RETURNS:**
`true` if the calling `Timestamp` object is later than the given `Timestamp` object; `false` if they are equal or the calling `Timestamp` object is earlier than the given `Timestamp` object.

**EXAMPLE:**
```
Timestamp ts = new Timestamp(100, 0, 1, 15, 45, 0, 999999999);
Timestamp ts2 = new Timestamp(100, 0, 1, 15, 45, 0, 999999999);
boolean b = ts2.after(ts); // b = false
```

**OVERRIDES:**
`java.util.Date.after` to include the fractional seconds component of a `Timestamp` object.

### before

```
public boolean before(Timestamp ts)
```

Tests the calling `Timestamp` object to see if it is before `ts`.

**PARAMETERS:**

`ts`                 a `Timestamp` object with which to compare the calling `Timestamp` object.

**RETURNS:**
`true` if the calling `Timestamp` object is before the given `Timestamp` object; `false` if they are equal or the calling `Timestamp` object is after the given `Timestamp` object.

**EXAMPLE:**
```
Timestamp ts = new Timestamp(100, 0, 1, 15, 45, 0, 0);
Timestamp ts2 = new Timestamp(100, 0, 1, 15, 45, 0, 999999999);
boolean b = ts2.before(ts); // b = false
```

**OVERRIDES:**
java.util.Date.before to include the fractional seconds component of a
Timestamp object.

## equals

```
public boolean equals(Timestamp ts)
```

Tests the calling Timestamp object to see if it is equal to ts.

**PARAMETERS:**

ts                      a Timestamp object with which to compare the calling
                        Timestamp object.

**RETURNS:**
true if the two Timestamp objects are equal; false if they are not equal.

**EXAMPLE:**
```
Timestamp ts = new Timestamp(100, 0, 1, 15, 45, 0, 999999999);
Timestamp ts2 = new Timestamp(100, 0, 1, 15, 45, 0, 999999999);
boolean b = ts2.equals(ts); // b = true
```

**OVERRIDES:**
java.util.Date.equals to include the fractional seconds component of a
Timestamp object.

## getNanos

```
public int getNanos()
```

Retrieves the number of nanoseconds stored in the nanoseconds component of the calling Timestamp object.

**RETURNS:**
a Java int indicating the number of nanoseconds stored in the calling Timestamp object.

**EXAMPLE:**
```
Timestamp ts = new Timestamp(100, 0, 1, 15, 45, 0, 999999999);
int n = ts.getNanos(); // n = 999999999
```

## setNanos

```
public void setNanos(int n)
```

Sets the nanosecond value to *n*.

**PARAMETERS:**

*n*                    the new fractional seconds component.

**EXAMPLE:**
```
Timestamp ts = new Timestamp(100, 0, 1, 15, 45, 0, 999999999);
ts.setNanos(123456);
int n = ts.getNanos(); // n = 123456
```

## toString

```
public String toString()
```

Formats the calling `Timestamp` object as a `String` object with the format yyyy-mm-dd hh:mm:ss.f . . . . The method `Timestamp.toString` overrides the method `Date.toString`.

**RETURNS:**
a `String` object with the format "yyyy-mm-dd hh:mm:ss.f . . . ".

**EXAMPLE:**
```
Timestamp ts = new Timestamp(100, 0, 1, 15, 45, 0, 999999999);
String s = t.toString(); // s is "2000-01-01 15:45:00.999999999"
```

**OVERRIDES:**
```
java.util.Date.toString
```

## valueOf

```
public static Timestamp valueOf(String s)
```

Converts *s*, a formatted string, to a `Timestamp` object. The method `Timestamp.valueOf` overrides the method `Date.valueOf`.

**PARAMETERS:**

| | |
|---|---|
| *s* | a `String` object in the format "yyyy-mm-dd hh:mm:ss.f . . . ", where yyyy is year, mm is month, dd is day, hh is hours, mm is minutes, ss is seconds, and f is nanoseconds. |

**RETURNS:**

a `Timestamp` object representing the year, month, day, hours, minutes, seconds, and nanoseconds specified in the `String` object *s*.

**EXAMPLE:**

```
String s = new String("2000-01-01 15:45:00.999999999");
java.sql.Timestamp ts = java.sql.Timestamp.valueOf(s);
// ts contains a Timestamp object initialized with the values
// 100, 0, 1, 15, 45, 0, 999999999
```

**OVERRIDES:**

```
java.util.Date.valueOf
```

# CHAPTER 20

# Types

## 20.1 Overview of Class Types

THE class Types is simply a list of constants that are used to identify generic SQL types. These generic SQL type identifiers are called JDBC types, which distinguishes them from database-specific SQL types. See the overview section of "Mapping SQL and Java Types" on page 379 for a discussion of JDBC types and local DBMS types.

The class Types is never instantiated.

### 20.1.1 Using the Constants in Class Types

The constants defined in the class Types are used in various ways. They can be arguments supplied to methods or values returned in ResultSet objects.

For instance, one of the constants in java.sql.Types must be supplied as the second argument to the method CallableStatement.registerOutParameter. This method will register the specified OUT parameter with the given JDBC type. The value that the database assigns to this parameter must have the same JDBC type that is registered to this parameter. For example, if *cstmt* is a CallableStatement object, the following code registers the second parameter of its stored procedure as a JDBC SMALLINT. The value that the database assigns to the second output parameter will have a JDBC type of SMALLINT.

```
cstmt.registerOutParameter(2, Types.SMALLINT);
```

Note that in the definition of Types, SMALLINT is assigned the value 5, which is an int. Either SMALLINT or 5 can be used as the argument to a method, but it is generally considered good programming practice to use the name, which makes the meaning clear.

The method `DatabaseMetaData.supportsConvert` provides another example of using the constants in `Types` as method arguments. In this case, the two arguments represent the JDBC types to convert to and to convert from.

Another use of a `Types` constant is as a column value in the `ResultSet` object returned by a `DatabaseMetaData` method. For example, each row in the `ResultSet` object returned by the method `getTypeInfo` contains a `Types` constant and a description of that type as supported by a particular database.

### 20.1.2  Using the Constant OTHER

The constant `java.sql.Types.OTHER` indicates that the data type is not one of the standard JDBC types, but rather, an SQL type used only by this particular database. If an output parameter is registered with a JDBC type of `java.sql.Types.OTHER`, the value assigned to it gets mapped to a Java object, which can be accessed using the `CallableStatement.getObject` method.

This constant is one component of JDBC's support for dynamic database access. See "Dynamic Data Access" on page 391.

## 20.2  Types Class Definition

The class `Types` defines constants that are used to identify generic SQL types. The actual type constant values are equivalent to those in the X/Open CLI.

Since the class definition already contains complete information about its variables, they are not listed again in a separate "Fields" section.

```
package java.sql;
public class Types {
    public final static int BIT        = -7;
    public final static int TINYINT    = -6;
    public final static int SMALLINT   = 5;
    public final static int INTEGER    = 4;
    public final static int BIGINT     = -5;

    public final static int FLOAT      = 6;
    public final static int REAL       = 7;
    public final static int DOUBLE     = 8;
```

```
        public final static int NUMERIC       = 2;
        public final static int DECIMAL       = 3;

        public final static int CHAR          = 1;
        public final static int VARCHAR       = 12;
        public final static int LONGVARCHAR   = -1;

        public final static int DATE          = 91;
        public final static int TIME          = 92;
        public final static int TIMESTAMP     = 93;

        public final static int BINARY        = -2;
        public final static int VARBINARY     = -3;
        public final static int LONGVARBINARY = -4;

        public final static int NULL          = 0;

        public final static int OTHER         = 1111;
}
```

# CHAPTER 21

# Mapping SQL and Java Types

## 21.1 Overview

Since SQL datatypes and Java datatypes are not identical, there needs to be some mechanism for transferring data between an application using Java types and a database using SQL types.

To accomplish this, JDBC provides three sets of methods: (1) methods on the ResultSet class for retrieving SQL SELECT results as Java types, (2) methods on the PreparedStatement class for sending Java types as SQL statement parameters, and (3) methods on the CallableStatement class for retrieving SQL OUT parameters as Java types.

This section brings together information about datatypes affecting various classes and interfaces and puts all the tables showing the mappings between SQL types and Java types in one place for easy reference.

## 21.2 Mapping SQL Datatypes into Java

Unfortunately there are significant variations between the SQL types supported by different database products. Even when different databases support SQL types with the same semantics, they may give those types different names. For example, most of the major databases support an SQL datatype for large binary values, but Oracle calls this type LONG RAW, Sybase calls it IMAGE, Informix calls it BYTE, and DB2 calls it LONG VARCHAR FOR BIT DATA.

Fortunately, JDBC programmers will normally not need to concern themselves with the actual SQL type names used by a target database. Most of the time JDBC programmers will be programming against existing database tables, and they need not concern themselves with the exact SQL type names that were used to create these tables.

JDBC defines a set of generic SQL type identifiers in the class `java.sql.Types`. These types have been designed to represent the most commonly used SQL types. In programming with the JDBC API, programmers will normally be able to use these JDBC types to reference generic SQL types, without having to be concerned about the exact SQL type name used by the target database. These JDBC types are fully described in the next section.

The one major place where programmers may need to use SQL type names is in the SQL `CREATE TABLE` statement when they are creating a new database table. In this case programmers must take care to use SQL type names that are supported by their target databases. The table "Types Mapped to Database-specific SQL Types" on page 399 provides some suggestions for suitable SQL type names to be used for JDBC types for some of the major databases. We recommend that you consult your database documentation if you need exact definitions of the behavior of the various SQL types on a particular database.

If you want to be able to write portable JDBC programs that can create tables on a variety of different databases, you have two main choices. First, you can restrict yourself to using only very widely accepted SQL type names such as `INTEGER`, `NUMERIC`, or `VARCHAR`, which are likely to work for all databases. Or second, you can use the `java.sql.DatabaseMetaData.getTypeInfo` method to discover which SQL types are actually supported by a given database and select a database-specific SQL type name that matches a given JDBC type. This is what was done in the sample code application `SQLTypesCreate.java`. See "Getting Information about DBMS Types" on page 106 for an explanation of how to use the method `DatabaseMetaData.getTypeInfo`, and see "Sample Code 17 and 18" on page 117 for an explanation of `SQLTypesCreate.java`.

JDBC defines a standard mapping from the JDBC database types to Java types. For example, a JDBC `INTEGER` is normally mapped to a Java `int`. This supports a simple interface for reading and writing JDBC values as simple Java types.

The Java types do not need to be exactly isomorphic to the JDBC types; they just need to be able to represent them with enough type information to correctly store and retrieve parameters and recover results from SQL statements. For example, a Java `String` object does not precisely match any of the JDBC `CHAR` types, but it gives enough type information to represent `CHAR`, `VARCHAR`, or `LONGVARCHAR` successfully.

## 21.3  JDBC Types

This section describes the different JDBC datatypes and how they are related to standard SQL types and to Java types.

### 21.3.1  CHAR, VARCHAR, LONGVARCHAR

The JDBC types CHAR, VARCHAR, and LONGVARCHAR are closely related. CHAR represents a small, fixed-length character string, VARCHAR represents a small, variable-length character string, and LONGVARCHAR represents a large, variable-length character string.

The SQL CHAR type corresponding to JDBC CHAR is defined in SQL–92 and is supported by all the major databases. It takes a parameter that specifies the string length. Thus CHAR(12) defines a 12-character string. All the major databases support CHAR lengths up to at least 254 characters.

The SQL VARCHAR type corresponding to JDBC VARCHAR is defined in SQL–92 and is supported by all the major databases. It takes a parameter that specifies the maximum length of the string. Thus VARCHAR(12) defines a string whose length may be up to 12 characters. All the major databases support VARCHAR lengths up to 254 characters. When a string value is assigned to a VARCHAR variable, the database remembers the length of the assigned string and on a SELECT, it will return the exact original string.

Unfortunately there is no consistent SQL mapping for the JDBC LONGVARCHAR type. All the major databases support some kind of very large variable-length string supporting up to at least a gigabyte of data, but the SQL type names vary. See the table "Types Mapped to Database-specific SQL Types" on page 399 for some examples.

Java programmers do not need to distinguish among the three types of JDBC strings, CHAR, VARCHAR, and LONGVARCHAR. Each can be expressed as a Java String, and it is possible to read and write an SQL statement correctly without knowing the exact datatype that was expected.

CHAR, VARCHAR, and LONGVARCHAR could have been mapped to either String or char[], but String is more appropriate for normal use. Also, the String class makes conversions between String and char[] easy: There is a method for converting a String object to a char[] and also a constructor for turning a char[] into a String object.

One issue that had to be addressed is how to handle fixed-length SQL strings of type CHAR(n). The answer is that JDBC drivers (or the DBMS) perform appropriate padding with spaces. Thus, when a CHAR(n) field is retrieved from the data-base, the driver will convert it to a Java String object of length n, which may include some padding spaces at the end. Conversely, when a String object is sent to a CHAR(n) field, the driver and/or the database will add any necessary padding spaces to the end of the string to bring it up to length n.

The method ResultSet.getString, which allocates and returns a new String object, is recommended for retrieving data from CHAR, VARCHAR, and LONGVARCHAR fields. This is suitable for retrieving normal data, but can be unwieldy if the JDBC type LONGVARCHAR is being used to store multi-megabyte strings. To handle this case, two methods in the ResultSet interface allow programmers to retrieve a LONGVARCHAR value as a Java input stream from which they can subsequently read data in whatever size chunks they prefer. These methods are getAsciiStream and getUnicodeStream, which deliver the data stored in a LONGVARCHAR column as a stream of ASCII or Unicode characters.

## 21.3.2   BINARY, VARBINARY, LONGVARBINARY

The JDBC types BINARY, VARBINARY, and LONGVARBINARY are closely related. BINARY represents a small, fixed-length binary value, VARBINARY represents a small, vari-able-length binary value, and LONGVARBINARY represents a large, variable-length binary value.

Unfortunately, the use of these various BINARY types has not been standard-ized and support varies considerably among the major databases.

The SQL BINARY type corresponding to JDBC BINARY is a nonstandard SQL extension and is only implemented on some databases. It takes a parameter that specifies the number of binary bytes. Thus BINARY(12) defines a 12-byte binary type. Typically, BINARY values are limited to 254 bytes.

The SQL VARBINARY type corresponding to JDBC VARBINARY is a nonstandard SQL extension and is only implemented on some databases. It takes a parameter that specifies the maximum number of binary bytes. Thus VARBINARY(12) defines a binary type whose length may be up to 12 bytes. Typically, VARBINARY values are limited to 254 bytes. When a binary value is assigned to a VARBINARY variable, the database remembers the length of the assigned value and on a SELECT, it will return the exact original value.

Regrettably, there is no consistent SQL type name corresponding to the JDBC LONGVARBINARY type. All the major databases support some kind of very large vari-able length binary type supporting up to at least a gigabyte of data, but the SQL type names vary. See table "Types Mapped to Database-specific SQL Types" on page 399 for some examples.

BINARY, VARBINARY, and LONGVARBINARY can all be expressed identically as byte arrays in Java. Since it is possible to read and write SQL statements correctly without knowing the exact BINARY datatype that was expected, there is no need for Java programmers to distinguish among them.

The method recommended for retrieving BINARY and VARBINARY values is ResultSet.getBytes. If a column of type JDBC LONGVARBINARY stores a byte array that is many megabytes long, however, the method getBinaryStream is recommended. Similar to the situation with LONGVARCHAR, this method allows a Java programmer to retrieve a LONGVARBINARY value as a Java input stream that can be read later in smaller chunks.

### 21.3.3   BIT

The JDBC type BIT represents a single bit value that can be zero or one.

SQL–92 defines an SQL BIT type. However, unlike the JDBC BIT type, this SQL–92 BIT type can be used as a parameterized type to define a fixed-length binary string. Fortunately, SQL–92 also permits the use of the simple non-parameterized BIT type to represent a single binary digit, and this usage corresponds to the JDBC BIT type. Unfortunately, the SQL–92 BIT type is only required in "full" SQL–92 and is currently supported by only a subset of the major databases. Portable code may therefore prefer to use the JDBC SMALLINT type, which is widely supported.

The recommended Java mapping for the JDBC BIT type is as a Java boolean.

### 21.3.4   TINYINT

The JDBC type TINYINT represents an 8-bit unsigned integer value between 0 and 255.

The corresponding SQL type, TINYINT, is currently supported by only a subset of the major databases. Portable code may therefore prefer to use the JDBC SMALLINT type, which is widely supported.

The recommended Java mapping for the JDBC TINYINT type is as either a Java byte or a Java short. The 8-bit Java byte type represents a signed value from -128 to 127, so it may not always be appropriate for larger TINYINT values, whereas the 16-bit Java short will always be able to hold all TINYINT values.

### 21.3.5   SMALLINT

The JDBC type SMALLINT represents a 16-bit signed integer value between –32768 and 32767.

The corresponding SQL type, SMALLINT, is defined in SQL–92 and is supported by all the major databases. The SQL–92 standard leaves the precision of SMALLINT up to the implementation, but in practice, all the major databases support at least 16 bits.

The recommended Java mapping for the JDBC SMALLINT type is as a Java short.

### 21.3.6   INTEGER

The JDBC type INTEGER represents a a 32-bit signed integer value between –2147483648 and 2147483647.

The corresponding SQL type, INTEGER, is defined in SQL–92 and is widely supported by all the major databases. The SQL–92 standard leaves the precision of INTEGER up to the implementation, but in practice all the major databases support at least 32 bits.

The recommended Java mapping for the INTEGER type is as a Java int.

### 21.3.7   BIGINT

The JDBC type BIGINT represents a 64-bit signed integer value between –9223372036854775808 and 9223372036854775807.

The corresponding SQL type BIGINT is a nonstandard extension to SQL. In practice the SQL BIGINT type is not yet currently implemented by any of the major databases, and we recommend that its use should be avoided in portable code.

The recommended Java mapping for the BIGINT type is as a Java long.

### 21.3.8   REAL

The JDBC type REAL represents a "single precision" floating point number that supports seven digits of mantissa.

The corresponding SQL type REAL is defined in SQL–92 and is widely, though not universally, supported by the major databases. The SQL–92 standard leaves the precision of REAL up to the implementation, but in practice all the major databases supporting REAL support a mantissa precision of at least seven digits.

The recommended Java mapping for the REAL type is as a Java float.

### 21.3.9  DOUBLE

The JDBC type DOUBLE represents a "double precision" floating point number that supports 15 digits of mantissa.

The corresponding SQL type is DOUBLE PRECISION, which is defined in SQL–92 and is widely supported by the major databases. The SQL–92 standard leaves the precision of DOUBLE PRECISION up to the implementation, but in practice all the major databases supporting DOUBLE PRECISION support a mantissa precision of at least 15 digits.

The recommended Java mapping for the DOUBLE type is as a Java double.

### 21.3.10  FLOAT

The JDBC type FLOAT is basically equivalent to the JDBC type DOUBLE. We provided both FLOAT and DOUBLE in a possibly misguided attempt at consistency with previous database APIs. FLOAT represents a "double precision" floating point number that supports 15 digits of mantissa.

The corresponding SQL type FLOAT is defined in SQL–92. The SQL–92 standard leaves the precision of FLOAT up to the implementation, but in practice all the major databases supporting FLOAT support a mantissa precision of at least 15 digits.

The recommended Java mapping for the FLOAT type is as a Java double. However, because of the potential confusion between the double precision SQL FLOAT and the single precision Java float, we recommend that JDBC programmers should normally use the JDBC DOUBLE type in preference to FLOAT.

### 21.3.11  DECIMAL and NUMERIC

The JDBC types DECIMAL and NUMERIC are very similar. They both represent fixed-precision decimal values.

The corresponding SQL types DECIMAL and NUMERIC are defined in SQL–92 and are very widely implemented. These SQL types takes precision and scale parameters. The precision is the total number of decimal digits supported, and the scale is the number of decimal digits after the decimal point. The scale must always be less than or equal to the precision. So for example, the value "12.345" has a precision of 5 and a scale of 3, and the value ".11" has a precision of 2 and a scale of 2. JDBC requires that all DECIMAL and NUMERIC types support both a precision and a scale of at least 15.

The sole distinction between DECIMAL and NUMERIC is that the SQL–92 specification requires that NUMERIC types be represented with exactly the specified precision, whereas for DECIMAL types, it allows an implementation to add additional precision beyond that specified when the type was created. Thus a column created with type NUMERIC(12,4) will always be represented with exactly 12 digits, whereas a column created with type DECIMAL(12,4) might be represented by some larger number of digits.

The recommended Java mapping for the DECIMAL and NUMERIC types is java.math.BigDecimal, a Java type that also expresses fixed-point numbers with absolute precision. The java.math.BigDecimal type provides math operations to allow BigDecimal types to be added, subtracted, multiplied, and divided with other BigDecimal types, with integer types, and with floating point types.

The method recommended for retrieving DECIMAL and NUMERIC values is ResultSet.getBigDecimal. JDBC also allows access to these SQL types as simple Strings or arrays of char. Thus, Java programmers can use getString to receive a DECIMAL or NUMERIC result. However, this makes the common case where DECIMAL or NUMERIC are used for currency values rather awkward, since it means that application writers have to perform math on strings. It is also possible to retrieve these SQL types as any of the Java numeric types.

### 21.3.12  DATE, TIME, and TIMESTAMP

There are three JDBC types relating to time:

- The JDBC DATE type represents a date consisting of day, month, and year. The corresponding SQL DATE type is defined in SQL–92, but it is implemented by only a subset of the major databases. Some databases offer alternative SQL types that support similar semantics.

- The JDBC TIME type represents a time consisting of hours, minutes, and seconds. The corresponding SQL TIME type is defined in SQL–92, but it is implemented by only a subset of the major databases. As with DATE, some databases offer alternative SQL types that support similar semantics

- The JDBC TIMESTAMP type represents DATE plus TIME plus a nanosecond field. The corresponding SQL TIMESTAMP type is defined in SQL–92, but it is implemented by only a very small number of databases.

Because the standard Java class java.util.Date does not match any of these three JDBC date/time types exactly (it includes both DATE and TIME information but has no nanoseconds), JDBC defines three subclasses of java.util.Date to correspond to the SQL types. They are:

- java.sql.Date for SQL DATE information. The hour, minute, second, and millisecond fields of the java.util.Date base class are set to zero.

- java.sql.Time for SQL TIME information. The year, month, and day fields of the java.util.Date base class are set to 1970, January, and 1. This is the "zero" date in the Java epoch.

- java.sql.Timestamp for SQL TIMESTAMP information. This class extends java.util.Date by adding a nanosecond field.

All three of the JDBC time-related classes are subclasses of java.util.Date, and as such, they can be used where a java.util.Date is expected. For example, internationalization methods take a java.util.Date object as an argument, so they can be passed instances of any of the JDBC time-related classes.

A JDBC Timestamp object has its parent's date and time components and also a separate nanoseconds component. If a java.sql.Timestamp object is used where a java.util.Date object is expected, the nanoseconds component is lost. However, since a java.util.Date object is stored with a precision of one millisecond, it is possible to maintain this degree of precision when converting a java.sql.Timestamp object to a java.util.Date object. This is done by converting the nanoseconds in the nanoseconds component to whole milliseconds (by dividing the number of nanoseconds by 1,000,000) and then adding the result to the java.util.Date object. Up to 999,999 nanoseconds may be lost in this conversion, but the resulting java.util.Date object will be accurate to within one millisecond.

The following code fragment is an example of converting a java.sql.Timestamp object to a java.util.Date object that is accurate to within one millisecond:

```
Timestamp t = new Timestamp(100, 0, 1, 15, 45, 29, 987245732);
java.util.Date d;
d = new java.util.Date(t.getTime() + (t.getNanos() / 1000000));
```

## 21.4   Examples of Mapping

In any situation where a Java program retrieves data from a database, there has to be some form of mapping and data conversion. In most cases JDBC programmers will be programming with knowledge of their target database's schema. In other words, they know, for example, what tables the database contains and the datatype for each column in those tables. They can therefore use the strongly typed access methods in the interfaces ResultSet, PreparedStatement, and CallableStatement. This section presents three different scenarios, describing the data mapping and conversion required in each case.

### 21.4.1   Simple SQL Statement

In the most common case, a user executes a simple SQL statement and gets back a ResultSet object with the results. Each value returned by the database and stored in a ResultSet column will have a JDBC datatype. A call to a ResultSet.getXXX method will retrieve that value as a Java datatype. For example, if a ResultSet column contains a JDBC FLOAT value, the method getDouble will retrieve that value as a Java double. Table 21.6 on page 398 shows which getXXX methods may be used to retrieve which JDBC types. (A user who does not know the type of a ResultSet column can get that information by calling the method ResultSet.getMetaData.)

### 21.4.2   SQL Statement with IN Parameters

In another possible scenario, the user sends an SQL statement that takes input parameters. In this case, the user calls the PreparedStatement.setXXX methods to assign a value to each input parameter. For example, PreparedStatement.set-Long(1, 2345678) will assign the value 2345678 to the first parameter as a Java long. The driver will convert 2345678 to a JDBC BIGINT in order to send it to the database. Which JDBC type the driver sends to the database is determined by the standard mapping from Java types to JDBC types, shown in Table 21.2 on page 394.

### 21.4.3   SQL Statement with INOUT Parameters

In yet another scenario, a user wants to call a stored procedure, assign values to its INOUT parameters, retrieve values from a ResultSet, and retrieve values from the parameters. This case is rather uncommon and more complicated than most, but it gives a good illustration of mapping and data conversion.

In this scenario, the first thing to do is to assign values to the INOUT parameters using `PreparedStatement.setXXX` methods. In addition, since the parameters will also be used for output, the programmer must register each parameter with the JDBC type of the value that the database will return to it. This is done with the method `CallableStatement.registerOutParameter`, which takes one of the JDBC types defined in the class `Types`. A programmer retrieves the values stored in the output parameters with `CallableStatement.getXXX` methods.

The XXX type used for `CallableStatement.getXXX` must map to the JDBC type registered for that parameter. For example, if the database is expected to return an output value whose type is JDBC REAL, the parameter should have been registered as `java.sql.Types.REAL`. Then to retrieve the JDBC REAL value, the method `CallableStatement.getFloat` should be called (the mapping from JDBC types to Java types is shown in Table 21.1 on page 393). The method `getFloat` will return the value stored in the output parameter after converting it from a JDBC REAL to a Java `float`. To accommodate various databases and make an application more portable, it is recommended that values be retrieved from `ResultSet` objects before values are retrieved from output parameters.

The following code demonstrates calling a stored procedure named `getTestData`, which has two parameters that are both INOUT parameters and which also returns a normal JDBC `ResultSet`. First the `Connection` object *con* creates the `CallableStatement` object *cstmt*. Then the method `setByte` sets the first parameter to 25 as a Java byte. The driver will convert 25 to a JDBC TINYINT and send it to the database. The method `setBigDecimal` sets the second parameter with an input value of 83.75. The driver will convert this Java `BigDecimal` object to a JDBC NUMERIC value. Next the two parameters are registered as OUT parameters, the first parameter as a JDBC TINYINT and the second parameter as a JDBC NUMERIC with two digits after the decimal point. After *cstmt* is executed, the values are retrieved from the `ResultSet` object using `ResultSet.getXXX` methods. The method `getString` gets the value in the first column as a Java `String` object, `getInt` gets the value in the second column as a Java `int`, and the second `getInt` gets the value in the third column as a Java `int`.

Then `CallableStatement.getXXX` methods retrieve the values stored in the output parameters. The method `getByte` retrieves the JDBC TINYINT as a Java byte, and `getBigDecimal` retrieves the JDBC NUMERIC as a Java `BigDecimal` object with two digits after the decimal point. Note that when a parameter is both an input and an output parameter, the `setXXX` method uses the same Java type as the `getXXX` method (as in `setByte` and `getByte`). The `registerOutParameter` method

registers it to the JDBC type that is mapped from the Java type (a Java byte maps
to a JDBC TINYINT, as shown in Table 21.2 on page 394).

```
CallableStatement cstmt = con.prepareCall(
                                "{call getTestData(?, ?)}");
cstmt.setByte(1, 25);
cstmt.setBigDecimal(2, 83.75);
// register the first parameter as a JDBC TINYINT and the second
// as a JDBC NUMERIC with two digits after the decimal point
cstmt.registerOutParameter(1, java.sql.Types.TINYINT);
cstmt.registerOutParameter(2, java.sql.Types.NUMERIC, 2);
ResultSet rs = cstmt.executeQuery();
// retrieve and print values in result set
while (rs.next()) {
    String name = rs.getString(1);
    int score = rs.getInt(2);
    int percentile = rs.getInt(3);
    System.out.print("name = " + name + ", score = " + score);
    System.out.println(", percentile = " + percentile);
}
// retrieve values in output parameters
byte x = cstmt.getByte(1);
java.math.BigDecimal n = cstmt.getBigDecimal(2, 2);
```

To generalize, the XXX in CallableStatement.getXXX and CallableState-
ment.setXXX methods is a Java type. For setXXX methods, the driver converts the
Java type to a JDBC type before sending it to the database (using the standard
mappings shown in Table 21.2 on page 394). For getXXX methods, the driver converts the JDBC type returned by the database to a Java type (using the standard
mappings shown in Table 21.1 on page 393) before returning it to the getXXX
method.

The method registerOutParameter always takes a JDBC type as an argument, and the method setObject may take a JDBC type as an argument.

Note that if a JDBC type is supplied in its optional third argument, the method
setObject will cause an explicit conversion of the parameter value from a Java
type to the JDBC type specified. If no target JDBC type is supplied to setObject,
the parameter value will be converted to the JDBC type that is the standard mapping from the Java type (as shown in Table 21.2 on page 394). The driver will perform the explicit or implicit conversion before sending the parameter to the
database.

## 21.5   Dynamic Data Access

In most cases, the user wants to access results or parameters whose datatypes are known at compile time. However, some applications, such as generic browsers or query tools, are compiled with no knowledge of the database schema they will access. For this reason, JDBC provides support for fully dynamically typed data access in addition to static datatype access.

Three methods and one constant facilitate accessing values whose datatypes are not known at compile time:

- `ResultSet.getObject`

- `PreparedStatement.setObject`

- `CallableStatement.getObject`

- `java.sql.Types.OTHER` (used as an argument to `CallableStatement.regis-terOutParameter`)

If, for example, an application wants to be able to accept a variety of types as results in a `ResultSet` object, it can use the method `ResultSet.getObject`.

The methods `ResultSet.getObject` and `CallableStatement.getObject` retrieve a value as a Java `Object`. Since `Object` is the base class for all Java objects, an instance of any Java class can be retrieved as an instance of `Object`. However, the following Java types are built-in "primitive" types and are therefore not instances of the class `Object`: `boolean`, `char`, `byte`, `short`, `int`, `long`, `float`, and `double`. As a result, these types cannot be retrieved by `getObject` methods. However, each of these primitive types has a corresponding class that serves as a wrapper. Instances of these classes are objects, which means that they can be retrieved with the methods `ResultSet.getObject` and `CallableStatement.getObject`. Table 21.3 on page 395 shows the mapping from a JDBC type to a Java `Object` type. This table differs from the standard mapping from JDBC type to Java type in that each primitive Java type is replaced by its wrapper class, except that JDBC `TINYINT` and JDBC `SMALLINT` are mapped to the Java class `Integer`.

The method `getObject` can also be used to retrieve user-defined Java types. With the advent of abstract datatypes (ADTs) or other user-defined types in some database systems, some vendors may find it convenient to use `getObject` for retrieving these types.

## 21.6   Tables for Type Mapping

This section contains the following tables relating to JDBC and Java datatypes:

Table 21.1—JDBC Types Mapped to Java Types

Table 21.2—Java Types Mapped to JDBC Types

Table 21.3—JDBC Types Mapped to Java `Object` Types

Table 21.4—Java `Object` Types Mapped to JDBC Types

Table 21.5— Conversions by `setObject` from Java `Object` Types to JDBC  Types

Table 21.6—JDBC Types Retrieved by `ResultSet.getXXX` Methods

Table 21.7—JDBC Types Mapped to Database-specific SQL Types

### 21.6.1 JDBC Types Mapped to Java Types

| JDBC Type | Java Type |
|---|---|
| CHAR | String |
| VARCHAR | String |
| LONGVARCHAR | String |
| NUMERIC | java.math.BigDecimal |
| DECIMAL | java.math.BigDecimal |
| BIT | boolean |
| TINYINT | byte |
| SMALLINT | short |
| INTEGER | int |
| BIGINT | long |
| REAL | float |
| FLOAT | double |
| DOUBLE | double |
| BINARY | byte[] |
| VARBINARY | byte[] |
| LONGVARBINARY | byte[] |
| DATE | java.sql.Date |
| TIME | java.sql.Time |
| TIMESTAMP | java.sql.Timestamp |

**Table 21.1: JDBC Types Mapped to Java Types**

### 21.6.2   Java Types Mapped to JDBC Types

Table 21.2 shows the reverse mapping of Table 21.1, from Java types to JDBC types.

| Java Type | JDBC Type |
|---|---|
| String | CHAR, VARCHAR or LONGVARCHAR |
| java.math.BigDecimal | NUMERIC |
| boolean | BIT |
| byte | TINYINT |
| short | SMALLINT |
| int | INTEGER |
| long | BIGINT |
| float | REAL |
| double | DOUBLE |
| byte[] | BINARY, VARBINARY or LONGVARBINARY |
| java.sql.Date | DATE |
| java.sql.Time | TIME |
| java.sql.Timestamp | TIMESTAMP |

**Table 21.2:  Standard Mapping from Java Types to JDBC Types**

These are the conversions used for IN parameters before they are sent to the DBMS.

The mapping for String will normally be VARCHAR but will turn into LONGVAR-CHAR if the given value exceeds the driver's limit on VARCHAR values. The same is true for byte[] and VARBINARY and LONGVARBINARY values.

In most cases, the choice between CHAR and VARCHAR is not significant. In any case, drivers will just make the right choice. The same is true for the choice between BINARY and VARBINARY.

### 21.6.3  JDBC Types Mapped to Java Object Types

This table shows the mapping from JDBC types to Java object types that is used by the `getObject/setObject` methods.

| JDBC Type | Java Object Type |
|---|---|
| CHAR | String |
| VARCHAR | String |
| LONGVARCHAR | String |
| NUMERIC | java.math.BigDecimal |
| DECIMAL | java.math.BigDecimal |
| BIT | Boolean |
| TINYINT | Integer |
| SMALLINT | Integer |
| INTEGER | Integer |
| BIGINT | Long |
| REAL | Float |
| FLOAT | Double |
| DOUBLE | Double |
| BINARY | byte[] |
| VARBINARY | byte[] |
| LONGVARBINARY | byte[] |
| DATE | java.sql.Date |
| TIME | java.sql.Time |
| TIMESTAMP | java.sql.Timestamp |

**Table 21.3:  Mapping from JDBC Types to Java Object Types**

## 21.6.4  Java Object Types Mapped to JDBC Types

| Java Object Type | JDBC Type |
|---|---|
| String | CHAR, VARCHAR or LONGVARCHAR |
| java.math.BigDecimal | NUMERIC |
| Boolean | BIT |
| Integer | INTEGER |
| Long | BIGINT |
| Float | REAL |
| Double | DOUBLE |
| byte[] | BINARY, VARBINARY or LONGVARBINARY |
| java.sql.Date | DATE |
| java.sql.Time | TIME |
| java.sql.Timestamp | TIMESTAMP |

**Table 21.4:  Mapping from Java Object Types to JDBC Types**

Note that the mapping for String will normally be VARCHAR but will turn into LONGVARCHAR if the given value exceeds the driver's limit on VARCHAR values. The case is similar for byte[] and VARBINARY and LONGVARBINARY values.

### 21.6.5   Conversions by `setObject`

| | TINYINT | SMALLINT | INTEGER | BIGINT | REAL | FLOAT | DOUBLE | DECIMAL | NUMERIC | BIT | CHAR | VARCHAR | LONGVARCHAR | BINARY | VARBINARY | LONGVARBINARY | DATE | TIME | TIMESTAMP |
|---|---|---|---|---|---|---|---|---|---|---|---|---|---|---|---|---|---|---|---|
| String | x | x | x | x | x | x | x | x | x | x | x | x | x | x | x | x | x | x | x |
| java.math.Big Decimal | x | x | x | x | x | x | x | x | x | x | x | x | x | | | | | | |
| Boolean | x | x | x | x | x | x | x | x | x | x | x | x | x | | | | | | |
| Integer | x | x | x | x | x | x | x | x | x | x | x | x | x | | | | | | |
| Long | x | x | x | x | x | x | x | x | x | x | x | x | x | | | | | | |
| Float | x | x | x | x | x | x | x | x | x | x | x | x | x | | | | | | |
| Double | x | x | x | x | x | x | x | x | x | x | x | x | x | | | | | | |
| byte[] | | | | | | | | | | | | | | x | x | x | | | |
| java.sql.Date | | | | | | | | | | | x | x | x | | | | x | | x |
| java.sql.Time | | | | | | | | | | | x | x | x | | | | | x | |
| java.sql.Time-stamp | | | | | | | | | | | x | x | x | | | | x | x | x |

**Table 21.5:  Conversions Performed by `setObject` Between Java Object Types and Target JDBC Types**

An "x" means that the given Java object type may be converted to the given JDBC type. Note that some conversions may fail at runtime if the value presented is invalid.

### 21.6.6   Types Retrieved by `ResultSet.getXXX` Methods

| | TINYINT | SMALLINT | INTEGER | BIGINT | REAL | FLOAT | DOUBLE | DECIMAL | NUMERIC | BIT | CHAR | VARCHAR | LONGVARCHAR | BINARY | VARBINARY | LONGVARBINARY | DATE | TIME | TIMESTAMP |
|---|---|---|---|---|---|---|---|---|---|---|---|---|---|---|---|---|---|---|---|
| getByte | **X** | x | x | x | x | x | x | x | x | x | x | x | x | | | | | | |
| getShort | x | **X** | x | x | x | x | x | x | x | x | x | x | x | | | | | | |
| getInt | x | x | **X** | x | x | x | x | x | x | x | x | x | x | | | | | | |
| getLong | x | x | x | **X** | x | x | x | x | x | x | x | x | x | | | | | | |
| getFloat | x | x | x | x | **X** | x | x | x | x | x | x | x | x | | | | | | |
| getDouble | x | x | x | x | x | **X** | **X** | x | x | x | x | x | x | | | | | | |
| getBigDecimal | x | x | x | x | x | x | x | **X** | **X** | x | x | x | x | | | | | | |
| getBoolean | x | x | x | x | x | x | x | x | x | **X** | x | x | x | | | | | | |
| getString | x | x | x | x | x | x | x | x | x | x | **X** | **X** | x | x | x | x | x | x | x |
| getBytes | | | | | | | | | | | | | | **X** | **X** | x | | | |
| getDate | | | | | | | | | | | x | x | x | | | | **X** | | x |
| getTime | | | | | | | | | | | x | x | x | | | | | **X** | x |
| getTimestamp | | | | | | | | | | | x | x | x | | | | x | x | **X** |
| getAsciiStream | | | | | | | | | | | x | x | **X** | x | x | x | | | |
| getUnicodeStream | | | | | | | | | | | x | x | **X** | x | x | x | | | |
| getBinaryStream | | | | | | | | | | | | | | x | x | **X** | | | |
| getObject | x | x | x | x | x | x | x | x | x | x | x | x | x | x | x | x | x | x | x |

### Table 21.6:  Use of `getXXX` Methods to Retrieve JDBC Datatypes

An "x" means that the method can retrieve the JDBC type. An "X" means that the method is recommended for that JDBC type.

### 21.6.7  Types Mapped to Database-specific SQL Types

There is considerable variation among the different SQL types supported by the different databases. Table 21.7 shows for various major databases the database-specific SQL types that best match the JDBC types. The presence of a database-specific type name indicates that the given type can be used to achieve the semantics of the corresponding JDBC type, though the database-specific type may also provide additional semantics.

Notes and Lamentations:

1. Some databases provide extra precision for some integral and floating-point types.

2. Some databases provide a DATE or DATETIME type that can be used to contain either a DATE or a TIME or both.

3. VARCHAR and VARCHAR2 are currently synonyms in Oracle7.

4. For LONGVARCHAR, DB2 also supports "CLOB(n)" with a limit of 2 gigabytes.

5. For LONGVARBINARY, DB2 also supports "BLOB(n)" with a limit of 2 gigabytes.

6. Handling of BINARY, VARBINARY, and LONGVARBINARY literals in SQL statements varies widely among databases. We recommend using PreparedStatement.setBytes to set values in a portable way.

7. Handling of DATE, TIME, and TIMESTAMP literals in SQL statements varies widely among databases. We recommend using the JDBC SQL escape syntax for dates and times (see "SQL Escape Syntax in Statement Objects" on page 345) to set Date, Time, and Timestamp values in a portable way.

## Table 21.7: JDBC Types Mapped to Database-specific SQL Types

| JDBC Type Name | Oracle 7.2 | Sybase 11.0 | Informix 7.12 | IBM DB2 2.1 | Microsoft SQL Server 6.5 | Microsoft Access 7.0 | Sybase SQL Anywhere 5.5 |
|---|---|---|---|---|---|---|---|
| BIT | | BIT | | | BIT | BIT | BIT |
| TINYINT | | TINYINT | | | TINYINT | BYTE | TINYINT |
| SMALLINT | SMALLINT | SMALLINT | SMALLINT | SMALLINT | SMALLINT | SMALLINT | SMALLINT |
| INTEGER | INTEGER | INTEGER | INTEGER | INTEGER | INTEGER | INTEGER | INTEGER |
| BIGINT | | | | | | | |
| REAL | REAL | REAL | REAL | | REAL | REAL | REAL |
| FLOAT | FLOAT | FLOAT | FLOAT | FLOAT | FLOAT | FLOAT | FLOAT |
| DOUBLE | DOUBLE PRECISION | DOUBLE PRECISION | DOUBLE PRECISION | DOUBLE PRECISION | DOUBLE PRECISION | DOUBLE | DOUBLE PRECISION |
| NUMERIC(p,s) | NUMERIC(p,s) | NUMERIC(p,s) | NUMERIC(p,s) | NUMERIC(p,s) | NUMERIC(p,s) | | NUMERIC(p,s) |
| DECIMAL(p,s) | DECIMAL(p,s) | DECIMAL(p,s) | DECIMAL(p,s) | DECIMAL(p,s) | DECIMAL(p,s) | | DECIMAL(p,s) |
| CHAR(n) | CHAR(n) n <= 255 | CHAR(n) n <= 255 | CHAR(n) n <= 32767 | CHAR(n) n <= 254 | CHAR(n) n <= 255 | CHAR(n) n <= 255 | CHAR(n) n <= 32,767 |
| VARCHAR(n) | VARCHAR(n) n <= 2000 | VARCHAR(n) n <= 255 | VARCHAR(n) n <= 255 | VARCHAR(n) n <= 4000 | VARCHAR(n) n <= 255 | VARCHAR(n) n <= 255 | VARCHAR(n) n <= 32,767 |
| LONGVARCHAR | LONG VARCHAR limit is 2 Gigabytes | TEXT limit is 2 Gigabytes | TEXT limit is 2 Gigabytes | LONG VARCHAR limit is 32,700 bytes | TEXT limit is 2 Gigabytes | LONGTEXT limit is 1.2 Gigabytes | LONG VARCHAR limit is 2 Gigabytes |
| BINARY(n) | | BINARY(n) n <= 255 | | CHAR(n) FOR BIT DATA n <= 254 | BINARY(n) n <= 255 | BINARY(n) n <= 255 | BINARY n <= 32,767 |
| VARBINARY | RAW(n) n <= 255 | VARBINARY(n) n <= 255 | | VARCHAR(n) FOR BIT DATA n <= 4000 | VARBINARY(n) n <= 255 | VARBINARY(n) n <= 255 | |
| LONGVARBINARY | LONG RAW limit is 2 Gigabytes | IMAGE limit is 2 Gigabytes | BYTE limit is 2 Gigabytes | LONG VARCHAR FOR BIT DATA limit is 32,700 bytes | IMAGE limit is 2 Gigabytes | LONGBINARY limit is 1.2 Gigabytes | IMAGE limit is 2 Gigabytes |
| DATE | DATE | DATETIME | DATE | DATE | | DATE | DATE |
| TIME | DATE | DATETIME | | TIME | | TIME | TIME |
| TIMESTAMP | | | | TIMESTAMP | DATETIME | | TIMESTAMP |

# For Driver Writers

T HIS appendix contains information of interest mainly to driver developers.

As far as possible, there should be a standard JDBC API that works in a uniform way across all databases. To this end, JDBC imposes some requirements that apply to all drivers. However, it is unavoidable that different databases support different SQL features and provide different semantics for some operations. Consequently, JDBC allows some variations in particular situations.

Appendix A outlines JDBC requirements and allowed variations, addresses some implementation issues, and lists security responsibilities of drivers.

## A.1   Requirements for All Drivers

### A.1.1   Implement All Methods in the Interfaces

All of the methods in the interfaces contained in the package `java.sql` must be implemented so that they support at least ANSI SQL–92 Entry Level. These interfaces are listed below in alphabetical order:

- `java.sql.CallableStatement`
- `java.sql.Connection`
- `java.sql.DatabaseMetaData`
- `java.sql.Driver`
- `java.sql.PreparedStatement`
- `java.sql.ResultSet`
- `java.sql.ResultSetMetaData`
- `java.sql.Statement`

The fully implemented classes in the JDBC API are listed here for reference:

- `java.sql.DataTruncation`
- `java.sql.Date`
- `java.sql.DriverManager`
- `java.sql.DriverPropertyInfo`
- `java.sql.SQLException`
- `java.sql.SQLWarning`
- `java.sql.Time`
- `java.sql.Timestamp`
- `java.sql.Types`

A test suite is provided with the JDBC API to help driver developers test whether their drivers conform to JDBC requirements. Only drivers that pass the tests in this suite can be designated JDBC Compliant.

In addition to implementing all of the methods in the interfaces, a JDBC driver must also comply with the requirements presented in the following sections.

### A.1.2   Implement a Special Static Section

Every `Driver` class should contain a static section that does two things when it is loaded:

- creates an instance of itself.

- registers the newly created instance by calling the method `DriverManager.registerDriver`.

This is demonstrated in the following code fragment:

```
public class MyDriver implements java.sql.Driver {
    static {
        java.sql.DriverManager.registerDriver(new MyDriver());
    }
      . . .
}
```

When the driver is implemented to do these two things, a user can load and register a driver simply by calling the method `Class.forName` with the driver class name as the argument. See the section "Loading and Registering a Driver" on page 257 for more information.

### A.1.3   Support Extensions to SQL–92 Entry Level

Certain SQL features beyond SQL–92 Entry Level are widely supported and are desirable to include as part of the JDBC compliance definition so that applications can depend on the portability of these features. However, SQL–92 Transitional Level, the next higher level of SQL compliance defined by ANSI, is not widely supported. Even where Transitional Level semantics are supported, the syntax is often different across DBMSs.

Therefore, JDBC defines two kinds of extensions to SQL–92 Entry Level that must be supported by a JDBC Compliant driver:

- Selective Transitional Level syntax and semantics. Currently the only feature at this level that is required for JDBC compliance is the command `DROP TABLE`.

- An escape syntax that supports the Selective Transitional Level semantics. A driver should scan for and translate this escape syntax into DBMS-specific syntax. Note that these escapes need only be supported where the underlying database supports the corresponding Transitional Level semantics. Where appropriate, an escape syntax must be included for stored procedures, time and date literals, scalar functions, `LIKE` escape characters, and outer joins. These escapes are described in the section "SQL Escape Syntax in Statement Objects" on page 345.

JDBC supports the same DBMS-independent escape syntax as ODBC for stored procedures, scalar functions, dates, times, and outer joins. By mapping this escape syntax into DBMS-specific syntax, a driver allows portability of application programs that require these features.

This ODBC-compatible escape syntax is in general *not* the same as has been adopted by ANSI in SQL–92 Transitional Level for the same functionality. In cases where all of the desired DBMSs support the standard SQL–92 syntax, the user is encouraged to use that syntax instead of these escapes. When enough DBMSs support the more advanced SQL–92 syntax and semantics, these escapes should no longer be necessary. In the meantime, however, JDBC drivers should support them.

An ODBC driver that supports ODBC Core SQL as defined by Microsoft complies with JDBC SQL as defined here.

### A.1.4    Support Scalar Functions

Support for scalar functions needs some extra explanation. JDBC supports numeric, string, time, date, system, and conversion functions on scalar values. For those who want more detail than is provided in the section "SQL Escape Syntax in Statement Objects" on page 345, the X/Open CLI specification provides more information on the semantics of the scalar functions. The functions supported are listed below for reference.

If a DBMS supports a scalar function, the driver should also. Because scalar functions are supported by different DBMSs with slightly different syntax, it is the driver's job either to map them into the appropriate syntax or to implement the functions directly in the driver.

A user should be able to find out which functions are supported by calling metadata methods. For example, the method `DatabaseMetaData.getNumericFunctions` should return a comma separated list of the names of the numeric functions supported. Similarly, the method `DatabaseMetaData.getStringFunctions` should return a list of string functions supported, and so on.

The scalar functions are listed by category:

## NUMERIC FUNCTIONS

| Function Name | Function Returns |
|---|---|
| `ABS(number)` | Absolute value of `number` |
| `ACOS(float)` | Arccosine, in radians, of `float` |
| `ASIN(float)` | Arcsine, in radians, of `float` |
| `ATAN(float)` | Arctangent, in radians, of `float` |
| `ATAN2(float1, float2)` | Arctangent, in radians, of `float2` / `float1` |
| `CEILING(number)` | Smallest integer >= `number` |
| `COS(float)` | Cosine of `float` radians |
| `COT(float)` | Cotangent of `float` radians |
| `DEGREES(number)` | Degrees in `number` radians |
| `EXP(float)` | Exponential function of `float` |
| `FLOOR(number)` | Largest integer <= `number` |
| `LOG(float)` | Base e logarithm of `float` |
| `LOG10(float)` | Base 10 logarithm of `float` |
| `MOD(integer1, integer2)` | Remainder for `integer1` / `integer2` |
| `PI()` | The constant `pi` |
| `POWER(number, power)` | `number` raised to (integer) power |

| | |
|---|---|
| RADIANS(number) | Radians in number degrees |
| RAND(integer) | Random floating point for seed integer |
| ROUND(number, places) | number rounded to places places |
| SIGN(number) | -1 to indicate number is $< 0$; <br> 0 to indicate number is $= 0$; <br> 1 to indicate number is $> 0$ |
| SIN(float) | Sine of float radians |
| SQRT(float) | Square root of float |
| TAN(float) | Tangent of float radians |
| TRUNCATE(number, places) | number truncated to places places |

## STRING FUNCTIONS

| Function Name | Function Returns |
|---|---|
| ASCII(string) | Integer representing the ASCII code value of the leftmost character in string |
| CHAR(code) | Character with ASCII code value code, where code is between 0 and 255 |
| CONCAT(string1, string2) | Character string formed by appending string2 to string1; if a string is null, the result is DBMS-dependent |
| DIFFERENCE(string1, string2) | Integer indicating the difference between the values returned by the function SOUNDEX for string1 and string2 |
| INSERT(string1, start, length, string2) | A character string formed by deleting length characters from string1 beginning at start, and inserting string2 into string1 at start |
| LCASE(string) | Converts all uppercase characters in string to lowercase |
| LEFT(string, count) | The count leftmost characters from string |
| LENGTH(string) | Number of characters in string, excluding trailing blanks |
| LOCATE(string1, string2[, start]) | Position in string2 of the first occurrence of string1, searching from the beginning of string2; if start is specified, the search begins from position start. 0 is returned if string2 does not contain string1. Position 1 is the first character in string2. |
| LTRIM(string) | Characters of string with leading blank spaces removed |

| | |
|---|---|
| REPEAT(string, count) | A character string formed by repeating string count times |
| REPLACE(string1, string2, string3) | Replaces all occurrences of string2 in string1 with string3 |
| RIGHT(string, count) | The count rightmost characters in string |
| RTRIM(string) | The characters of string with no trailing blanks |
| SOUNDEX(string) | A character string, which is data source-dependent, representing the sound of the words in string; this could be a four-digit SOUNDEX code, a phonetic representation of each word, etc. |
| SPACE(count) | A character string consisting of count spaces |
| SUBSTRING(string, start, length) | A character string formed by extracting length characters from string beginning at start |
| UCASE(string) | Converts all lowercase characters in string to uppercase |

## TIME and DATE FUNCTIONS

| **Function Name** | **Function Returns** |
|---|---|
| CURDATE() | The current date as a date value |
| CURTIME() | The current local time as a time value |
| DAYNAME(date) | A character string representing the day component of date; the name for the day is specific to the data source |
| DAYOFMONTH(date) | An integer from 1 to 31 representing the day of the month in date |
| DAYOFWEEK(date) | An integer from 1 to 7 representing the day of the week in date; 1 represents Sunday |
| DAYOFYEAR(date) | An integer from 1 to 366 representing the day of the year in date |
| HOUR(time) | An integer from 0 to 23 representing the hour component of time |
| MINUTE(time) | An integer from 0 to 59 representing the minute component of time |
| MONTH(date) | An integer from 1 to 12 representing the month component of date |
| MONTHNAME(date) | A character string representing the month component of date; the name for the month is specific to the data source |
| NOW() | A timestamp value representing the current date and time |

| | |
|---|---|
| QUARTER(date) | An integer from 1 to 4 representing the quarter in date; 1 represents January 1 through March 31 |
| SECOND(time) | An integer from 0 to 59 representing the second component of time |
| TIMESTAMPADD(interval, count, timestamp) | A timestamp calculated by adding count number of interval(s) to timestamp; interval may be one of the following: SQL_TSI_FRAC_SECOND, SQL_TSI_SECOND, SQL_TSI_MINUTE, SQL_TSI_HOUR, SQL_TSI_DAY, SQL_TSI_WEEK, SQL_TSI_MONTH, SQL_TSI_QUARTER, or SQL_TSI_YEAR |
| TIMESTAMPDIFF(interval, timestamp1, timestamp2) | An integer representing the number of interval(s) by which timestamp2 is greater than timestamp1; interval may be one of the following: SQL_TSI_FRAC_SECOND, SQL_TSI_SECOND, SQL_TSI_MINUTE, SQL_TSI_HOUR, SQL_TSI_DAY, SQL_TSI_WEEK, SQL_TSI_MONTH, SQL_TSI_QUARTER, or SQL_TSI_YEAR |
| WEEK(date) | An integer from 1 to 53 representing the week of the year in date |
| YEAR(date) | An integer representing the year component of date |

## SYSTEM FUNCTIONS

| **Function Name** | **Function Returns** |
|---|---|
| DATABASE() | Name of the database |
| IFNULL(expression, value) | value if expression is null; expression if expression is not null |
| USER() | User name in the DBMS |

**CONVERSION FUNCTIONS**

| Function Name | Function Returns |
|---|---|
| CONVERT(value, SQLtype) | value converted to SQLtype where SQLtype may be one of the following SQL types: BIGINT, BINARY, BIT, CHAR, DATE, DECIMAL, DOUBLE, FLOAT, INTEGER, LONGVARBINARY, LONGVARCHAR, REAL, SMALLINT, TIME, TIMESTAMP, TINYINT, VARBINARY, or VARCHAR |

### A.1.5   Provide Locks for Positioned Updates and Deletes

JDBC provides simple cursor support. When a query is executed with the method executeQuery, the result is a ResultSet object with a cursor pointing above the first row. This cursor will remain valid until the ResultSet object or its parent Statement object (the query that generated the result set) is closed. A call to the method ResultSet.getCursorName will provide the name of the cursor associated with the current ResultSet object. This cursor name can then be used in positioned update or positioned delete statements.

Not all DBMSs support positioned updates and positioned deletes. An application can use the JDBC methods DatabaseMetaData.supportsPositionedUpdate and DatabaseMetaData.supportsPositionedDelete to determine whether or not a particular connection supports them. Since many DBMSs do not support "for update" in a SELECT statement (as in SELECT FOR UPDATE), drivers for these DBMSs will have to scan for this phrase and implement the intended semantics. The purpose of this syntax is to signal that the result set generated from a query will be used in a positioned update or positioned delete.

When positioned updates and deletes are supported, the DBMS/driver must ensure that rows selected are properly locked so that positioned updates do not result in update anomalies or other concurrency problems.

### A.1.6   Support Multithreading

All operations on java.sql objects are required to be multithread safe. They must be able to cope correctly with having several threads simultaneously calling the same object. In other words, a statement execution in one thread should not block an execution in another thread. In particular, JDBC drivers should operate correctly when used from multiple threads.

An example of a specific use of multithreading is the way a long-running statement can be cancelled. This is done by using one thread to execute the statement and a second one to cancel it with the method Statement.cancel.

Even though it is expected that in practice most JDBC objects will be accessed in a single-threaded way, there needs to be support for multithreading.

Some database APIs, such as ODBC, provide mechanisms for allowing SQL statements to execute asynchronously. This allows an application to start up a database operation in the background and then handle other work (such as managing a user interface) while waiting for the operation to complete.

Since Java is a multithreaded environment, there seems to be no real need to provide support for asynchronous statement execution. Java programmers can easily create a separate thread if they wish to execute statements asynchronously with respect to their main thread.

Some drivers may allow more concurrent execution than others, but developers should be able to assume fully concurrent execution. If the driver requires some form of synchronization, then the driver should provide it. In this situation, the only difference visible to the developer should be that applications run with reduced concurrency.

For example, two `Statement` objects on the same connection can be executed concurrently, and their `ResultSets` can be processed concurrently (from the perspective of the developer). Some drivers will provide this full concurrency. Others may execute one statement and wait until it completes before sending the next one.

### A.1.7   Throw Exceptions for Truncated Input Parameters

If input parameters are truncated, a `DataTruncation` exception should be thrown.

See "DataTruncation" on page 247 for general information about data truncation warnings and exceptions.

## A.2   Permitted Variants

Because of the variation in database functionality and syntax, JDBC allows some variation in driver implementations. The actual SQL used by one database may vary from that used by other databases. For example, different databases provide different support for outer joins. The `java.sql.DatabaseMetaData` interface provides a number of methods that can be used to determine exactly which SQL features are supported by a particular database. Similarly, the syntax for a number of SQL features may vary between databases and can also be discovered from `java.sql.DatabaseMetaData` methods.

### A.2.1    When Functionality Is Not Supported

Some variation is allowed for drivers written for databases that do not support certain functionality. For example, some databases do not support OUT parameters with stored procedures. In this case, the `CallableStatement` methods that deal with OUT parameters (`registerOutParameter` and the various `getXXX` methods) would not apply, and they may be written so that when they are called, they raise an `SQLException`.

### A.2.2    Variation in Fundamental Properties

Variation is also permitted in some fundamental properties, such as transaction isolation levels. The default properties of the current database and the range of properties it supports can be obtained by calling `DatabaseMetaData` methods.

### A.2.3    Adding Functionality

Database vendors who wish to expose additional functionality that is supported by their databases may create subclasses of existing JDBC classes and provide additional methods in the new subclasses. Thus the Foobah corporation might define a new Java type `foobah.sql.FooBahStatement` that inherits from the standard `java.sql.Statement` type but adds some new functionality.

## A.3    Security Responsibilities of Drivers

Because JDBC drivers may be used in a variety of different situations, it is important that driver writers follow certain simple security rules to prevent applets from making illegal database connections.

These rules are unnecessary if a driver is downloaded as an applet because the standard security manager will prevent an applet driver from making illegal connections. However, JDBC driver writers should bear in mind that if their drivers are "successful," then users may start installing them as trusted parts of the Java environment, and must make sure that they are not abused by visiting applets. We therefore urge all JDBC driver writers to follow the basic security rules.

These rules apply at connection open time. This is the point when the driver and the virtual machine should check that the current caller is really allowed to connect to a given database. After connection open, no additional checks are necessary.

Only native code drivers need to verify database access prior to connecting. Pure Java drivers can rely on the security manager.

The sections that follow discuss the basic security measures that drivers need to address.

### A.3.1 Check Shared TCP Connections

If a JDBC driver attempts to open a TCP connection, then the open will be automatically checked by the Java security manager. The security manager will check to see if there is an applet on the current call stack and if so, will restrict the open to whatever set of machines that applet is allowed to call. So normally a JDBC driver can leave TCP open checks up to the Java virtual machine.

However, if a JDBC driver wants to share a single TCP connection among several different database connections, then it becomes the driver's responsibility to make sure that each of its callers is really allowed to talk to the target database. For example, if a TCP connection is opened to the machine foobah for applet A, this does not mean that applet B should automatically be allowed to share that connection. Applet B may have no right whatsoever to access machine foobah.

Therefore, before allowing someone to re-use an existing TCP connection, the JDBC driver should check with the security manager that the current caller is allowed to connect to that machine. This can be done with the following code fragment:

```
SecurityManager security = System.getSecurityManager();
if (security != null) {
    security.checkConnect(hostName, portNumber);
}
```

The `SecurityManager.checkConnect` method will throw a `java.lang.SecurityException` if the connection is not permitted.

### A.3.2 Check All Local File Access

If a JDBC driver needs to access any local data on the current machine, then it must ensure that its caller is allowed to open the target files. The following code fragment illustrates this:

```
SecurityManager security = System.getSecurityManager();
if (security != null) {
```

```
    security.checkRead(fileName);
}
```

The `Security.checkRead` method will throw a `java.lang.SecurityException` if the current caller is an applet that is not allowed to access the given file.

As with TCP connections, the driver need only be concerned with these security issues if file resources are shared among multiple calling threads and the driver is running as trusted code.

### A.3.3  Assume the Worst

Some drivers may use native methods to bridge to lower-level database libraries. In these cases, it may be difficult to determine what files or network connections will be opened by the lower level libraries.

In these circumstances the driver must make worst-case security assumptions and deny all database access to downloaded applets unless the driver is completely confident that the intended access is innocuous.

For example, a JDBC-ODBC bridge might check the meaning of ODBC data source names and only allow an applet to use those ODBC data source names that reference databases on machines to which the applet is allowed to open connections. But for some ODBC data source names, the driver may be unable to determine the hostname of the target database and must therefore deny downloaded applets access to these data sources.

In order to determine if the current caller is a trusted application or applet (and can therefore be allowed arbitrary database access), the JDBC driver can check to see if the caller is allowed to write an arbitrary file:

```
Security Manager security = System.getSecurityManager();
if (security != null) {
    security.checkWrite("foobah");
}
```

## A.4  SQLExceptions

As just stated, if a DBMS does not support certain functionality, a method may be implemented so that it throws an `SQLException`.

There are cases where a Java `RunTimeException` and an `SQLException` might overlap. For example, if a method expects an argument to be a `java.sql.Types` constant and something else is supplied, the exception thrown could be an `IllegalArgumentException` or an `SQLException`. In such cases, it is recommended that the `SQLException` be thrown because that gives JDBC more consistent control over errors.

## A.5   Suggested Implementations

### A.5.1   Prefetch Rows

JDBC provides methods for retrieving individual columns within individual rows, a field at a time. It does not at present provide the means for prefetching rows in larger chunks. However, in order to reduce the number of interactions with the target database, it is recommended that drivers normally prefetch rows in suitable chunks.

### A.5.2   Provide "Finalize" Methods for Applets

Users are advised to call the method `close` on `Statement` and `Connection` objects when they are done with them. However, some users will forget, and some code may get killed before it can close these objects. Therefore, if JDBC drivers have state associated with JDBC objects that need to get explicitly cleared up, they should provide `finalize` methods to take care of them. The garbage collector will call these `finalize` methods when the objects are found to be garbage, and this will give the driver a chance to close (or otherwise clean up) the objects. Note, however, that there is no guarantee that the garbage collector will ever run. If that is the case, the finalizers will not be called.

Driver writers should look carefully at the semantics used for finalization in Java. A good source of information on this is *The Java Language Specification*, by James Gosling, Bill Joy, and Guy Steele. Some care is required to ensure that the finalization process occurs in the right order regardless of the order in which the garbage collector deals with a driver's objects.

### A.5.3   Avoid Implementation-dependent States

Some databases have restrictions that result in hidden dependencies between JDBC objects. For instance, two `Statement` objects may be open, but while the `ResultSet` object of one is in use, the other `Statement` object cannot be executed. This implies that an implementation-defined `Statement` state exists that is controlled via another `Statement` object.

JDBC does not define such states, and if at all possible, JDBC implementations should not introduce them. They hinder portability, and implementations containing them are not fully JDBC Compliant.

# JDBC Design

$W$E have covered a great deal of JDBC design and API details in this book, without explaining how and why JDBC came about the way it did. For readers curious about the history or motivation for the design, we have included some background in this appendix. We hope that you can learn something from our experience with both the politics and the technical design of JDBC. Failing that, we hope that you can at least understand why we did the design this way, especially if it differs from what you would have done.

## B.1   A Bit of History

This first section covers the history of the work. The later sections cover design rationale and design issues we hope to address in the future.

### B.1.1   How It Started

We conceived of the JDBC idea in September 1995. Most of the early work on JDBC was done by Graham, who joined JavaSoft earlier that year as part of the JavaOS team. During this time Rick attempted to consult on the design while continuing to work in SunSoft. Moonlighting for a "start-up" leaves one spread pretty thin, so he gave up and joined Graham full-time in December.

We were both quite enamored with Java as a programming language, not just as a web page scripting language. We had both spent too much of our lives chasing memory clobbers, memory leaks, and misuses of void* (mostly in other peoples' code, of course ;-)). Java was easy to read, easy to write, and easy to debug. Admittedly, we had both used programming languages comparable to Java before in earlier academic and research experience (CLU, Cedar, and others), but these languages had failed to gain the critical mass for libraries and tools necessary for real success. Finally we had found a programming language that was *reasonable* and also *popular!* When Netscape, IBM, Apple, HP, and finally Microsoft licensed Java, its success was looking quite clear to us.

It was also clear to us that some kind of database connectivity was needed for Java, since a great deal of the industry's applications are database applications. We were concerned that developers would define their own database APIs for Java, and that applications written for one company's drivers would not work with another company's drivers.

This concern turned out to be well-founded. When we started, we knew of only one company (WebLogic) that had worked on Java database connectivity. When we approached companies with our proposed JDBC API in January of 1996, half a dozen conflicting APIs and product plans were already underway at different companies. Fortunately, everyone was very cooperative and understanding of our desire to make drivers plug-compatible; the industry quickly aligned itself with the JDBC effort. If we had taken just a couple of months longer, this might have been much more difficult.

We went through many iterations of the design, and got a lot of good ideas from people who knew more about the problem than we did. Visigenic, Intersolv, and IBM probably deserve credit for the most voluminous input, but a dozen other companies contributed in dozens of meetings in December 1995 through the announcement in March 1996.

Mark Hapner joined our team in March, and he has provided valuable feedback as well as being the key player in delivering the JDBC implementation we eventually shipped. Hundreds of other people provided input by email during the public review that we conducted in March through the end of May, when we finalized the API.

Maydene Fisher joined our team in June. Over the ensuing months, with collaboration from the rest of the team, she transformed the JDBC specification into the much more complete book you see here.

## B.1.2    What Can Be Learned from Our Experience?

We had a lot going in our favor with JDBC. Everyone wanted to work with Java-Soft; it seemed to boost a company's stock price by several points at that time just to announce a JavaSoft partnership. Rick had a lot of friends in the database industry. We had a programming language that made prototyping fast and easy. However, in retrospect there are numerous ways that we could and probably would have failed had we done things differently. In our opinion there are a number of key points here:

1. We are both impatient people and have a bent toward doing things quickly; if we had not moved in "web time," we most certainly would have been superseded by too many incompatible existing implementations in the field.

2. Successful industry standards are almost never created by a committee; consider UNIX, NFS, SQL, Windows, and virtually every other widely adopted API. Standards are created by a small number of people who are in the right place to capture industry mindshare. They are *later* adopted by committees that incrementally improve them. Rick had written an article on this theme based on earlier experience,[1] and Graham likewise believed strongly in the benefits of meeting with companies one at a time. This approach avoids creating competitive tensions and lessens the "committee thinking" problem.

3. A proven, timely implementation is essential; again, this is true of successful standards. If Graham had not implemented a JDBC–ODBC bridge prototype early on, other companies would not have taken us seriously and we would have made a lot of mistakes in the API design for lack of understanding of implications for applications.

4. We maintained an attitude of cooperation with partners and tried to present a win-win proposition for everyone. We were surprised by the enthusiastic reciprocation. More than one company offered to give us an implementation of JDBC in exchange for the "press" value of working with us. We chose to work with Intersolv on the bridge and test suites, but tried to be fair in our dealings with everyone.

5. We didn't try to do too much. We started with accepted industry APIs and tried to put together something simple that met our design criteria. We tried to build on what was there.

We and our colleagues at JavaSoft used these principles successfully in a number of efforts that followed JDBC in 1996 and afterward.


## B.2   Evolution of JDBC

Although the basic goals of JDBC have remained constant, there have been various API changes as JDBC evolved into what it is today.

---

[1.] Cattell, R., Experience with the ODMG Standard, *ACM Standard View*, September 1995.

### B.2.1    `ResultSet.getXXX` Methods

In earlier versions, the getXXX methods took no argument; they simply returned the next column value in left-to-right order. This seemed simpler to us, but it made the resulting example code difficult to read. We frequently found ourselves having to count through the various getXXX calls in order to match them up with the columns specified in the SELECT statement. Using the column number as an argument to the getXXX methods greatly improved readability.

Then, several developers who were using early specifications requested that they be able to use the name of a column as the argument to the getXXX methods. We initially resisted this because it doubled the number of getXXX methods: we are minimalists. However, it is often more meaningful and more convenient to use a name rather than a column index, and it is less error-prone. In the end, the ease of using column names won out.

### B.2.2    `PreparedStatement.setXXX` Methods

Initially, there was only one method for setting parameter values: setParameter. This method was overloaded with different argument types, and that determined the type to which a parameter was being set. Our reviewers found this confusing, particularly in cases where the mapping between SQL types and Java types is ambiguous. So in the end, each type had its own set method, as in setByte, setBoolean, and so on.

### B.2.3    `CallableStatement.registerOutParameter` Method

We did not want JDBC to require a registerOutParameter method. We felt that drivers should be able to determine the OUT parameter types from the database metadata or from the setXXX calls made by the programmer, instead of requiring this redundancy. However the parameter type is required by at least one widely used DBMS before the setXXX calls are executed, and the performance impact of database metadata calls seemed an excessive penalty to pay for each stored procedure call. Feedback from early reviewers convinced us that it was better to require the use of the method registerOutParameter.

### B.2.4    Support for Large OUT Parameters

We considered supporting OUT parameters that are very large and decided against it. It would probably have consisted of allowing programmers to register

java.io.OutputStreams into which the JDBC runtime could send the OUT parameter data when a statement executed. This seemed harder to explain than it was
worth, given that there is already a mechanism for handling large results as part of a
ResultSet object.

### B.2.5    isNull versus wasNull

We had some difficulty in determining a good way of handling the type JDBC NULL.
By JDBC 0.50 we had designed a ResultSet.isNull method that seemed fairly
pleasant to use. The isNull method had the advantage that it could be called on any
column to check for NULL before (or after) reading the column.

```
if(!ResultSet.isNull(3)) {
    count += ResultSet.getInt(3);
}
```

Unfortunately, harsh reality intervened and it emerged that isNull could not
be implemented reliably on all databases. Some databases have no separate means
for determining if a column is null other than by reading the column, and they
would permit reading a given column only once. We looked at reading the column
value and "remembering" it for later use, but this caused problems when data conversions were required.

After examining a number of different solutions, we reluctantly decided to
replace the isNull method with the wasNull method. The method wasNull merely
reports whether the last value read from the given ResultSet or CallableStatement object was of type JDBC NULL.

### B.2.6    Java Type Names or JDBC Type Names

Originally, the getXXX and setXXX methods used JDBC types. For example, there
were getChar and setSmallInt. Since it is Java programmers who use JDBC, however, it seemed that the meaning of each method would be clearer if the methods
used Java types instead. Consequently, getChar became getString, and setSmall-
Int became setShort. Using Java type names also avoids potential confusion in
those cases where the local type names used by a DBMS differ from the generic
JDBC type names.

### B.2.7    Scrollable Cursors

We considered including scrollable cursors in JDBC, which would have provided a previous method as well as a next method in the interface ResultSet. The problem is that most DBMSs do not implement scrollable cursors. To include them, JDBC driver writers would have had to implement scrollable cursors themselves, and we did not want to impose that burden on them. We feel that the best solution is to have scrollable cursors implemented on top of JDBC.

## B.3    Post 1.0 Changes

We tried *very* hard not to make any changes after the 1.0 specification was finalized, but gave in to two modifications in merging JDBC into the JDK. The first was made necessary by a change in the Java API. Given that change, we reluctantly made a second one that had repeatedly been requested by our reviewers.

### B.3.1    Numeric to Bignum to BigDecimal

In an ongoing effort to offer the best possible API for extended-precision fixed point numbers, there have been changes in the Java API that necessitated some corresponding changes in the JDBC API.

Originally, JDBC provided the class java.sql.Numeric to handle extended-precision fixed point numbers, so early specifications used that class. For example, the ResultSet and CallableStatement getXXX methods included getNumeric, and PreparedStatement included the method setNumeric.

The JDBC class java.sql.Numeric was incorporated into Java and became java.lang.Bignum with the result that getNumeric became getBignum and setNumeric became setBignum. JDBC version 1.1 used java.lang.Bignum; it is the JDBC version that is compatible with version 1.0.2 of the JDK.

Subsequently, the facilities of java.lang.Bignum were divided up into the two classes, java.math.BigDecimal and java.math.BigInteger. The class java.math.BigInteger deals with the security-oriented integer operations, and since neither JDBC nor typical drivers or users reference this functionality, java.math.BigInteger does not need to appear in the JDBC API. The class java.math.BigDecimal, on the other hand, replaced those operations of java.lang.Bignum that JDBC does reference, so it was necessary for java.math.BigDecimal to replace java.lang.Bignum in the JDBC API. In JDBC version 1.2, getBignum became getBigDecimal, and setBignum became setBigDecimal. JDK versions 1.1 beta3 and later use java.math.BigDecimal and `java.math.BigInteger`, so JDBC version 1.2 must be used with them to be compatible.

Note that JDBC version 1.2 is part of the JDK1.1 release and does not need to be installed separately. Users who have a driver that references `java.lang.Bignum`, however, will need to install JDBC1.1 manually. It is available from the JDBC web page (`http://www.javasoft.com/products/jdbc/`).

### B.3.2   AutoClose Mode Dropped

One of the basic design considerations for JDBC was that simple things be kept simple. Originally, a connection was set up so that in its default mode, statements and cursors would be automatically closed when the statement was committed, thus making it easier for the programmer and ensuring that statements were properly closed without waiting for the garbage collector.

It became evident, however, that this strategy to keep simple things simple was making life more difficult for sophisticated users. For example, in order to keep a `PreparedStatement` object open so that it could be executed multiple times, `autoClose` mode had to be disabled. Further, the effects of disabling and enabling `autoClose` mode could sometimes get quite complicated.

We were also concerned early on that some DBMS drivers *required* auto-Close as a result of the way they were implemented. Certainly we wanted a default case that could be implemented. Fortunately, this turned out not to be a problem for any major DBMS.

In the end, after much prompting from developers, it seemed better just to drop `autoClose` mode.

## B.4   The Future of JDBC

At the time of this writing in early 1997, JDBC has been much more successful than we imagined just a year ago. JDBC drivers have appeared throughout the industry, including a number of innovative and pure Java drivers. The JDBC design has been widely adopted despite its relative simplicity; no competition has emerged. So, what now?

Of course, higher-level APIs and tools can be developed on top of JDBC, including automatic forms/application construction tools, embedded SQL, and object/relational mappings, as mentioned in chapter 1. All of these products are under way at various places. However, none of them obviate the need for the basic

JDBC API that makes them possible. So, we believe that JDBC has a long future to come.

At this point, we are examining a number of directions for JDBC 2.0 and beyond.

Probably the most likely direction is an expansion of the `ResultSet` idea, probably through a class implemented on top of `ResultSet`. There are several kinds of functionality that we'd like to provide:

1. the ability to move both forward and backwards through the set of rows

2. the ability to conveniently read and write the current row in the set

3. the ability to temporarily "disconnect" the set from the database (On re-connection, the driver must determine that the updates are still valid or abort the transaction.)

Another area we are considering is extensions for SQL3 functionality that we were hesitant to add before these were better understood and agreed upon.

We have encouraged JDBC driver writers to experiment with extensions. We require that these be made through subclassing or new classes rather than modifying the existing JDBC classes; this provides consistency and backward compatibility. We may adopt some of these vendor extensions into future JDBC classes.

Suggestions for future JDBC directions should be sent to:

```
jdbc@wombat.eng.sun.com
```

Constructive suggestions with attention to specifics and implications are likely to receive the closest attention.

# Glossary

**API** Application Programming Interface. In the case of Java, this is a set of classes and interfaces that specify a particular functionality, for example, the JDBC API.

**Applet** A Java program that can be downloaded over the network and executed by a browser. Java applets can be contrasted to Java applications, which are loaded from a disk, as are programs in other programming languages.

**Attribute** A column of a table. This term is also applied to a "column" of just one row of the table (a field).

**Bytecodes** Executable Java programs are represented in an intermediate form called bytecodes. This is higher level than machine code, so that it runs on multiple platforms, but lower level than source code, so it is efficient to move around, execute, or compile into machine code.

**Catalog** A name space mechanism for databases, used to keep people from tripping over each other. Database schemas are grouped into catalogs. Each catalog is a separate name space. Some DBMSs have called catalogs "users".

**Class** Java's basic type mechanism. If you are looking up this term in the glossary, you will need to read a Java tutorial before going beyond chapter 1.

**Commit** A commit operation causes all of the updates made during a transaction to be permanently written into the database, completing the transaction. If a transaction is explicitly or implicitly aborted (rolled back), it is incomplete and all changes made are backed out, as if the transaction never happened.

**Concurrency** Concurrency refers to multiple users or programs simultaneously sharing the same database. Transactions and locks are used to give each of these a consistent view of the database.

**Connection** A connection is a session with a database opened by a JDBC application program, so-called because it represents a connection between the program and a (usually remote) database. At any one time, only one transaction can be associated with a connection.

**Cursor**  A cursor is used to reference the current position in a result set. SQL defines a cursor mechanism that can be used through JDBC to do positioned updates and deletes. See Appendix B of the book for further plans here.

**Database**  A database is a set of data that conforms to a particular schema. In the case of JDBC, the database is generally a set of tables. Occasionally, the term database is used loosely to refer to the software that stores the database (a DBMS).

**Database system**  A shorter term for database management system (DBMS).

**DBMS**  (DataBase Management System) Software used to manage databases. In a client/server environment, this software runs on a different machine than the database application program. A JDBC driver usually is designed to work with only one DBMS.

**DDL**  (Data Definition Language) A subset of SQL commands dealing with database objects. The most common DDL commands are CREATE TABLE and DROP TABLE.

**Deadlock**  A condition that can occur when two or more users are all waiting for each other to give up locks. More advanced DBMSs do deadlock detection and abort one of the user transactions when this happens.

**Dirty read**  A dirty read happens when a transaction reads data from a database that has been modified by another transaction, and that data has not yet been committed. If dirty reads are not desired, one must specify a higher isolation level (possibly resulting in lower performance).

**Driver**  A JDBC driver is a Java (or partly Java) program that implements the JDBC interface. It is loaded by the JDBC driver manager.

**Error**  An error is a problem that is not recoverable. A JDBC error results in an exception.

**Escape character/syntax**  Escape characters are special characters that JDBC drivers scan for in SQL strings before passing the SQL on to the underlying DBMS. They are used to delimit special DBMS-independent syntax that the driver must translate into DBMS-specific syntax, generally used where DBMSs are not standardized in the SQL they support.

**Finalization**  Before the Java garbage collector deletes an object that is no longer in use, the object is given a chance to finalize itself, to clean up loose ends.

For example, a `Connection` object must ensure that the underlying DBMS connection is closed before going away.

**Foreign key**  A foreign key is an attribute (or group of attributes) of a table that is used to refer to rows of another table (more precisely, to the primary key of another table). For example, an employee table may contain an attribute that is the employee's department number. The department number is used to look up the correct row of the department table.

**HTTP**  HyperText Transfer Protocol. The standardized protocol used by browsers to get information for servers over the network.

**Index**  It would be very inefficient for a DBMS to look at every row of a table or tables in order to find the information requested by a query. An index is a data structure on disk that allows rows of tables to be found quickly based on the values of one or more attributes. Multiple indexes can be defined on a table or a database, and the SQL processor will pick the best ones to use to execute a query.

**Interface**  Java uses classes to define object types and implementations just like other object-oriented languages. Interfaces allow functionality to be defined (as a set of methods, just like classes) without defining how the methods are implemented. A class can support multiple interfaces.

**Intranet**  Multiple local area networks (LANs) within one company.

**Isolation level**  When you use a DBMS with other concurrent users, you must choose a compromise between performance and a slightly inconsistent view of data (because the data is being updated concurrently by other users). Unless you choose the highest level of isolation (full serializability), your program may see such anomolies as dirty reads or phantom reads.

**JDBC**  The `java.sql` package, which is a set of classes and interfaces that make it possible to access databases from Java.

**JDBC Compliant**  A JDBC driver for a DBMS is JDBC Compliant if it passes the test suite that JavaSoft provides. The driver/DBMS must support SQL–92 Entry Level and all of the JDBC methods defined in this book.

**JDK**  Java Development Kit. The software released by JavaSoft to support the Java environment. The JDK includes the Java compiler and interpreter, and many Java libraries.

**Join** The basic relational operator that allows data from more than one table to be combined. A join matches rows of two tables based on columns with common values. For example, the employee table may contain a column specifying the department number for each employee. The department number is also a column of the department table. Rows of the employee table can be matched up (joined) with the department table based on these values.

**Lock** Locks allow a database transaction to mark data (for example, rows or tables) it is using in order to exclude a concurrent user from performing certain operations on the same data. There are different kinds of locks; for example, an exclusive (write) lock disallows all other users, while a read lock allows other concurrent readers.

**Metadata** Metadata describes the kind of functionality a DBMS provides (for example, whether it supports specific SQL features) and the types of data in the database (that is, the database schema).

**Method** A procedure associated with a class or interface, defining one of the legal operations on instances of the class or interface.

**MIS** Management Information Services. An MIS department is in charge of the corporate information on computers, like inventory and payroll, and usually determines which computers (Windows, Solaris, Macintosh) are used by administrative personnel.

**Multithreading** Multithreading allows more than one concurrent thread of control within one address space (or Java Virtual Machine). This is useful, for example, when writing a service that responds to requests from multiple client programs on a network. JDBC supports multithreading.

**Native code** Code written in a language other than Java (usually C) and compiled to machine code. Mixing Java and native code in an application requires use of the JNI (Java Native Interface) to allow calls from Java to native code. It is generally good to avoid native code in applications because many of the benefits of Java (for example, machine independence and automatic installation over the network) are lost.

**Network protocol** The convention for encoding of data and commands over the network between a client and server. HTTP and FTP are protocols. Most DBMSs have a proprietary protocol they have evolved for communicating between clients and their database servers. Two-tier JDBC drivers can speak these protocols directly to the DBMS.

**Non-repeatable read**  Data returned by an SQL query that would be different if the query were repeated within the same transaction. Non-repeatable reads can occur when other users are updating the same data you are reading. They can be avoided by specifying a higher isolation level, in exchange for some performance loss.

**Null**  A data value that is unknown or unspecified. Java has a distinguished `null` object value, and SQL has a distinguished `null` value that represents the absence of an actual value.

**ODBC**  Open Database Connection. An API defined by Microsoft, a derivative of the X/Open CLI API.

**Phantom read**  This occurs when your program fetches a tuple that has been inserted by another user's transaction, and the other transaction subsequently aborts, erasing the tuple you fetched.

**Positioned update/delete**  A mechanism to update or delete the row at the current position through an SQL cursor.

**Precision**  In SQL, the total number of digits in a numeric value, for example 243.24 has a precision of 5.

**Prepared statement**  An SQL statement that has been compiled for efficiency. The SQL processor parses and analyzes the query, decides which indexes to use to fetch tuples, and produces an execution plan for the prepared statement.

**Primary key**  An attribute or set of attributes that are unique among rows of a table. A table's primary key is used to refer to rows of the table. For example, an employee ID attribute uniquely identifies the rows (employees) in an employee table.

**Protocol**  A convention for communication between programs. See network protocol.

**Pseudo-column**  A column that is not actually stored, but that appears as an ordinary column in a table to the user or application program.

**Pure Java**  An adjective referring to a program that is written entirely in Java, with no native code.

**Query**  An SQL SELECT statement.

**RDBMS**  Relational Database Management System. There is some debate in the database literature about what is truly "relational," but generally a DBMS that supports the SQL standard is considered relational.

**Record**  A row of a table or a row of the result set returned by a query.

**Referential integrity**  Correctness of foreign keys. A DBMS maintains referential integrity by ensuring that there exists a row in the referenced table for every reference to the table. For example, if employee records refer to department records through a department ID attribute, there should be a valid department record for each employee.

**Relation**  A table, the basic data structure of the relational model.

**Rollback**  Undoing the changes made by a transaction. This can be initiated in a JDBC application by explicitly calling the Connection method rollback, and in some cases, a rollback can be spontaneously generated by the DBMS due to an error or unresolvable deadlock between transactions.

**Runtime exception**  A Java exception that does not need to be explicitly declared in a method that throws it.

**Scalar value**  A single entry in a table, at the intersection of a row and column. Scalar functions operate on scalar values, as opposed to an aggregate of values.

**Scale**  The number of decimal digits after the decimal point in numeric values.

**Schema**  A description of the tables in a database and their attributes. Every database is an instance of some schema. A schema name is a way of qualifying a table name within a catalog.

**Server**  A machine providing services of some kind to client machines on the network. In a two-tier approach, a database server is called directly by JDBC drivers on client machines. In a three-tier approach, client programs make calls (through RMI, IIOP, HTTP, or some other protocol) to services on a separate machine, which in turn make JDBC calls to the database server.

**SQL**  A standardized database language for specifying queries and updates to databases. ANSI X3H2 is the U.S. organization responsible for SQL; see http//www2.x3.org/ncits/ for more information. ISO is the corresponding international body.

**SQL–92**  The version of SQL standardized by ANSI in 1992. Sometimes called SQL2.

**SQL–92 entry level**  A subset of full SQL–92 specified by ANSI/ISO that is supported by nearly all major DBMSs today. This subset unfortunately is not complete enough to allow portability of non-trivial database applications; in particular, it does not specify a full set of standard data types. JDBC compliance requires entry level SQL compliance and defines escape syntax and metadata routines for more advanced features.

**SQL–92 intermediate level** A subset of full SQL–92 specified by ANSI/ISO that contains more functionality than SQL–92. Hopefully most DBMSs will support this soon.

**Static method**  A method that is associated with a class rather than operating on a specific object of the class.

**Stored procedure**  Major DBMS vendors' SQL as well as SQL3 provide a mechanism to write programming-language-style procedures with arguments and procedural code that are stored in and executed in the DBMS server. These are called stored procedures.

**Synchronized**  An attribute of a Java method that provides concurrency control among multiple threads sharing an object by locking the object during execution of the method.

**Three-tier JDBC driver**  A driver that implements the JDBC API by making calls to a "middle tier" server that translates the calls into DBMS-specific protocols and makes the calls to the DBMS server.

**Transaction**  A sequence of SQL/JDBC calls that constitute an atomic unit of work. Transactions provide ACID properties: atomicity, consistency, integrity of data, and durability of database changes.

**Tuple**  A row of a table.

**Two-tier JDBC driver**  A JDBC driver that translates JDBC calls directly into a DBMS vendor's on-the-wire protocol. Ideally, a two-tier driver is all-Java, but for the short term many include native code from existing client-side DBMS libraries.

**Unicode**  A character encoding used in Java strings to support multiple language character sets.

**URL**  Universal Resource Locator. First used on the WorldWideWeb to identify HTML documents. A specialized form of URL is used by JDBC to identify databases and drivers.

**Warning**  An exceptional condition that does not interrupt execution of an application program, such as truncation of data values. JDBC provides a getWarnings method to obtain this information.

**X/Open CLI**  X/Open is an international standards organization. It has defined a database Call-Level Interface (CLI) for C that allows SQL strings to be passed to a DBMS and results to be returned. JDBC is based on X/Open CLI, but with different design goals (using Java instead of C, more focus on ease of use, object-orientation).

# Index

# D

# H

# I

# The Addison-Wesley Java™ Series

### The Java™ Programming Language
Ken Arnold and James Gosling
ISBN 0-201-63455-4

### The Java™ Tutorial
*Object-Oriented Programming for the Internet*
Mary Campione and Kathy Walrath
ISBN 0-201-63454-6

### The Java™ Class Libraries
*An Annotated Reference*
Patrick Chan and Rosanna Lee
ISBN 0-201-63458-9

### The Java™ Language Specification
James Gosling, Bill Joy, and Guy Steele
ISBN 0-201-63451-1

### The Java™ Application Programming Interface, Volume 1
*Core Packages*
James Gosling, Frank Yellin, and The Java Team
ISBN 0-201-63453-8

**The Java™ Application Programming Interface, Volume 2**
*Window Toolkit and Applets*
James Gosling, Frank Yellin, and The Java Team
ISBN 0-201-63459-7

**JDBC™ Database Access with Java™**
*A Tutorial and Annotated Reference*
Graham Hamilton, Rick Cattell, and Maydene Fisher
ISBN 0-201-30995-5

**The Java™ FAQ**
Jonni Kanerva
ISBN 0-201-63456-2

**Concurrent Programming in Java™**
*Design Principles and Patterns*
Doug Lea
ISBN 0-201-69581-2

**The Java™ Virtual Machine Specification**
Tim Lindholm and Frank Yellin
ISBN 0-201-63452-X

Please see our web site (http://www.awl.com/cp/javaseries.html) for more information on these and other forthcoming titles.

# JDBC Quick Reference

```
Connection con = DriverManager.getConnection(url, login, password);
Statement stmt = con.createStatement();
ResultSet rs = stmt.executeQuery("select COF_NAME, SALES from COFFEES");
while (rs.next()) {
        String coffeeName = rs.getString("COF_NAME"); // or rs.getString(1);
        int amountSold = rs.getInt("SALES"); // or rs.getInt(2);
}
int n = stmt.executeUpdate(
                "update COFFEES set SALES = 50 where COF_NAME = 'Espresso'");

PreparedStatement pstmt = con.prepareStatement(
                      "update COFFEES set SALES = ? where COF_NAME like ?");
pstmt.setInt(1, 50);
pstmt.setString(2, "Espresso");
int updateCount = pstmt.executeUpdate();

CallableStatememt cstmt = con.prepareCall("{call myProcedure}");
ResultSet rs = cstmt.executeQuery(); // if myProcedure returns a result set
int n = cstmt.executeUpdate(); // if myProcedure is an update or DDL statement
```

| JDBC Type | Java Type |
|-----------|-----------|
| CHAR | String |
| VARCHAR | String |
| LONGVARCHAR | String |
| NUMERIC | java.math.BigDecimal |
| DECIMAL | java.math.BigDecimal |
| BIT | boolean |
| TINYINT | byte |
| SMALLINT | short |
| INTEGER | int |
| BIGINT | long |
| REAL | float |
| FLOAT | double |
| DOUBLE | double |
| BINARY | byte[] |
| VARBINARY | byte[] |
| LONGVARBINARY | byte[] |
| DATE | java.sql.Date |
| TIME | java.sql.Time |
| TIMESTAMP | java.sql.Timestamp |

**JDBC Types Mapped
to Java Types**

| Java Type | JDBC Type |
|-----------|-----------|
| String | CHAR, VARCHAR or LONGVARCHAR |
| java.math.BigDecimal | NUMERIC |
| boolean | BIT |
| byte | TINYINT |
| short | SMALLINT |
| int | INTEGER |
| long | BIGINT |
| float | REAL |
| double | DOUBLE |
| byte[] | BINARY, VARBINARY or LONGVARBINARY |
| java.sql.Date | DATE |
| java.sql.Time | TIME |
| java.sql.Timestamp | TIMESTAMP |

**Standard Mapping from Java Types
to JDBC Types**

| | TINYINT | SMALLINT | INTEGER | BIGINT | REAL | FLOAT | DOUBLE | DECIMAL | NUMERIC | BIT | CHAR | VARCHAR | LONGVARCHAR | BINARY | VARBINARY | LONGVARBINARY | DATE | TIME | TIMESTAMP |
|---|---|---|---|---|---|---|---|---|---|---|---|---|---|---|---|---|---|---|---|
| getByte | **X** | x | x | x | x | x | x | x | x | x | x | x | x | | | | | | |
| getShort | x | **X** | x | x | x | x | x | x | x | x | x | x | x | | | | | | |
| getInt | x | x | **X** | x | x | x | x | x | x | x | x | x | x | | | | | | |
| getLong | x | x | x | **X** | x | x | x | x | x | x | x | x | x | | | | | | |
| getFloat | x | x | x | x | **X** | x | x | x | x | x | x | x | x | | | | | | |
| getDouble | x | x | x | x | x | **X** | **X** | x | x | x | x | x | x | | | | | | |
| getBigDecimal | x | x | x | x | x | x | x | **X** | **X** | x | x | x | x | | | | | | |
| getBoolean | x | x | x | x | x | x | x | x | x | **X** | x | x | x | | | | | | |
| getString | x | x | x | x | x | x | x | x | x | x | **X** | **X** | x | x | x | x | x | x | x |
| getBytes | | | | | | | | | | | | | | **X** | **X** | x | | | |
| getDate | | | | | | | | | | | x | x | x | | | | **X** | | x |
| getTime | | | | | | | | | | | x | x | x | | | | | **X** | x |
| getTimestamp | | | | | | | | | | | x | x | x | | | | x | x | **X** |
| getAsciiStream | | | | | | | | | | | x | x | **X** | x | x | x | | | |
| getUnicodeStream | | | | | | | | | | | x | x | **X** | x | x | x | | | |
| getBinaryStream | | | | | | | | | | | | | | x | x | **X** | | | |
| getObject | x | x | x | x | x | x | x | x | x | x | x | x | x | x | x | x | x | x | x |

## Use of ResultSet.getXXX methods to retrieve JDBC types.

An "x" indicates that the getXXX method may legally be used to retrieve the given JDBC type.
An "X" indicates that the getXXX method is recommended for retrieving the given JDBC type.